W9-AHO-499

SAFE SCHOOLS
A Security and Loss Prevention Plan

SAFE SCHOOLS

A Security and
Loss Prevention Plan

J. Barry Hylton, Ph.D., CFE

Butterworth—Heinemann
Boston   Oxford   Johannesburg   Melbourne   New Delhi   Singapore

Library of Congress Cataloging-in-Publication Data

Hylton, J. Barry (James Barry), 1946–
    Safe schools: a security and loss prevention plan / by J. Barry
  Hylton.
      p. cm.
    Includes bibliographical references and index.
    ISBN 0-7506-9759-8 (alk. paper)
    1. Public schools—United States—Safety measures.   2. School
violence—United States—Prevention.   I. Title.
LB2864.5.H95   1996
371.7´7´0973—dc20   96-3323
                                                 CIP

British Library Cataloging-in-Publication Data

A catalogue record for this book is available from the British Library.
The publisher offers discounts on bulk orders of this book.
For information, please contact:
Manager of Special Sales
Butterworth—Heinemann
313 Washington Street
Newton, MA 02158-1626
Tel: 617-928-2500
Fax: 617-928-2620

For information on all Security publications available, contact our World Wide Web home page at: http://www.bh.com/bh/

10 9 8 7 6 5 4 3 2 1

Printed in the United States of America

Contents

Preface

Violence among young people and in our schools has increased at an alarming and unacceptable rate in recent years, and school districts are struggling to find ways to cope with and manage the problem.[1] Some school districts have their own proprietary security or police forces. Some have a city or county police officer (a school resource officer) assigned to their schools, and some hire private security personnel. Other school districts have no police or security presence at all on campus. The current trend in the United States is for public school systems to establish their own district police departments like those on college campuses or in cities.[2] Whatever structure they choose, school districts, like other organizations, must have a plan to proactively manage, rather than react to, crises.

This book addresses school security issues, perceptions, and security program design and provides a model security and loss prevention plan. School districts can use this model plan to establish regulation, provide examples and guidance, and set forth uniform standards for security, physical security, and loss prevention measures intended to safeguard buildings, materials and equipment, and individuals on school property. The information and guidelines set forth in this book and model plan are intended to deter, reduce, and, in most instances, remove the opportunity for crime, violence, and related problems. It is hoped that they will set the stage for effective crime prevention, create safer schools, and reduce workplace violence.

However, the guidelines and recommendations offered here are not intended to be all-encompassing or to supply all answers to all questions and problems. There are many approaches and innovative measures that can provide good security in a school. Most depend on the philosophy of service and administrators and security professionals working to bridge the gap between the different roles of education and security. Safer schools require a broad spectrum of programs, including not only fundamental policing and physical security programs, but also programs that take into consideration the characteristics of students and staff and the social and cultural environment of the school. Crime and violence will grow in a school where it is tolerated and where students feel entitled to use violent behavior to deal with problems or conflict.

There is no guarantee that crime will be prevented as a result of implementing some or all of the recommendations in this book. Effective security depends on many variables. A security program must be directed by a professional security manager or executive with support from the nonsecurity leadership at all levels of the school district.

The education community must develop less parochial views regarding the need for professionally run security programs in public schools. Security operations must be viewed as the primary duty of a security force, and security personnel should not be used inappropriately for other purposes. If public school systems do not develop and maintain professional and systematic security programs, security-related litigation will eventually force them to acknowledge a reality check and to come out of any cocoon of naiveté and well-cultivated routines of resistance to change.

In today's climate of increasing security litigation, we must always be mindful that few jurors are ever impressed solely by the combat preparedness of a security force. They relate more readily to an organization's written crime-prevention policy and how security personnel operate and are trained and supervised.

Every symptom of violence recognized by school staff should be seen as an opportunity to form school and community action groups to deal better with the symptoms and prevent or reduce future violence. After all, violence is a learned behavior, and as such, it can also be unlearned in time with appropriate deterrent security programs, professional staff development, education, and the development of community partnerships. To that end, I suggest that you use this plan as an example when organizing and operating an effective, responsible, and professional school security program.

ABOUT THE AUTHOR

The views expressed in this book are based on more than 28 years of training, experience, knowledge, and leadership of the author in the field of law enforcement and security management. Dr. Hylton is a retired special agent of the U.S. Secret Service and former director of security for naval air stations, aircraft, and aircraft carriers in the Atlantic and on the East Coast where he directed security, police operations, and anti-terrorism security measures. Since 1991, Dr. Hylton has been the director of security services for a large inner-city school district on the East Coast. He is a recognized expert on anti-terrorism security measures, crime prevention, and school security. Dr. Hylton also provides security and crime prevention consulting services to public and private school districts across the country and a wide range of other clientele. He also routinely gives presentations to many public and professional organizations on security, crime prevention, and school-oriented policing and security. He is currently an adjunct professor at The University of Virginia and LaSalle University.

NOTES

1. Mary Tobias Weaver, "Gazing into a Crystal Ball," *School Safety* (Winter 1994): 8.
2. Diane M. Rotondo, "Curbing Crime," *American School and University* (October 1992): 48.

Introduction

THE PROBLEM: VIOLENCE AND CRIME IN OUR SCHOOLS

The issues in school security today are not much different from the issues with which most police departments and communities are dealing except that they involve children in the eyes of the law. School campuses, once "islands of safety," now face violence every day. It is only natural that the types of violence that take place everywhere in the community should spill over into the schools.

We are living in an increasingly violent society. Violence is contagious and is transmitted in overt, subtle, and often unintentional ways.[1] People act out their feelings more today—not just the young, but also adults. Violence in the adult workplace is also increasing at an alarming rate.

What images and messages are adults sending to the young people in our society? Parents, friends, officials, and strangers are lying, cheating, being unfaithful, stealing, and back-stabbing one another. They are displaying an increasing amount of both verbal and physical violence. Special treatment and the unequal application of the law appear to be given to certain groups or individuals based on money and influence. Our children note the appearance of cover-ups and deception on the part of our top officials down to local governments and, school officials and businesses. They see violence on television and in their movies, music, and video games. Many children experience poverty and family unemployment; they have no hope for the future and little or no family support. A child today can make more from selling drugs than most parents make working a regular job. What kids are saying is that they don't trust us or the system, and we are not setting a very good example for them to follow! They are asking who *we* are to preach to *them*, when all they see is abusive and inharmonious relationships, the lack of concern for one another, the lack of consequences, and the lack of personal values.

Violence among young people and in our schools has increased at an alarming and unacceptable rate. School districts and communities are reacting to the ground swell of concern over violence. It is not a matter of *whether* crime will occur in a school district, but *when* it will occur and how serious it will be. Unlike the generations of children before them, children today have become increasingly more violent. Although only a small percentage of these children are problematic, they have a tremendous influence on other children, and the disruptions they cause waste a tremendous amount of time and labor. Arguments that were once settled with knives or fists are now settled with guns, and these arguments are growing increasingly trivial in nature.

In dealing with children and violence from a personal perspective, a number of parents and educators believe that there is no bad kid. Many parents have a difficult time bringing themselves to accept the fact that their young or teenage children did something that was criminal or violent. Many believe that any kid can be saved. Whether that is true or not is open to debate, but this mentality presents a problem for school security professionals—a problem that requires flexibility and the professional application of traditional and innovative security practices. Many parents foster the school-against-us attitude, perhaps as a result of their own unpleasant experiences in the educational system. Compounding the problem is the number of children who are having children.

Education is one of the elements that has an influence on crime. In addition to the quality of education offered in the schools, the following have an important effect on crime rates: the quality of moral education offered in the home; family stability and cohesiveness; the mobility of society and the dislocation of family members; and whether the society teaches that citizens are subordinate to authority, to manners, and to respect for people or celebrates and rules in favor of self-expression, individual freedom, and resistance to authority. Crime may be the price we pay for the individualism that our culture reveres.

Not a day goes by without a mention in the media about how serious safety and security problems in school have become. The media will report on what's taking place in the community, and schools are now increasingly experiencing media coverage and exposure involving incidents that are uncomfortable to address and require deliberate actions on the part of school administrators. The news coverage of school violence has increased more than 300 percent in the past two years.[2] According to a survey by the Center for Media and Public Affairs, the network evening newscasts doubled their coverage of crime and violence in 1993, and the coverage of murder was three times as high as in 1992.[3] The three major networks aired 1,632 domestic crime stories in 1993 and 830 in 1992.[4] The schools, however, are not the chaotic jungles that they are often portrayed or perceived to be, but we can easily come under the influence of our expectations and perceptions. Still, the increasing coverage of crime in the media is contagious, and with it comes the necessary justification for school districts to shift some resources from academic and educational purposes to increased security-related programs and personnel.

Safety and security issues continue to influence the way the nation's schools are operated, designed, and constructed. These issues are no longer ancillary issues, but top concerns that are reinforced by statistical realities. According to a 1993 national survey by the Center for Disease Control and Prevention, one in twenty students carried a gun to school at least once a month.[5] According to the National Education Goals Report in 1991, one in four high school seniors reported that they had been threatened with violence, and 14 percent said that they had been injured in school.[6] In a 1993 survey of sixty-five thousand students across the nation, 550 of the students in grades ten to twelve knew that weapons were regularly brought to school. Nearly 80 percent said that violence often results from something as simple as bumping into someone and that students, as a rule, do not feel safe from violence in school.[7] A Justice Department study reported that every day in American schools at least 35,000 students bring a gun to classes, 160,000 students skip classes because they fear physical harm, forty students are hurt or killed by firearms, 6,250 teachers are threatened with bodily injury, and 260 teachers are physically assaulted.[8] According to Handgun Control, Inc., and the Center to Prevent Handgun Violence an average of fourteen children and teenagers are killed with guns each day, the leading cause of death for both black and white teenage boys is gunshot wounds, and firearms kill more people between the ages of fifteen and twenty-four than all natural causes combined.[9] The good news is that according to another study done in New York City, students reported that weapons possession, fighting, and threats are less likely to occur on school campuses than in other community settings,[10] perhaps because schools are beginning to do a better job of promoting awareness and attention to security, supervising students, and having a more visible security presence.

WORKING TOGETHER TO SOLVE THE PROBLEM

Clearly, we cannot achieve excellence in education without order and discipline in the schools. We must begin by establishing clear and consistent discipline policies, installing new and appropriate security devices, instituting stricter security measures, locking school doors, and hiring and training school security professionals. We must also simultaneously pay attention to the established principles of effective education because it will take both approaches working together to bridge the gap and noticeably improve education and society.

The challenge is learning how to quickly and permanently reduce crime and violence in the schools to a manageable or acceptable level. Changes in attitudes and cooperation must take place. Educators must embrace the use of security principles and methodologies and must recognize the value of security professionals and criminal justice involvement in the school environment. They must treat security as a requisite component of education and an integral part of the school infrastructure. They must consider the important role that school climate and environment play in influencing how students, staff, principals, and parents relate, solve problems, and interact with one another. They must also understand that educators and security have different roles and both must be respectful and mutually supportive of those roles.

The violence we are confronting in the schools is not solely a school problem, but a problem that must be addressed by communities, houses of worship, businesses, and parents as well as educators. Today, school districts are probably doing more than their share of addressing and attempting to correct the problem. They are employing numerous strategies, both long and short term. Some require little resources; others require resources that school districts often cannot afford. Some strategies demand a change in habits; others involve a change in perceptions. Together, these strategies will probably have a significant effect on solving the problem of crime and violence in the schools, but most will take time and consistent reinforcement by all segments of society. For our schools and communities to be safe for our young people, we must first work on making them safe, decent, and nurturing places in which students can live, play, interact, and have hope.

The obligation to provide a safe and secure environment is often complicated by the increasingly wide range of after-school activities and public events that occur on school property. It is relatively easy to design tightly controlled physical environments; it is more difficult to balance the need for security against the need for an accepting educational environment. These competing goals require difficult choices. If we react too quickly or do not react quickly enough to include professional security programs and management in educational administration, schools could easily appear to become interchangeable with prisons or instead become a comfortable and warm environment that is reasonably safe and secure for education to take place.

THE NEED TO ACT NOW

School districts today are confronted with the ultimate public relations challenge ever—school crime and violence. They must do more than stick their heads in the sand and deny the problem, give it only lip service, or put up smoke and mirrors in order to confuse the real issues.

In the words of British statesman Edmund Burke, "The only thing necessary for the triumph of evil is that good men do nothing." Too often, school officials and community leaders talk about the problem of crime and violence in the schools but really do nothing. School districts must also cease intimidating employees who come forward with the truth about irregular and manipulative procedures administrators become a part of. They must become accountable by becoming truly proactive instead of reactive when it comes to planning for and managing education and security/law enforcement needs together.

Survival politics and imagery play a key role in school districts' public relations programs. What school district can or should say that security is not one of its top goals for the year? Saying and doing are two different things, however. Most school districts across the country are not large. Most have fewer than ten thousand students and only a small number of schools. They, understandably, do not have the financial resources needed to make changes, especially with declining or stagnant budgets.

Educators are sometimes apprehensive about collecting and maintaining actual data about crime that occurs on school grounds for fear that the results will reflect negatively or even sometimes accurately on a school's reputation or on an administrator's management skills. However, educators must realize that only by acknowledging and analyzing the problem can they begin to target the assets and support they need to solve or minimize the problem.

School administrators who have personal knowledge of safety- and security-related problems and do not take affirmative action or who act contrary to professional security and law enforcement recommendations may ultimately be found to be negligent or in violation of the standard of "deliberate indifference." They place their districts and their personal assets at risk.

TAKING THE FIRST STEPS

It is not too late to start thinking about and implementing security strategies. The best time to make security a requisite component of a school district's successful educational mission was probably ten years ago. The second best time, however, is now! Even school districts that cannot afford to spend the money required to secure a school physically according to current industry standards and to protect its students, employees, and visitors as desired can certainly work on planning for and implementing changes that will make them measurably more secure or at least psychologically secure.

The first giant step in providing good school security is to devise a written security and loss prevention plan for the school district and to implement professional security operations and supervision. Not only does school crime and violence affect education, but sooner or later, dwindling property assets due to lack of good security and loss prevention planning will also have an effect on the quality of education that a school district can afford to provide. The security plan should be realistic in what can be accomplished, concentrating on short- and long-range strategic initiatives.

Once security professionals have identified deficiencies and recommended improvements, action plans should be set in motion, monitored, and adjusted until the recommended changes or upgrades are accomplished. If recommendations are based not only on available security technology and professional standards, but also on budget and labor constraints, improvement will be possible. When the recommended measures cannot be instituted, the school district must have a strong employee security awareness training program and must be strict about enforcing security procedures. Security must be stressed as a requisite component of education and an integral part of the school infrastructure. It should also be emphasized that improving security means changing habits and possibly being inconvenienced by new procedures. All employees should be made to understand that they must accept change and that school security is everyone's responsibility. When all employees accept this concept, the results will be a reduction of crime and violence and a greater protection of people and property.

POPULAR STRATEGIES IN USE TODAY

Some of the strategies being used today are necessarily educational in nature, and this is appropriate because we must change behavior. We have tried incarcerating criminals, but this hasn't stemmed the growth of crime. The United States has succeeded in locking up more criminals than any other nation, even more than the so-called police states. We now incarcerate 455 people per 100,000, compared to 97 in England and 40 in the Netherlands. We seem to believe that criminal sanctions will win the "war on drugs" and solve our other problems. Arrests, convictions, and imprisonment for drug offenses, as one example, have risen sharply, but what does this really show? It does not necessarily indicate a change in behavior, but rather a change in the patterns of enforcement and punishment in the criminal justice system. This approach has not lead to a noticeable improvement in the drug problem.[11] Statistics show that the use of drugs among young people is again on the rise.[12]

A number of school districts across the United States have implemented educational and behavioral programs and strategies in attempts to counter the rise of crime and violence in the schools. Some of these programs work well; others are still being evaluated. Most will need time, reinforcement, and participation to have an effect on the root problems. Here are some of the programs that schools are trying out:

- Alternative programs or schools
- Multicultural curricula
- Human/ethnic sensitivity training
- Implementing and enforcing discipline policies consistently and fairly
- Teaching conflict resolution and problem solving to students and teachers
- Drug education programs
- In-school suspension
- Truancy abatement programs
- Partnerships
- Parental support and involvement programs
- Peer mediation training
- Life skills training (empirical data shows great promise)
- Anger management
- Saturday detention
- On-site probation officers
- Student courts
- Adopt-a-student programs
- Mentoring programs
- After-school activities
- Intramural sports in middle/junior high schools
- Community involvement initiatives
- Strengthened relationships with juvenile courts, human services, and law enforcement
- Educating the community about school problems
- Educating the media about problems and proactive efforts by schools
- Establishing zero-tolerance policies
- Teaching more effective classroom management skills
- Teaching nonverbal message skills
- Reporting, collecting, and analyzing incident data

Let's turn now to a few of the security-related programs and practices that some schools are using. *Integration* is a popular buzzword in the security industry today. It often has to do with combining an alarm system with other systems, such as energy management, access control, identification badging, and closed-circuit television.[13] We must also look at integrating security into the school setting and making security a requisite component of education.

We have to make changes from our old comfortable ways. The Crime Prevention through Environmental Design (CPTED) process is a good start. Many schools were designed years before security became a necessary concern. The CPTED process analyzes the design of a structure and its intended use in relation to the area in which it is located. It identifies everything about the building's design, placement, or use that might create an opportunity for crime to occur. Having identified these vulnerabilities, the next step is to determine ways to modify these elements to reduce or eliminate security risks and to increase the quality of life of the user of the space. The CPTED process is best incorporated into the design, review, and construction of new buildings.[14] This is the best time to reduce or eliminate the opportunity for criminal behavior through design modification. Although it is less costly than modifying an existing building, declining budgets often cannot accommodate the desired CPTED process.

The standard security approaches of locks, lights, alarms, and awareness education can help mitigate crime-related problems, and often these do not have to be budget-busting techniques or fixes. By surveying the site and getting input from administrators and employees, schools can make small, cost-effective modifications (even things as simple as notice signs) that help increase the appearance of security and control on school buildings and grounds. We must get away from the old-fashioned concept of welcoming everyone, no matter what. We must instead say, "Welcome, but here are the rules, and we expect them to be followed." An image of having a security presence and control helps deter crimes of opportunity. Criminals will choose to act somewhere else if they believe that they will be unsuccessful on school property. In addition, a strong security image goes a long way in encouraging those who use the facility to cooperate with desired school procedures and policies.

This security concept also applies in schools. Administrators, teachers, and security or police personnel must have high visibility and presence. Not only is this a great deterrent, but it also allows for a quick and effective response to serious incidents, which results in less disruption. Students and their parents see this response, and they believe that the schools are safer. There is little evidence that "getting tough" with children deters crime, whereas prevention programs have proven effectiveness.

The following are some of the security-related programs in place today in an increasing number of schools:

- Using metal detectors in a district administrative random inspection program
- Increasing the number and use of radios for security and other staff
- Increasing staff presence in halls and on the grounds
- Implementing security volunteer programs involving parents and others
- Developing and exercising plans to deal with crisis situations
- Consistently enforcing and applying discipline for violations of the law or school rules and regulations
- Informing and showing students and parents that disruption will not be tolerated and that students will be held accountable for their actions
- Reporting and documenting all incidents and analyzing what's happening, where, and when
- Developing strategies to reduce, eliminate, or even relocate the problem incidents
- Using drug- and explosive-detection dogs or other detection methods and equipment
- Keeping field testing kits for drugs and alcohol
- Posting visitor notice signs at all entrances and on the grounds
- Controlling personnel movement and limiting access

- Instituting an employee and visitor identification badging program throughout the system and enforcing the program
- Installing appropriate access-control, intrusion-detection, and related equipment (locks, card readers, alarm systems, and so on)
- Using closed-circuit television (CCTV) or portable video cameras to deter and assess unwanted activity on buses, in parking lots, halls, cafeterias, stairwells, at athletic events, and so on (There are many CCTV systems on the market, but they are expensive and require extra effort. Portable security cameras cost less, are inexpensive to install, and can be used as a deterrent with little additional effort.)
- Devising gang prevention programs and strategies
- Using physical security surveys and assessments by security professionals to identify vulnerabilities and solutions
- Using security personnel for security duties only; having them patrol with security in mind and respond in a professional manner
- Adding call-back communications between office and classrooms, including portable classrooms
- Instituting district-wide standardized procedures for security personnel
- Devising a written security and loss prevention plan for the district
- Conducting security operations and management from a district central location/department

THE ROLE OF SECURITY IN THE SCHOOLS

The field of public school security has only recently come into its own. However, it plays a very relevant and important role in almost everyone's personal life and in society because of the traumatic increase in criminal acts and violence committed by young people in schools and in the community. Crime and violence have been so commonplace and frequent in schools across our country—whether urban, suburban, or rural—that a school security or police presence is not only required but expected to maintain good discipline and control and to reduce incidents of crime and violence.

Security personnel in public schools must be more than cops. They must also be educators and counselors. This is truly school oriented policing in action. The school oriented policing concept is one where the officer (police/security) is involved in activity that allows for greater flexibility and use of discretion to interact with students and teachers and coordinate activities with other police, public agencies, and community members within the area they operate. In this role, the officer becomes more proactive in forming the type of partnerships that will be effective in preventing and deterring violent and criminal incidents in the school and the surrounding community.

Crime prevention and security awareness are more effective and less costly than reacting to criminal incidents, particularly when considering effective public relations.[15] Regardless of the size of the school district, a definite set of security objectives must be defined. However, there is only one bottom-line objective for security: the maintenance and improvement of the school district's health. It is similar to the advice given in *The Wealthy Barber*[16] on how to plan for a comfortable financial future. It's a monthly purchase plan involving dollar cost averaging, forced savings, long-term growth, and a low PITA (pain in the—). Good planning, similarly, is necessary for a school district's future.

The importance of school security and law enforcement management has never before been as obvious or as recognized as in today's complex and turbulent society. The work of security and police professionals is often concerned with human behavior, and helping people exercise social control is a ceaseless job.[17] This includes children, who have constitutional rights and face legal consequences when they violate the law. The popular approach of the past concentrated on enforcement. Today, however, in a society where inattention, lack of accountability, changing values, and inharmonious relationships seem to be the norm, security and law enforcement professionals must be innovative and proactive, employing traditional and nontraditional security techniques when dealing with public schools and our youth, or they must accept the fact that violent crime will continue to increase. Community- and school-oriented policing concepts are a relevant approach because security and law enforcement cannot do the job alone. To reduce crime in the schools, they must work with citizens, parents, houses of worship, schools, businesses, other governmental agencies, and also students to form partnerships and promote awareness.

THE NEED FOR PROFESSIONAL SECURITY MANAGEMENT

Whether a school district has a school police department, a school security department, or contract security personnel, the security function must be operated and managed by a career security professional according to established security and police procedures. You wouldn't expect anyone but a licensed pilot to fly a passenger jet, and you wouldn't expect anyone but a certified teacher to lead a class, so why would a school district even consider operating security or police personnel with anyone but a security or police management professional? Security programs are only effective when they are managed and operated by professional security managers or executives with years of prevention and enforcement experience, with organizational knowledge, and with tactful and effective people skills.

The security program must address planning, training, written procedures, supervision, reinforcement, and monitoring. It must also be flexible in adjusting security measures and initiatives because security is a very fluid and dynamic profession where the only constant is change. The security force must be centrally organized and operated, with proper professional management and supervision. In addition, properly documented training, yearly refresher training, and written orders and standard operating procedures must be in place.

The solution to meeting the challenge of providing safe schools for our children depends on the professional security managers, supervisors, and leaders of a school district—and on their ability to accept the need for change, to do their jobs, and work together. They will ultimately determine the quality and effect of the rank-and-file security or police officers, the security program itself, and how the program is supported by nonsecurity employees. Professional security leaders and school administration leaders both must understand the need for, and not be afraid to empower and properly train, all security supervisors and officers. However, at the same time, they must insist on strong supervision and aggressive individual action, and they must not tolerate unprofessional conduct and appearances.

CONCLUSION

Many kids today live like orphans. There is not much that educators and security professionals can do to significantly improve their quality of life. However, we can provide a safe and secure environment where they can receive the education they deserve. The finest gift we can give our children is a good education.

NOTES

1. Joseph D. Dear, Kathleen Scott, and Dorie Marshall, "An Attack on School Violence," *School Safety* (Winter 1994): 7.
2. Ibid., p. 5.
3. Ellen Edwards, "Coverage on Crime, Violence Has Doubled," *Norfolk Virginian-Pilot*, March 7, 1994: A1.
4. Ibid.
5. Walt Landen, "Violence and Our Schools: What Can We Do?" *Updating School Board Policy* 23 (February 1992): 1.
6. Ibid.
7. Mary Tobias Weaver, "Gazing into a Crystal Ball," *School Safety* (Winter 1994): 8.
8. Keith Baker, "Can Leopards Change Their Spots?" *The Quarterly,* Magazine of the National Association of School Safety and Law Enforcement Officers (March 1993): 3.
9. Bob Herbert, "Firearm Death Toll Last Year: 38,317," *Norfolk Virginian-Pilot*, March 7, 1994: A2.
10. Michael Furlong, "Evaluating School Violence Trends," *School Safety* (Winter 1994): 27.
11. Edwin Yoder, "Lock 'em-up Plans Aren't Going to Work," *Norfolk Virginian-Pilot*, February 2, 1994: B4.
12. "Growing Use of Illicit Drugs, Alcohol, Cigarettes among Intermediate and High School Students," *School Security Report* vol. 10, no. 5 (1994): 8.
13. ———James Keener, "Integrated Systems: What They Are and Where They Are Heading," *Security Technology and Design*, vol. 4, no. 4 (May 1994): 6.
14. Timothy Crowe, "Safer Schools by Design," *Security Management* (September 1991): 81.
15. Mark Beaudry, "A Unified Approach to Crime Prevention?" *Security Management* (March 1993): 98.
16. David Chilton, *The Wealthy Barber* (Rockland, Calif.: Prima Publishing, 1991).
17. Patrick V. Murphy, "Policing and Effective Law Enforcement," *Intergovernmental Perspectives* 19, no. 2 (Spring 1993): 26.

How not to solve your school district security problem
"School crime and violence: The ultimate PR and Liability Challenge"

Chapter 1

Introduction

To be effective, a security and loss prevention program must receive attention and support from all echelons within an organization. Not only does there have to be a written plan or policy to deal with day to day activities in a school—for preventing, deterring, or handling violent and criminal incidents—but also a plan to deal with crises, the foreseeable, and the unexpected. In order to be prepared and responsible, these functions must be carried out by professionally trained, organized, and operated personnel.

Definitions

For the purpose of this manual, the following definitions apply.

Activity, Facility, or Location.   A real property entity consisting of one or more of the following: a building or a structure with a utility system, pavement, or underlying land (for example, a schoolhouse, warehouse, or transportation facility).

Administrative Inspection.   A cursory inspection of a person or the contents of a vehicle or package with the full consent of the person, operator, or owner of the vehicle or package. Administrative inspections are conducted with prior written notice and authorization, and they follow predetermined procedures.

Administrative Officer.   A person in charge of or responsible for an activity, facility, or program operation. Includes assistant superintendents, principals, directors, department heads, and so on.

Exception.   A written, approved, long-term (two years or longer) or permanent deviation from a specific provision of this instruction. Exceptions require compensatory or equivalent security measures.

Installation.   A group of facilities located in the same vicinity that supports a particular function (for example, school plant facilities/transportation/warehouse on one site).

Loss Prevention.   The part of an overall facility security program that deals with the resources, measures, and tactics devoted to the care and protection of property. Loss prevention includes identifying and reporting missing, lost, stolen, and recovered property, including documents and computer media, and developing trend analyses to plan and implement reactive and proactive loss prevention measures.

Physical Security.   The part of a facility's security program that is concerned with physical measures designed to safeguard personnel; prevent unauthorized access to equipment, facilities, material, computer media, and documents; and safeguard these against damage, theft, and other criminal acts.

Physical Security and loss prevention Program.   Part of the overall security program at an activity. Physical security and loss prevention measures include instructions, procedures, plans, policies, agreements, systems, and resources committed to safeguard personnel, protect property, and prevent losses. Physical security is concerned with the means and measures designed to safeguard personnel and protect property by preventing, detecting, and confronting acts of unauthorized access, wrongful destruction, malicious damage, theft, pilferage, and so on.

Loss prevention is particularly concerned with preventing loss of supplies, tools, equipment, or other material while it is being issued, used, stored, or transported. Not only does loss prevention focus on the threat of criminal activity and acts of wrongdoing by individuals outside the activity, but it also specifically addresses internal threats: theft and pilferage by those who have authorized access, inattention to physical security practices and procedures, and disregard for property controls and accountability.

Physical Security Audit.   An examination of the physical security and loss prevention programs of an activity to determine compliance with physical security policy. A physical security audit is conducted by the coordinator or director of security (or another appropriate person). Follow-up action to correct noted deficiencies is advised.

Physical Security Survey/Assessment.   A specific on-site examination and evaluation of an activity's physical security and loss prevention programs by the office of security or other security professional to determine the activity's vulnerabilities and compliance with physical security policies. Survey results are used primarily as a management tool by the surveyed activity and the coordinator of security to "harden" the school as a target and improve security.

Property.   All assets, including real property, facilities, funds, and negotiable instruments; tools and equipment; material and supplies; communications towers and antennas and power transformers; computer software and hardware; and information in the form of documents and other media, whether categorized as routine or special, unclassified or confidential, nonsensitive or sensitive, critical, valuable, or precious.

Security Force.   The portion of a security organization in a school district that comprises security, police, contract guard personnel, or a combination, that is tasked to provide security, physical security, or law enforcement. The size and composition of the security force depends on the district's and activity's size, geographic location, criticality of assets, and vulnerability and accessibility, as determined by the administration, activity administrative officer, the director of security, as well as on budgetary constraints.

Special Reaction Team. A small element of the local law enforcement agency that is organized, trained, and equipped to provide rapid armed response to critical incidents beyond the normal scope of the law enforcement agency.

Theft. The taking of property without the owner's consent with the intent to deprive the owner of the value of the property and to appropriate it to the use or benefit of the person taking it. Theft is a common name for larceny and pilferage. (Refer to Appendix 5 for a more detailed discussion on pilferage and its prevention.)

Purpose

The purpose of this manual is to establish regulations and to standardize requirements for physical security and loss prevention at _____ activities. Specifically, this manual:

- Establishes uniform minimum standards
- Provides guidance for evaluating, planning, and implementing the Physical Security and Loss Prevention Program
- Relates physical security measures to physical security interests
- Provides a basis for determining cost-effective physical security measures and upgrades through standardized practices
- Assists those responsible for physical security in their efforts to carry out their assigned tasks

Scope

This manual covers responsibilities for physical security, security/law enforcement, and loss prevention. It classifies various security hazards, details protective measures, and distinguishes between recommended physical security measures and required measures. Directive words, such as *should, will,* and *must,* indicate that the physical security measure is mandatory or strongly advised.

This manual applies to all _____ activities.

This manual places specific emphasis on measures to assist in identifying, analyzing, reducing, and eliminating loss of property. Improvement of physical security is essential to loss prevention.

The uniformity and compatibility of security requirements and the elimination of conflicting guidance are primary objectives of this manual. The Physical Security and Loss Prevention Program addresses the protection of personnel and property. Such protection is accomplished by identifying the property requiring protection, assessing the threat, committing resources, and determining jurisdiction and boundaries; by establishing perimeters, barriers, and access control; by providing the means to detect efforts to remove wrongfully, damage, or destroy property; and by employing a professional security force sufficient to protect, react to, and confront situations that threaten personnel and property. When property has special characteristics, such as when it is confidential or sensitive, additional physical security requirements are necessary, and measures will be tailored to the needs of the property and the organizational unit dealing with it.

THE SECURITY PROBLEM

The security problem is influenced by the mission of the activity, the type and jurisdiction of the property, the geographic location and size of the activity, the topography of the area, the economic, political, and community atmosphere, potential and existing threats, past problems, and the logistical and operational support provided by other organizations, elements, or school staff.

Leased Space (Real Property) Security

Activities located within leased-space facilities confront unique physical security issues, such as commercial firms or contractors located in the building, public facilities, shared entranceways, and common spaces. When applicable, activities will use the guidance and policies contained in Chapter 3 in determining security and protective measures deemed essential for their particular spaces, areas, and buildings. Liaison with appropriate authorities, building administrators, lessors, and so on, is essential to delineate specific security measures that are necessary for the protection of lives and property and are tailored to the individual characteristics of the leased space. All lease agreements should address security as appropriate and consultation should be made with the office of security.

This manual applies to all _____ spaces. Many security standards contained here, however, cannot be implemented at leased locations for various unique reasons. Physical security standards that cannot be met, either temporarily or permanently, must be identified, and an exception request must be submitted to the office of security. Compensatory security measures implemented or planned must also be identified in all such requests.

SECURITY RESPONSIBILITIES

Security is the direct, immediate, and moral responsibility of everyone in the employment of _____. Specific responsibilities are set forth in the following sections. The willingness to support change and the acceptance of responsibility for personal involvement usually result in greater protection for people and property.

Director of Security

The director of security (DOS) will oversee implementation of _____ security, physical security, law enforcement, and loss prevention policy and programs. His or her responsibilities include conducting compliance audits; providing advice, assessment, and assistance to activity administrative officers; assisting in the development of plans for security upgrades and enhancement; and coordinating and directing security force activities.

Specifically, the DOS will do the following:

- Plan, manage, implement, direct, and supervise the _____ security, physical security, law enforcement, and loss prevention program, including developing and maintaining comprehensive district physical security instructions and regulations
- Determine the adequacy of the physical security and loss prevention programs, identify areas that need improvement, and recommend such improvement to the superintendent/deputy superintendent and building administrators as appropriate
- Develop and maintain a current physical security plan
- Conduct security surveys/assessments, audits, and investigations
- Identify and prioritize the real property, structures, and assets to be protected
- Assess the threat to activities
- Determine and identify the resources needed to implement effective security and loss prevention programs
- Recognize constraints in resource application
- Determine and recommend the establishment of barriers and points of ingress and egress as they pertain to access control
- Develop and maintain personnel identification and access-control systems as required
- Coordinate the security requirements of the activities and ensure that those requirements are addressed and considered in security planning and operations
- Provide technical assistance on all security matters
- Ensure that liaison concerning mutual security responsibilities is maintained with local, state, and federal agencies
- Develop security aspects of crisis management; participate in the planning, direction, coordination, and implementation of procedures for managing situations that pose a threat to the security of activities; and act as a crisis manager and a primary staff adviser during any security-related crisis
- Identify through surveys, audits, and budget submissions, physical security procedures, equipment, and security upgrades that will detect, delay, deter, and/or prevent wrongful removal, damage, destruction, or compromise of protected property or will endanger students, employees, or visitors
- Identify other security and physical security measures and procedures necessary to accomplish the security mission
- Establish and maintain records relating to property loss, violations, and breaches of security measures and procedures (these records will be retained for at least three years)
- Establish and maintain liaison and working relationships and agreements with federal, state, and local law enforcement agencies
- Serve as facilitator of and be responsible for the minutes and records of the Security Advisory and Awareness Council (SAAC) or similar purpose council when established
- Maintain contact with and solicit advice from the state/city/commonwealth attorney concerning the legal aspects of security and law enforcement

- Develop, maintain, and administer an ongoing security awareness program encompassing security, crime prevention, loss prevention, and local threats
- Develop and maintain a loss prevention program and supporting loss prevention plan that
  - Identifies and prioritizes by likelihood of loss assigned property susceptible to theft or pilferage
  - Establishes procedures for adequate internal and external investigative measures and for the review and trend analysis of losses
  - Establishes functional areas and designates personnel to be active in and responsible for loss reporting, review, trend analysis, and investigative requests
  - Helps establish procedures for ensuring that all losses and gains, inventory adjustments, and property surveys are reported
  - Monitors legal, disciplinary, and administrative procedures and remedies applicable to individuals who are found responsible and liable for losses
- Organize, train, and operate the security force
- Prepare post orders, standard operating procedures (see Appendix 11), and training plans for the security force, including jurisdiction, use of force, apprehension and temporary detention of intruders and violators, and other appropriate law enforcement and security-related topics
- Develop written security orders or directives to cover all phases of security operations

Administrative Officer

The administrative officer (AO) of an activity (school, transportation, warehouse, food services, school plant facilities, and so on) is responsible for security at that activity. He or she will establish and maintain a physical security and loss prevention program in cooperation with and in support of the office of security. The AO will provide sufficient resources to implement, manage, and execute an effective physical security and loss prevention program, including providing appropriate space with the necessary supplies and office equipment where security officers are assigned.

ORGANIZATION OF THE OFFICE OF SECURITY

The office of security will be organized in the following manner (specific districts may vary). The director of security (DOS) will report to the superintendent or deputy superintendent on all matters pertaining to security, physical security, law enforcement, and loss prevention at each of the activities. All other administrative and department heads will provide sufficient material and support to maintain an adequate security and loss prevention posture.

The office of security will have at least five divisions: Staff, Operations, Physical Security, Training, and Investigations. Other associated security functions may be added as divisions or as staff members of the office of security as needed.

Staff Division

The Staff Division will consist of the DOS, security secretary, Division heads, and others as deemed necessary to operate and provide leadership for the office of security. It is the mission of the Staff Division to coordinate and direct security activities, execute planning, handle financial matters, provide guidance, ensure policies and regulations are complied with, and establish regulations and supervision as relates to the operation of security force personnel.

Operations Division

The Operations Division will be responsible for all security and law enforcement patrol functions. The Operations Division officer will report directly to the DOS and be responsible for the performance of duties assigned. This is a "chain-of-command" statement which means that the person who has this job will be responsible for those described functions and will report to the DOS directly for guidance and accountability of the functions. Assigned duties could be said another way: as assigned functional responsibilities and duties; or as duties assigned.

Physical Security Division

The Physical Security Division will be responsible for all administrative functions normally associated with a security operation, including loss prevention, crime prevention, badge control, access control, plans, surveys, intrusion detection, and assessment. The Physical Security Division officer will report to the DOS for the performance of assigned duties.

Training Division

The Training Division will be responsible for the training of the security force and for the security awareness training of all employees. The Training Division officer will report to the DOS for the performance of duties assigned.

Investigations Division

The Investigations Division will be responsible for investigating all cases of a criminal, serious, or disruptive nature and any other cases assigned. The division will maintain effective liaison with local, state, federal, and other law and regulatory enforcement and intelligence agencies. The Investigations Division officer will report directly to the DOS and be responsible for the performance of duties assigned.

SECURITY ADVISORY AND AWARENESS COUNCIL

The principal of each school, along with the directors of transportation, food services, school plant facilities, warehouse, and other stand-alone physical sites, will designate, in writing, a person to be on the Security Advisory and Awareness Council. Members of the council will advise and assist in applying the standards of and implementing the program for physical security and loss prevention set forth in this manual. The members of the council will:

- Assist in determining the requirements for and evaluating the security afforded to areas of their activity
- Review physical security and loss prevention plans and recommended changes when appropriate
- Review reports of significant losses or breaches of security and recommend improvements to the Security and Loss Prevention Program
- Serve as a vehicle for employee security awareness and reindoctrination training at their activity

Membership

The SAAC will, as a minimum, include the following members:

- The director of security (or designated representative)
- Each office of security division head
- An investigator or security officer from each school assigned
- Designated representative from each school and other administration departments

Meetings and Minutes

Council members or their representatives will meet as required, but at least annually. Minutes of the meeting will be made a matter of record, and such records will be retained a minimum of three years. Meetings may be held in conjunction with other meetings as appropriate.

FACILITIES

Crime Prevention through Environmental Design

The Crime Prevention Through Environmental Design (CPTED) process, as explained by Timothy Crowe, addresses the idea that the proper design and effective use of the built environment can lead to a reduction in crime and the fear of crime and an improvement in the quality of life. The CPTED process emphasizes the physical environment, human behavior, the productive use of space, and the resulting crime and loss prevention. There are many strategies involved in the CPTED process. School design directly affects the behavior patterns of students, teachers, and visitors alike. The CPTED process helps school administrators understand how the constructed environment can affect behavior. (See Appendix 13.)

New Construction

New construction will comply with the requirements of this manual and appropriate physical security design and principles. Plans for new construction, incorporating physical security features, will be reviewed by the office of security or a designated representative during the design process and the various review stages. It is the responsibility of the office of school planning to include the office of security in construction planning and review processes to help prevent crime through the use of CPTED principles. The CPTED School Security Survey Forms found in Appendix 13 should be used as a guide.

Facility Modifications

Physical security enhancement modifications (new intrusion-detection alarm system equipment, security fencing, security lighting, locks, and so on) to existing buildings, facilities, or sites will be reviewed by the office of security during the design process and review stages or when enhancements are considered. Modification requests will be forwarded to the office of school planning via the office of security, which will ensure that changes are consistent with applicable security criteria and the CPTED process.

Chapter 2

Security and Loss Prevention Planning

GENERAL

Security planning is a constant process carried out both in advance of and concurrently with security operations. Normally, the planning for any security operation will follow a typical pattern: the estimate, the plan, and implementation in the administrative plan or appendixes. The security estimate, with its analysis of the mission and the situation (courses of action and decision), provides the basis for the security plan. Each activity will develop and publish a security and loss prevention plan, as set forth in Chapter 1. The office of security will be available to facilitate and assist with this plan. The security plan will contain standard operating procedures that detail the required crisis management actions with separate appendixes for fires, disturbances, major accidents, hostage situations, bomb threats, natural disasters, and other appropriate foreseeable crises.

SECURITY PLANS

Orders or directives will be established to cover all phases of security operations. They will be disseminated to everyone who is charged with security responsibilities. Such orders or directives must provide instruction relative to individual security responsibilities, authority, and procedures for handling and reporting incidents. These directives must be current and must reflect the routine needs of the activity as well as unusual situations that require special security measures. Plans should be realistic, focusing on what can actually be accomplished, not what looks or sounds good. Contingency plans will contain provisions for reinforcement of the security force when necessary.

FORMAT

A sample physical security plan is included in Appendix 1. Each physical security plan, however, should be written in the format that is most applicable to the relevant activity. For small activities, a chapter or memorandum in the school improvement plan that discusses physical security, defines access controls, establishes a lock and key control program and a loss prevention program, and implements the overall security plan may suffice. For moderate-size activities, a letter-type directive with enclosures addressing specialized subjects, such as crisis management, loss prevention, access-control procedures, and emergency responses, may be adequate, particularly if it is well integrated with a comprehensive disaster preparedness instruction. For large activities, a physical security plan that is written as a manual (with appendixes) may be more appropriate. Regardless of format, the plan must be a user's instruction that clearly delineates how users should conduct day-to-day security and how they should respond to security incidents. It should not be philosophical or a verbatim reiteration of this manual. It should reflect the detailed implementation of true practices at the activity.

SECURITY CONSIDERATIONS

The following security measures will be considered when developing physical security plans:

- Personnel screening and indoctrination/security training
- Protection for vulnerable points and assets within the activity
- Security force organization, training, operation, and supervision
- Personnel identification and movement control systems
- Installation of physical security hardware (for example, intrusion-detection systems, barriers, access-control systems)
- Key and lock control
- Coordination with other agencies via the office of security
- Appropriate crisis measures (for example, hostage plans)

CALCULATED RISK

The concept of calculated risk dictates that when there are limited resources available for protection, possible loss or damage to some supplies or to a portion of the activity is risked to ensure a greater degree of security to the remaining supplies or activity concerns. Each activity should prioritize such risks taking into account existing manpower availability, alternative or creative use of existing manpower, and existing physical security measures in place.

CRISIS SITUATIONS

In evaluating the need for physical protection and the extent to which it is required, the possibility of injury to security force and administrative personnel must be considered. This is especially relevant when addressing security measures to be taken during crises (for example, bomb threats, fires, criminal incidents, natural catastrophes, hostage situations) to protect assets and personnel, to limit damage and provide emergency services to contain the incident, and to restore the activity to normal operation.

Situations that present unique and growing physical security concerns are the handling of bomb threats and criminal incidents as well as any change to the school climate that creates conditions for violence to take place. Bomb threat planning should be coordinated and cross-referenced with disaster preparedness and fire plans and should include preventive measures to reduce the opportunity for the introduction of bombs and other items, procedures for evaluating and handling threatening messages, a policy on evacuation and the safety of personnel, search procedures, procedures for obtaining assistance and support from law enforcement agencies, procedures to follow in the event that a bomb is found on the premises or in the event of an explosion or detonation. (See Appendix 2 for a discussion of bomb threats and procedures and Appendix 10 for barricaded captor/hostage situations.)

PHYSICAL SECURITY SURVEY

A physical security survey/assessment differs from an audit or review in that it covers a formal assessment of an activity's total physical security and crime prevention program. Each survey includes a complete reconnaissance, study, and analysis of the physical security of each activity's property and operation. Physical security surveys are designed to show the administration, administrative officer, and office of security what security measures are in effect and what areas need improvement and to provide a basis for determining priorities for funding and accomplishing the work.

The administrative officer, in cooperation with and in support of the office of security representative, will conduct a detailed physical security survey at least triennially (every three years) or as appropriate. Appendixes 6 and 13 will be used as a guide to this instruction, but they are not meant to be all-inclusive. Results of physical security surveys will be retained at least three years.

The office of security will also conduct a videotaped survey of each activity. This survey will show and discuss all major areas of the activity and will identify specifically known problem areas and other areas that have a potential for crisis related incidents. The office of security will maintain a library of such video assessments for use in a crisis (i.e., hostage situation, etc.).

THREAT ASSESSMENT

Oftentimes, based on incidents in the community or timely information received, hostile, violent, or criminal activity may take place in or around a school or school sponsored activity, and an administrative officer may desire to have a threat assessment conducted. These assessments can, after a preliminary investigation and evaluation, support or disprove the likelihood of these activities to occur and can further provide a basis for whether or not security countermeasures are needed.

Evaluation

Based on available information, each activity will determine the active short- and long-term threat. The office of security will supply these threat evaluations on request. Such information must be carefully analyzed to determine what additional physical security measures are necessary when the existing physical security requirements are not adequate. Possible attempts by hostile groups or criminals to penetrate the security is a matter of concern. Accordingly, the office of security will provide, upon request, an area threat assessment with the support of local law enforcement agencies.

Liaison with Law Enforcement Agencies

The office of security will maintain liaison with federal, state, and local law enforcement and intelligence agencies and will disseminate, by the most expeditious means, known threat information affecting the security of a particular activity. If an activity detects or perceives a threat, the office of security and the police will be promptly notified. Follow-up action generally consists of attempting to obtain amplifying details or intelligence regarding the perceived threat and coordinating with law enforcement personnel.

Chapter 3

Security and
Loss Prevention Measures

SECURITY MEASURES

Security and loss prevention measures are actions taken to establish or maintain an adequate physical security and loss prevention posture at an activity. Incidents can be greatly reduced by limiting the following: opportunity, misinterpretation of theft, poor relationship between management and employees, and careless management.

Collectively, security measures create conditions favorable to the maintenance of an effective security posture. They are designed to develop habits and attitudes conducive to maintaining good security and loss prevention practices and eliminating existing or potential causes of security breaches and violations.

Corrective security measures deal with breaches of security. They correct conditions that might lead to further security breaches. Corrective security measures include identifying and apprehending security violators; investigating, analyzing, and reporting losses; and instituting disciplinary or administrative personnel action; and implementing additional prevention and deterrence measures.

LOSS PREVENTION MEASURES

A vigorous loss prevention program is essential at every activity. Losses of property may prevent the timely accomplishment of mission requirements and may cost thousands of dollars annually. Losses must be minimized through the application of a comprehensive loss prevention program consisting of loss analysis, inventories, proper use of available investigative and police resources, continuing employee loss prevention education, application of firm and corrective measures, administrative personnel actions and pursuit of prosecution, and other necessary loss prevention measures. These topics will be addressed during required meetings of the Security Advisory and Awareness Council, as appropriate. At a minimum, loss prevention measures will consist of the following.

Loss Analysis

To help identify trends and patterns of losses and gains, all incidents involving reportable property must be included in an ongoing program of analysis. A continuing loss analysis process should consider the types of material lost; geographic location; times and dates; proximity of specific personnel; proximity of doorways, passageways, loading docks and ramps, gates, parking facilities, and other activities adjacent to loss or gain locations; and material movement paths. At activities with extensive losses, the loss analysis process may require the application of data-processing resources to sort and analyze the data. The resulting analysis of loss and gain trends and patterns will be used to balance the allocation of resources available for crime prevention.

Investigative and Police Resources

To prevent or reduce opportunities for losses of property, activities must establish aggressive loss prevention programs employing available investigative and law enforcement resources. Patrols of pilferable or sensitive property areas should be stressed, and a preliminary investigative capability should exist. Local loss analysis program data should be used to program security resources to combat and limit losses.

Loss Prevention Equipment

Exterior doors and windows in schools, warehouses, storage buildings, office buildings, and other structures that contain high value, sensitive, or pilferable property, supplies, or office equipment will be afforded security protection commensurate with the value and sensitivity of the contents. At a minimum, hinges either will be nonremovable or will be provided with lock and hasp security systems that meet security standards and with inside hinge protection that prevents locked doors from opening even if the hinges are removed. The use of built-in combination or mechanical push button combination locks is acceptable and encouraged.

Security padlocks should be used to add protection for high-value, sensitive, and highly pilferable property. Heavy-duty security hardware that would provide added security is available commercially. When installing heavy-duty hardware, remember that a $60 padlock attached to a 50¢ hasp provides only 50¢ worth of security protection. A medium- or high-security padlock and hasp system realizes its full potential only when it is properly installed on a strong door with appropriate hardware.

Employee Education

All employees must be indoctrinated in local procedures for preventing asset losses as well as in their responsibility for the care and protection of property. This indoctrination will be included in the employee's initial security education briefing (that is, a copy of this manual, staff orientation, and so on) upon employment and annually thereafter. Loss prevention topics will be included in recurring district or school sponsored information, newsletters, and security publications. This will be closely coordinated with the office of security. (See Chapter 9.)

Financial Responsibility

Local procedures for issuing and controlling property will ensure that strict accountability is established for those who are responsible for property that is reported as missing, lost, or stolen. Recoupment action should be undertaken against an individual in each case in which the individual's negligence or noncompliance with established procedures, instructions, or statutes result in the reportable loss of property. This recoupment action is independent of and may be taken parallel to, or be exclusive of, any formal disciplinary action, criminal procedure, or prosecution arising from the same event.

Claims

Individuals who are accountable for property must be held responsible for negligent loss. An activity that has responsibility for reporting missing, lost, stolen, and recovered property may generate a claim action to recoup the value of the loss. The claims-collection procedure may result in civil court action independent of any disciplinary action or criminal prosecution that may arise from the same event. The involvement of risk managers and insurance carriers is appropriate.

Criminal Prosecution

The activity's examination of the facts may lead to referral to legal or law enforcement authorities for criminal prosecution for violations of law. Criminal prosecution is independent of disciplinary, recoupment, or claim action arising from the incident. The activity and the office of security, in conjunction with the state/city/commonwealth attorney's office and police (if appropriate), are responsible for ensuring that any security work on criminal cases (investigations, evidence, reports, statements, and so on) is handled properly and in sufficient detail to render them acceptable for prosecution in state and local courts. The office of security will also monitor the progress of criminal issues and maintain liaison with the prosecuting attorney and the responsible law enforcement or investigative agency to coordinate and facilitate effective prosecution.

LOSS REPORTING

Missing, Lost, Stolen, or Recovered (M-L-S-R) Property Reports will be submitted as required on Form _____ report. The office of security and property inventory and control are the activities focal points for M-L-S-R reporting. The activity will submit a report within twenty-four hours after becoming aware of M-L-S-R property.

The effective reporting of losses and the maintenance of loss trend analyses are basic to determining the scope of the loss prevention program that must be developed. When reviewing property losses, it is essential to know whether the expenditure of funds on physical security will be measurable in loss reductions. If actual losses are extremely low and involve only nonsensitive, low-value, or nonhazardous materials, absorbing such losses may be more cost effective than attempting to prevent them. Nevertheless, actual losses must be reported so that an accurate decision can be made. To this end, steps must be taken to ensure that reportable losses and accountable individuals are identified. This can be done by matching property inventories, requests for investigation, inventory adjustments, and so on, with the loss reports that are submitted. Many audit and inspection reports have shown that not all required reports are submitted and that actual losses have greatly exceeded reported losses.

The following definitions are provided to clarify the meaning of terms used in this instruction.

Missing (M).   A missing item is one that is not readily accounted for.

Lost (L).   A lost item is one that positively cannot be accounted for.

Stolen (S).   A stolen item is one that is either missing or lost under circumstances indicating the possibility of criminal activity.

Recovered (R).   A recovered item is material that is (1) gained by inventory, (2) found, (3) recovered after previously being reported missing, lost, or stolen, or (4) suspected to be the remainder of a loss due to theft or fraud.

Serialized Property.   Serialized property is any item that has an individual serial number affixed by the manufacturer or the user activity or that has a _____ inventory label issued by property and inventory control.

Unserialized Property.   Unserialized property is any item that does not have an individual serial number of any type.

Value

For M-L-S-R reporting purposes, the value of an item of property will equal the current cost of purchasing a new replacement on the open market (that is, the current market value) or the current list price, whichever is greater. Depreciated values will not be used for M-L-S-R reporting or for the purpose of reducing single-line item or aggregate item values.

Accountability

In each case of loss, theft, or destruction of property that is M-L-S-R reportable, efforts will be made to establish whether the event involved negligence or noncompliance with established procedures or policies for the handling and control of property. The individuals responsible will be determined whenever possible. Anyone who is found to have been negligent or to have failed to comply with established procedures or policies will be identified in the M-L-S-R or other reports.

Investigation

All incidents involving missing, lost, or stolen property, except stock inventory results where theft is not indicated, must be reported to the police and other approved personnel and on Form _____ for investigative consideration. _____ Computerized Equipment Inventory Manual was previously provided to all schools by property and inventory control which explains reporting procedures and formatting requirements.

Summary Information

Each M-L-S-R property incident will receive special attention and will be carefully described. Stock phrases will not be used to explain losses. Recurring M-L-S-R incidents involving the same type of material often indicate the lack of adequate crime prevention or inventory control procedures, the failure to observe existing property controls and loss prevention procedures, or the lack of enforcement when procedural violations occur.

Care must be taken to explain in detail the circumstances of a loss in the initial M-L-S-R report or to estimate the date when an explanation can be expected. Narrative comments provided in M-L-S-R reports must identify security problems or deficiencies related to the incident. This is especially crucial if the incident appears to be recurrent in nature. The early identification of security problems may allow correction before an excessive number of costly, avoidable losses occur.

Specific security measures taken as a result of the incident should refer to corrective physical security measures intended to reduce future similar losses. Improvement of loss prevention is dependent on effective physical security measures.

PERIMETER AND AREA PROTECTION AND CONTROL

Before deciding to employ particular security measures, a thorough risk and threat analysis must be performed to determine the degree of physical security required. Extensive and costly security measures may be necessary to protect certain items of security interest. However, in each case, the administrative officer of an activity is responsible for complying with established security requirements while working to achieve economy. To achieve this objective, higher security requirements must be clearly understood, and the relative criticality and vulnerability of the security interest must be evaluated in relation to potential threats. A specific level of security must be calculated to ensure the best possible cost-effective protection against potential threats. Only after these preliminary factors have been addressed can proper controls be instituted.

Activity or perimeter and area protective controls are the first step in providing actual protection against certain security hazards. These controls are obtained through the use of protective barriers and other security measures. They are intended to define the activity or area boundaries and are used to channel personnel and vehicular access. Security barriers may be natural or structural. (They are addressed in Chapter 6.)

Enclave ("Island") Security

Enclave security involves providing concentrated security measures at specific sites or smaller areas within an activity. It is the preferred method for securing relatively small but sensitive or problem areas. Segregating certain areas and assets and concentrating security measures and resources for these assets is generally more cost effective than fencing the entire perimeter. A sensitive area can be separately fenced, lighted, alarmed, or guarded, or the area may be separately "enclaved" without fencing the entire facility or installation perimeter with standard chain link/ornamental fencing.

Enclave security does not eliminate the need to identify and post installation or activity perimeters. This could be accomplished by installing alternate fencing or appropriate notice signs. Different areas and tasks require different degrees of security interest depending on their purposes, nature of the work performed within, and information or materials concerned. For similar reasons, different areas within an activity may have varying degrees of security importance or concerns. To address these situations, facilitate operations, and simplify the security system, a careful application of restrictions, controls, and protective measures commensurate with varying degrees or levels of security importance is essential. In some cases, the entire area of an activity may have a uniform degree of security importance, requiring only one level of restriction and control. In others, differences in the degree of security importance will require further segregation of certain security interests.

SIGNS AND POSTING OF BOUNDARIES

Doors (including exterior school building doors) and other entrances will be posted at regularly used points of ingress with notice signs approximately 8 by 4.5 inches with proportional lettering. Signs will read as shown in Figure 3.1. These notice signs are available through _____.

Building perimeter areas (particularly schools) will be posted as necessary with notice signs measuring approximately 9 by 12 inches or 24 by 36 inches, as appropriate, with proportional lettering. Signs will read as shown in Figure 3.2. These signs are available through _____. (See Appendix 4 for additional examples.)

NOTICE

**ONLY AUTHORIZED PERSONS AND STUDENTS PERMITTED.
ALL VISITORS MUST OBTAIN AUTHORIZATION AT SCHOOL OFFICE
UPON ENTERING THE GROUNDS.
TRESPASSERS WILL BE PROSECUTED.
AUTHORIZED ENTRY INTO THIS AREA CONSTITUTES CONSENT TO
INSPECTION OF PERSONS AND THE PROPERTY UNDER THEIR CONTROL.**

Figure 3.1   Sample Notice Signs for Building Perimeters

The interval between notice signs posted along perimeter boundaries will not exceed 200 feet (61 meters) unless otherwise appropriate. Signs will also be placed at obvious points of normal approach by visitors. All notice signs will be placed so as not to obscure the necessary lines of vision for security force personnel. The sign in Figure 3.2 may be used along perimeter boundaries.

Color Code

All signs will be color-coded to provide legibility from a distance of at least 100 feet (30.5 meters) during daylight under normal conditions. The following color codes are recommended for activity and area perimeter signs:

1.   All words except "NO TRESPASSING/NOTICE" should be black.
2.   The words "NO TRESPASSING/NOTICE" should be red.
3.   All wording should be on a white background for maximum color contrast.

**_____ PUBLIC SCHOOL PROPERTY
VISITORS REPORT TO OFFICE**

**NO TRESPASSING.
VIOLATORS WILL BE PROSECUTED**

Figure 3.2   Sample Notice Sign for Grounds/Property/Perimeter Boundaries

Replacing Notice Signs

Warning/notice signs that are not worded as prescribed herein must be replaced within one year from the date of this manual.

KEY AND LOCK CONTROL

Each activity must establish a strict key and lock control program to be managed and supervised by the activity administrative officer. All keys, locks, padlocks, and other locking devices used to protect or secure activity perimeters, security facilities, critical assets, confidential material, sensitive material, or supplies will be included in this program. Not included in this program are keys, locks, and padlocks used for convenience, privacy, or unclassified administrative or personal use. (A sample program is outlined in Appendix 12, which also contains a sample key receipt form.)

Key Control Officer

The key control officer will be designated in writing by the administrative officer (AO) and will be directly responsible for all security-related key and lock control functions. Normally, the key control officer is the AO, a custodian, or an office worker. The key control officer will conduct an annual inventory of all controlled, issued keys and will maintain appropriate logs, records, and receipts.

Key Custodian

The head of each major functional area within an activity (for example, department, directorate, and so on) will designate in writing a key custodian who will be responsible to the key control officer for all keys controlled by that functional area. Each custodian may have subcustodians as necessary to accomplish the mission. Each custodian will inventory keys issued to custodial and subcustodial key log accounts at least annually. The record of this inventory will be retained for at least three years.

Central Key Room

Duplicate keys, key blanks, padlocks (key and combination types), and key-making equipment will be stored in a central key room in a central location if appropriate. Access must be controlled, and the room must be secured when not in use. Duplicate keys will be provided protection that is equivalent to the asset or area that the original keys are used to secure. Controlled keys will not be duplicated, except by approved means, at any time for any reason, nor will they be removed from the activity without the prior written consent of the AO.

At activities where the security key and lock program is too small to warrant a central key room, a security container with a three-position combination lock or the equivalent may be used to protect duplicate keys, key blanks, and associated equipment. Under certain conditions, duplicate keys for special rooms may be stored in a sealed security container.

Rotation and Maintenance

Security locks, padlocks, and lock cores will be rotated (or will have their combination changed) from one location to another within areas of the same level of protection at least annually or as appropriate depending on the presence of an intrusion detection alarm system and so on. Rotation is designed to guard against the use of illegally duplicated keys. It also affords the opportunity for regular maintenance to avoid lockouts or security violations due to malfunction because of dirt, corrosion, or wear.

Criteria for Issuing Keys

Keys for security locks and padlocks must be issued based on need only to individuals approved by the activity AO. Convenience or status is not a sufficient criterion for issuing a security key. Certain categories of security assets have specific rules concerning the issue and control of keys affording access to them. The activity AO is responsible for developing and enforcing rules for key issue as part of the access-control function.

Key Control

Each key custodian and subcustodian must develop and maintain a system showing keys on hand, keys issued, to whom, the date and time the keys were issued and returned, and the signature of individuals drawing or returning a security key. The continuous accountability of keys is required.

Padlock Security

When a door, gate, or other equipment that a padlock is intended to secure is open or operable, the padlock will be locked into the staple, fence fabric, or other nearby securing point. This measure prevents someone from switching the padlock to facilitate a surreptitious entry at a later time.

Lock Control Seals

Inactive or infrequently used gates or entrances must be locked and have seals affixed. The preferred seal is the car ball end type seal but other types of seals may also be used.

Security personnel should be instructed that a lack of free play (approximately one-eighth inch) suggests the possibility of tampering and a follow-up examination of the seal should be conducted. Seals should be serialized and stored in the same manner as prescribed herein for keys. All unused seals will be inventoried annually. The activity AO will control the placement of entrance seals and will account for the seal numbers on hand, issued, and used.

Procurement of Locks and Padlocks

All locks and padlocks used for security applications will meet the minimum specifications for the level of security use. The activity AO or designated person responsible for that district must approve the procurement of all security locks and padlocks.

SECURITY SURVEYS AND INSPECTIONS

Each activity will establish a program to assess the degree of compliance with the security standards, requirements, and regulations contained in this manual. This security survey will take place triennially (once every three years). The security survey checklists contained in Appendix 6 should be used.

Inspections or special-purpose examinations of an activity's security program (for example, a physical security inspection, audit, or review) will be conducted by the office of security at least triannually (every three years). It will include the practical exercise of physical security, loss prevention, and crisis management plans to evaluate the overall adequacy of the security force and the activity's ability to protect against penetration of its barriers and unauthorized entry, to protect vital property, and to deal with other security situations.

SECURITY CHECKS

Each activity must establish a system for the daily after-hours checking of areas, facilities, containers, and barrier or building ingress and egress points to detect any deficiencies or violations of security standards. Security deficiencies or violations found during after-hour checks must be reported to the department involved and to the activity AO. The AO must follow up on each deficiency or violation, and a record must be kept of all actions taken (structural, security, disciplinary, administrative, and so on) by the responsible department or other organizational elements involved to resolve the present deficiency or violation and to prevent a recurrence. All security deficiencies, violations, breaches of security rules and regulations, and criminal incidents discovered, reported, or handled by the security force will be recorded. The appropriate alarm/false alarm reports will be made by responding personnel on Form _____ or other approved means.

PARKING OF PRIVATELY OWNED VEHICLES

As a general rule, employees will not park adjacent to work spaces. Privately owned vehicles will not be parked within 15 feet (4.5 meters) of doorways leading into or from schools or other buildings. Vehicle parking is prohibited within 15 feet (4.5 meters) of any building to minimize danger in the event of a fire or explosion and to deter loss/theft of property. Management of the parking assignment function is not the purpose of security, and the duties of security will not include parking assignments. The activity AO, supported by the office of security, is responsible for access and movement controls for all activity areas and for the activity loss prevention program and, thus, should be cognizant of all parking assignments and plans.

EQUIPMENT SECURITY

Office Equipment

Electric typewriters, personal computers, calculators, adding machines, and other items of office equipment will be secured to preclude pilferage. When an office or classroom space is vacant after hours, doors will be locked and access controlled, or these items of equipment will be secured in security containers or storage cabinets. As an alternative, computers and similar items may be secured to desks with commercially available anchor pads or similar securing devices.

Portable security gates should be placed in strategic locations throughout the school or facility hallways to reduce the accessibility of personnel during nonschool hours and after hours when the school or facility is open for authorized activities.

Audiovisual Equipment

Video recorders, televisions, film projectors, radio receivers, and similar items used for mission-related audio visual purposes will be stored in spaces where access is controlled during normal duty hours. After normal duty hours and during the summer, these items will be locked in a securable room with an alarm, if possible, and security measures will be implemented.

Equipment Custody and Tracking

Equipment that is inventoried through _____ Property Control will be tracked, whether permanent or temporary possession is authorized, with Form _____, Equipment Custody/Liability Change Authorization. When property is returned from temporary custody, the signature of both the receiving and transferring officials and the date of return will be noted on the original Form _____. Possession of equipment without completing Form _____ is not approved and may be considered theft.

Chapter 4

The Security Force

GENERAL

The security force constitutes one of the most important elements of an activity's physical security program. The security force consists of designated individuals specifically organized, trained, operated, supervised, and equipped to provide physical security and law enforcement for the activity. Properly used, it is one of the school district's and administrative officer's most effective and useful tools in a comprehensive, integrated security program.

Composition of the Security Force

Security forces at _____ activities may be composed of any one or a combination of the following:

- Investigators
- Security officers
- Substitute and part-time security officers
- Police officers
- Off-duty police officers

Functions of the Security Force

Regardless of the type of personnel employed, security force functions fall into four general categories:

- Deter, detect, and defeat criminal activity
- Prevent theft and other losses caused by fire, damage, accident, trespass, or criminal activity
- Protect life, property, and the rights of individuals
- Enforce laws, rules, regulations, and statutes

Size of the Security Force

The size of the security force depends on many factors, including the following:

- Size and location of the activity
- Assets to be protected
- Number, type, and size of areas
- Use of alternate security support measures and effectiveness of mechanical or electronic security measures and equipment
- Security force support provided by other agencies or school staff
- Total daily population of the activity and its composition
- Availability of resources

DIRECTOR OF SECURITY

The director of security (DOS), *in cooperation with* and supported by the administrative officer (AO), directs the security organization of an activity and, in this capacity, plans, implements, and supervises the entire security program. The director of security's specific duties are listed in Chapter 1.

SECURITY FORCE ORDERS

The DOS will publish and maintain security force orders pertaining to each post to which security officers are assigned. These orders give members of the security force written authorization to execute and enforce regulations.

The following guidelines concern security force orders:

1. All security force orders will specify the limits of the post, the hours the post is to be manned, and the special orders, duties, uniform, arms, and equipment prescribed for members of the security force. In addition, all orders will contain guidance in the use of force.
2. All security force orders will be concise, specific, and current. They will be written in clear and simple language. Security force orders will be reviewed continually and updated as required. The DOS will conduct a total detailed review at least annually.
3. Copies of security force orders will be given to each officer and will be readily available for reference by all security force personnel.
4. Security force orders will be approved and signed by the DOS and any others, as appropriate.

SELECTION OF SECURITY PERSONNEL

Care in the initial selection of security force personnel and in the elimination of the marginal performer during early training is important. Turnover in the security force is undesirable for several reasons. First, the release of personnel trained in sensitive operations creates a possible source of information for individuals seeking to discover vulnerable points of a security system. Second, the cost of training replacements is high. Finally, frequent turnover breaks the level of experience needed and the high number of officers required to be familiar with procedures, which results in reduced security and less effective protection.

General Requirements

In general, security force personnel should be physically agile, be mentally alert, and possess good judgment. Positions will be established on the basis of duties actually performed. Security force personnel must be proactive, flexible, self-motivated, and supportive of security policies and practices desired by the principal, and required by the office of security and the school administration.

SUPERVISION OF SECURITY PERSONNEL

A successful security program requires the close personal supervision of the security force. A supervisor will perform the following functions:

- Supervise the issue and recovery of all equipment
- Inspect security force personnel prior to posting
- Inform security force personnel of any special orders, instructions, or incidents and provide necessary roll-call training
- Inspect each security post or other security activity at least twice per shift to ensure that personnel and systems are functioning properly in accordance with procedures and security standards

POSTS

Because no two activities present the exact same degree of risk or contain identical situations, it is impractical to set fixed rules, outside of those involving professional standards and procedures, to apply to all activities. The administrative officer, in cooperation with the director of security, must ensure that an analysis of the activity is performed to determine the number and type of posts required to provide optimum and cost-effective protection. Consideration should be given to employing alternate security measures, such as additional electronic intrusion-detection systems, closed-circuit television, and the securing of nonessential doors to allow for more efficient deployment of security force personnel.

Types of Posts

There are three basic types of posts. As a result of fiscal restraints, a post may be a combination of two types.

Fixed.   In a fixed post, security personnel normally remain at one point or within a specific area—for example, at a gate or door or in a hallway. In schools, these posts should be kept to a minimum.

Mobile.   Mobile posts are used for perimeter surveillance, area patrols, and so on. The security forces may be on foot or in vehicles. Mobile posts are also known as roving patrols. These types of post are more effective in schools for preventing and deterring crime and violence.

Administrative.   These posts include the administrative personnel, dispatchers, alarm system monitoring personnel, locksmiths, security training specialists, investigators, clerks, stenographers, and others.

Post Requirements and Considerations

Gates and Doors.   Gates and doors will be limited to the minimum number required to permit the expeditious flow of traffic in and out of the activity. Except where justified by consistently heavy traffic throughout the day or by other security considerations, one officer at a main gate or door area will normally suffice. Rush-hour staff augmentation must be included in post calculations. Using personnel obtained temporarily from mobile posts to staff fixed posts reduces emergency response capability to alarms, accidents, criminal activity, and other potential problems that may arise.

Perimeter.   The need to prevent unauthorized entry justifies perimeter posts. If an activity requires inviolability at all costs, perimeter protection would call for a combination of approved fencing, protective lighting, and intrusion alarms, all supported by numerous fixed posts and with mobile patrols operating in relatively small areas. On the other hand, another activity may meet security requirements by using nothing more than a fixed or mobile post. The perimeter protection requirements for most activities will be found somewhere between these extremes. In most schools, perimeter protection is provided by roving patrols.

Area Posts.   The guarding of an area must be commensurate with the importance of the area and its assets and the seriousness of the threat of crime and violence.

Motorized Patrols.   One-person vehicular patrols are normally adequate as a deterrent or response. Members of the auxiliary security force may be used to comprise or augment motorized patrols.

Visitor Escorts.   It is normally not appropriate to establish full-time security posts to provide visitor escorts. After a visitor has checked in at the office and received a visitor identification badge, the person receiving the visitors or his or her representative should escort the person to and from the waiting area, if appropriate. Otherwise, badged visitors may move through the activity unescorted but with their badge displayed in open view.

SUPERVISORY STRENGTH

Each shift of security force personnel will have a professionally trained security supervisor. The ratio of security supervisors to security personnel will vary with the overall size of the security force, the extent of the operations, and the type and frequency of supervision desired.

SECURITY FORCE STRENGTH

The number of positions in the security force is normally based on the number of posts and the hours that they must be staffed. When this is known, the following guideline, or "staffing factor," can be used to determine the number of security personnel required:

A one-person post that operates twenty-four hours a day, seven days a week (168 hours per week) requires 5.63 nonadministrative security personnel.

Example

Post 1	1 individual, 24 hours, 7 days	= 168 hours
Post 2	1 individual, 10 hours, 5 days	= 50 hours
Post 3	1 individual, 2 hours, 5 days	= 10 hours
Post 4	2 individuals, 24 hours, 7 days	= 336 hours
Post 5	2 individuals, 16 hours, 7 days	= 224 hours
Post 6	1 individual, 8 hours, 2 days	= 16 hours
	Total hours: 804	

The total number of hours is 804 per week, which divided by 168 equals 4.78 posts. Multiplying 4.78 by the staffing factor of 5.63 yields 26.91, or 27, security personnel to staff the posts. When computation of the formula is complete, determine the most significant digit (two decimal places) and round up to the nearest whole number if more than .50 and down if .50 or less.

This factor includes the required 32 hours or more of refresher training per year/per person, normal days off for vacation, personal, and sick leave, as well as specialized in-service training. It does not reflect requirements for special details such as athletic events or miscellaneous assignments. Security force requirements can be adjusted if special assignments are valid and if security responsibilities and the staff requirements are consistent and can be gauged on the basis of "averages" indicated by past experience. If, however, such requirements are intermittent or generally of limited duration, consideration should be given to the use of overtime or doubling up of posts. Special details or miscellaneous assignments that are not valid security functions must be curtailed.

Post requirements for some supervisory personnel (such as one field supervisor required twenty-four hours per day, seven days per week to provide oversight and evaluation of security personnel effectiveness) may be included in post computations. Other administrative posts and supervisory requirements (for example, security supervisor or dispatcher) should be computed separately. In some cases, particularly those involving small security forces, the scheduling of work hours to give post coverage as it is needed may not be entirely practical if security force requirements are based on a strict minimum application of the aforementioned formula.

As a rule of thumb, in a school while students are present, one professional security officer assigned per 400 students enrolled is not unreasonable if the security personnel are properly used and supervised.

AUGMENTING THE SECURITY FORCE FOR EMERGENCIES

The crisis management portion of the security plan requires that plans be prepared for security force personnel to provide additional security, as required, during emergencies and for augmentation by the auxiliary security force and other additional personnel and equipment. These plans may also provide for the essential training of augmentation personnel and rapid identification and acquisition of emergency equipment and supplies.

Auxiliary Security Forces

The _____ is the duly constituted police force in the county/city of _____. It will be notified, when appropriate or as agreed on in a memorandum of understanding, of criminal activities identified on school property. It will support and reinforce all security investigations and law enforcement matters in the school district when requested or required by previous agreements.

Chapter 5

Personnel and Vehicle Movement Control

GENERAL

A system of personnel and vehicle movement control is a basic security measure required at most locations. Positive identification provides a means for visually establishing authorization for personnel movement and actions. The monitoring of movement by security operations personnel is facilitated by policies requiring the display or presentation of identification. The degree of control must be in keeping with the sensitivity, value, or operational importance of the area, and procedures must be simple.

PURPOSE

The purpose of establishing a system for personnel and vehicle movement control is to provide a visible means to identify and track authorized personnel and vehicles that have access to an area and to deny or make access difficult for unauthorized personnel and vehicles.

PERSONNEL IDENTIFICATION AND MOVEMENT CONTROL

The following systems may be used separately or collectively to provide the degree of security desired:

Personal Recognition. Personal recognition is the most positive method of identification in cases involving a small number of people (not exceeding twenty-five) and should be used wherever feasible.

Pass and Badge Systems. When the area to be secured is large or when there are more people than can be personally recognized by the staff or those who have been charged with security responsibility in the area, a pass and badge identification system will be used. Security badges will be used primarily for access control. Minimum standards for identification badges and passes are described later in this chapter.

Requirements of the System

The means of identification and control of personnel at a location will be included in written procedures in the security plan and will include the following:

- Description of identification media in use and authorization and limitations placed upon the bearer
- Identification mechanics for entering and leaving each area, as applied to both authorized personnel and visitors
- Details of where, when, and how badges will be issued, displayed, and returned
- Procedures to be followed in case of loss or damage to identification media
- Procedures for recovering issued passes or badges

Rebadging Criteria

An accurate monitoring system for determining the percentage of lost identification badges will be maintained. The procedures will include accurate records and bookkeeping accountability of all issued badges. Bookkeeping and records inventory will be conducted at least annually, and the results of this inventory will be maintained for at least three years. The following guidelines apply to the rebadging procedure:

1. The central administration will rebadge all regular district employees and other personnel with permanent picture badges every six years or when a loss of 10 percent is attained, whichever comes first.
2. A loss of 10 percent is the maximum acceptable standard for the reissue of permanent picture identification badges. To compute the percentage of lost permanent badges, divide the number of lost permanent badges by the number of permanent badges issued over a given period of time, normally from the beginning of the current six-year time period. Losses totaling 10 percent or more require rebadging.
3. New permanent picture badges will be distinctly different (for example, a new color for the paper stock) from those replaced.
4. The director of security, supported by _____, will maintain the central badging program.

Expiration

All issued security badges will bear an expiration date. The expiration date will be conspicuously displayed on the face of the badge and should be distinguishable from a distance of three feet during normal daylight hours.

Permanent Picture Badges.   All permanent picture badges issued during a six-year period to personnel should bear the same expiration date (incrementally, if appropriate) or known date badge is no longer needed. For example, badges issued during a six-year period ending in December 2001 would normally bear a December 2001 expiration date. If unscheduled rebadging is required during any six-year cycle, a new six-year cycle begins from the date of the unscheduled rebadging, and expiration would be six years from that date.

Contractor, Temporary Workers, Substitute Employee Picture Badges. Contractor, temporary worker, and substitute employee picture badges will expire at completion of the current contract or twelve months, whichever occurs first. If services or employment continues past the expiration date, another badge should be issued with a new expiration date.

Invalidation of Key Cards

Where card readers are used to control access, procedures for removing lost or no longer valid key cards from the system or invalidating them will be in place. Where digital key pads are used, procedures for changing or deleting personnel identification numbers will be in place.

Standards for Badges and Passes

General. The following guidelines apply when a pass or badge system of identification is used. _____ has adopted these guidelines into its identification badge program. Employee photographs for permanent identification badges will be taken in the office of security. The employee photo ID badge will be issued to the employee at that time. Temporary and visitor badges will be issued to the school by the office of security.

1. A facility's permanent identification badge for employees and visitors must contain the information set forth in this section as prescribed by district policy.
2. A temporary or visitor's badge need not contain all of the information set forth in this section because it only provides control of individuals who visit infrequently. However, the badges will be rigidly controlled and accounted for by individual serial number; will be distinctly different in color, style, and design from permanent badges or passes used at activities; will be color-coded differently for each school or facility; and will clearly indicate the period and limits of authorized use, if applicable. They will have the word "Temporary" or "Visitor," as applicable, boldly printed across the face.
3. Badges were designed by the administration with economy in mind. The design takes into consideration that the primary purpose of an identification system is to control access to specific areas and to alert personnel of the presence of unauthorized individuals in the area. Bold print, large and recent photographs, a distinctive design, and tamper-resistant structure are prime considerations.
4. The "exchange badge system," which requires the exchange of something for a badge, will be employed when visitor badges are issued. This will ensure return of the badge and allow for greater accountability.

5. The printer's plates for badges will be obtained and safeguarded to avoid compromise. When necessary, the badge system may be changed by reprinting in different colors or reformatting the badge.
6. The badge form for photo identification badges will be a continuous flow data card with each card having a consecutive serial number and the cards will be controlled and protected from theft. The administration will conduct an inventory of all serially numbered passes on hand at least annually and will establish written procedures for retrieving and destroying invalid passes from personnel whose access has been terminated or discounted by retirement or resignation.

Characteristics of Permanent Badges.   The characteristics of permanent badges are as follows. The _____ employee identification badge also follows this format:

1. The size of the pass is generally consistent with other standard identification cards (3 1/4 by 2 5/16 inches).
2. The badge will include a photograph with a minimum size of 2 3/4 by 1 3/4 inches. The maximum size will be consistent with economy, available equipment, and pass or badge design. The photograph will be in color, will stress facial features, and will not include the area below the neck. The background colors will be as follows:
   a. Blue—Central Office
   b. Red—Security/Law Enforcement
   c. Yellow—Transportation
   d. Green—School Plant Facilities
   e. Lavender—Food Service
   f. Orange—Warehouse
   g. Pink—Schools
   These colors in lieu of the name of the work location are for the sole identification of employees work locations to reduce the potential of employee stalking.
3. There will be a clear space at the top of the badge to place a hole that will facilitate an attachment device.
4. There will be a serial number for accountability.
5. The name of the holder, typewritten or printed, and the holder's signature will be on the badge.
6. If appropriate, the name and title of the validating officer, and a facsimile of his or her signature will be on the badge.
7. The expiration date of the badge will be so noted on the badge.

The statements shown in Figure 5.1 are required on the reverse side of the badge and may be incorporated in the design or may be an overlay before or after the lamination.

Construction.   The badge will be constructed with a heat-seal adhesive of the complete card to prevent photographic reproduction. An identifying logo or validation seal or initials will be manufactured into the lamination along with other positive security measures that will help prevent tampering. Identifying information must be clearly legible to security personnel at a distance of one meter in normal lighting conditions. Computer generated ID badging systems may also be considered.

POSTMASTER: Return Postage Guaranteed

_____

_____

_____

This card is the property of _____ and is issued to personnel
for identification. It should be worn at those times designated for your
department by the administration. If your card is lost, stolen, or
destroyed report it to the security office immediately. Upon termination
of employment, this card must be surrendered before final
compensation is made.

Figure 5.1   Required Badge Statements

Personnel Identification and Control Procedures

The following procedures will be followed to establish improving identification and control of personnel entering or departing facilities.

Regular Activity and District Employees.   Once an employee and visitor identification badging system is accepted and given attention to by all employees assigned to the facility and all district employees who conduct business in the facility, there will automatically be a sense of increased security. This will be because there is an increase in the number of personnel who feel that they have a responsibility and right to challenge anyone in the building not wearing a visitor's badge issued by the office. An identification badging program calls for a number of procedures to be considered:

- A method of establishing reason for entry
- A method of establishing the identity of personnel desiring entry
- A method of denying or challenging access to areas that an individual should not enter
- A method to recover badges when they are no longer valid (a log book of issued badges and a badge exchange system)

Visitors.   In this instruction, the term *visitor* includes all personnel who require infrequent access to a location and who have not been issued a permanent identification badge. In addition to the actions described above, the following will also be considered when establishing local controls for visitors:

- Using the district approved visitor's badge
- Providing an escort when appropriate
- Recording the area or person visited and reason for visit
- Time in and time out

Temporary.   In this instruction, the term *temporary* includes those personnel who are neither full-time nor full-time part-time employees but are acting in a staff capacity and should not be perceived as a visitor (for example, substitute teachers). Temporary badges may also be issued to a full-time employee who has lost his or her regular picture identification badge and is awaiting issue of a new badge or return of the old badge when and if it is found.

Contractor Employees.   Contractor employees performing work on school property are required to wear distinctive badges (with a *C* across the face of the badge). In a construction project or other project involving a considerable number of personnel over a long period of time, an effort should be made to fence off the work site from the rest of the area. When the contract work is comparatively brief and involves few contractor employees, escorts may be necessary if contractor personnel do not have the necessary access authorization. The use of Visitor or temporary badges should also be considered and the school custodian should be responsible for the accountability of contractor badges.

Utility and Maintenance Personnel.   Personnel who are working within an area at infrequent intervals or for a short period will be processed in the same manner as visitors. Personnel performing services within an area on a regularly scheduled or full-time basis will be processed the same as regular activity personnel (i.e., contracted services for the district such as Service Master, Marriott, etc.).

Application of Personnel Identification System

For a personnel identification system to be effective, it is important that security personnel, receptionists, teachers, and others in the facility carefully notice and watch to ensure all personnel are wearing the appropriate badges. To facilitate this, ingress and egress control points may be structured to encourage people to move in past or near supervised areas. Where the volume of traffic incidents is high, greater security and staff presence may be necessary or consideration might be given to relocating "safe activities" to this area. Close administrative supervision and spot checks of personnel charged with checking identification media are necessary. In schools in which students are not badged, "polite" challenges are appropriate for individuals in the facility who are not wearing identification badges.

The manufacture, storage, control, and issue of identification media by the administration will be carefully controlled to minimize the possibility of counterfeit or theft, to ensure return and destruction upon termination of employment, and to promptly invalidate lost, mutilated, or defective badges. Identification media will be controlled by rigid accountability procedures, and unissued "blanks" will be protected in locked containers with the keys or combinations to such containers under strict accountability. Lost badges will be replaced by badges with new serial numbers or other appropriate notation (a star added after the old serial number, for example) to facilitate the identification of lost and reissued badges.

Lost Badge Listing

A list of all lost badges should be maintained for use by the security force to guard against the unauthorized use of badges that have been reported lost. Upon notification of a lost badge, the lost badge listing will be immediately updated by the director of security. If a computerized badge list is used, it must be safeguarded against tampering. Lost badges will be reported on Form _____. There will be a $5 charge for lost badges to cover the administrative cost of issuing a new badge and to encourage badge accountability against losses. Badges damaged or showing wear will be replaced without cost, but the old badge will be destroyed upon issue of the new badge.

Enforcement of Movement Control

The enforcement of movement control systems rests primarily with the security force or other personnel at each location. However, it is essential that those charged with enforcing movement control have the full cooperation and participation of other personnel (see Chapter 9). All employees will be instructed to consider unidentified or improperly identified individuals as trespassers and to report them to their supervisor, to security personnel, or to other appropriate authority. Written procedures will be incorporated into the activity security plan to ensure attention to these requirements. These procedures will be tested during activity security drills of the security force and audits or other reviews of the physical security function by the director of security.

Upon the approval of the administration and the director of security, consideration may be given to the use of commercially available access-control systems to enhance movement controls within a facility. These systems prevent unimpeded admission through access points controlled by card readers. They meet security record-keeping requirements while reducing the number of security personnel assigned to fixed posts. The use of convex mirrors in halls, stairwells, and corners and simplex-type mechanical push button combination locks is encouraged.

VEHICLE IDENTIFICATION AND MOVEMENT CONTROL

The identification and control of people is also related to the identification and control of privately owned motor vehicles on activity property. The authority to determine the type of identification system used for privately owned vehicles rests with the activity administrative officer and the office of security. The instructions established should conform with applicable city and state laws. The vehicle identification method used serves as a rapid means of identifying the vehicle itself as having authority for being operated and parked on activity property. It will not be used to identify the driver or any occupant of the vehicle. The identification required of individuals traveling in motor vehicles will be the same as that required of pedestrians and employees, as appropriate.

Commercial Vehicles

Commercial vehicles, including buses, may be authorized entry by permanent registration or visitor control methods. Normal inspection and identification verification procedures and additional precautions, when needed, will be applied to prevent unauthorized material or personnel from being introduced into or removed from the activity.

Government-Owned Vehicles

The guidance and instructions contained in this chapter regarding motor vehicle identification do not apply to any government-owned vehicles that are provided with other means of identification.

Control and Review of Identification Media

A system must be established and records maintained to account for all vehicle identification media. This system will include a positive method for the return, destruction, or expiration of an identification medium when it is no longer authorized for use. Vehicle identification media may not be appropriate for most schools unless circumstances warrant.

Random Administrative Inspection of Vehicles

All vehicles on _____ property may be subject to random administrative inspections according to the procedures authorized by the superintendent. As ordered and directed, security personnel may, while performing their assigned duties to provide for a safe and secure school environment, administratively inspect vehicles entering or leaving the activity. Such inspections are deemed reasonably necessary to protect the premises, material, and personnel from loss, damage, destruction, or injury. Because important constitutional questions are involved, no person or group may be exempted from or singled out for such inspections. This instruction will be coordinated in advance of implementation of the program with the school board attorney's office to ensure strict adherence to a sound policy with structured random inspection patterns.

At a minimum, security personnel must be instructed that incoming individuals or their vehicles may not be inspected over their objections. However, those who refuse to permit inspection will not be allowed to enter the premises. Those who enter should be advised in advance that they and their vehicles are liable to inspection while on activity property and upon departure. A properly worded notice sign to this effect, prominently displayed in front of the access point, will suffice. Anyone who refuses to submit a vehicle to an authorized inspection while on the activity or upon departure may be issued a letter barring future entrance to the activity or such other action as may be appropriate.

(Inspection programs regarding personnel, weapons, and so on, are addressed in Appendix 3. They include the use of metal detectors and dogs trained to seek out drugs or explosives.)

Security and Law Enforcement Vehicles.   Accredited security and law enforcement personnel, vehicles used by them in the course of official business, and all occupants therein are exempt from administrative inspection upon the presentation of a badge or credential when entering and leaving the activity.

Honoring Vehicle Identification

Because _____ employees will generally need to enter nearby activities in their private automobiles for personal or official reasons, vehicle identification media issued by other school activities will be honored.

SPECIAL PRECAUTIONS

Personnel responsible for implementing personnel and vehicle control procedures will at all times be watchful for the unauthorized introduction to or removal from the activity of city or school board property. This surveillance will encompass all personnel and means of transportation, including official, private, and commercial vehicles.

Chapter 6

Barriers and Openings

PURPOSE

Physical barriers control, deny, impede, delay, and discourage access to an area by unauthorized or undesirable persons. They accomplish this by:

- Defining the perimeter of areas of special concern
- Establishing a physical and psychological deterrent to entry and providing notice that entry is not permitted
- Optimizing the use of security forces
- Enhancing detection and apprehension opportunities by authorized personnel in areas of special concern
- Channeling the flow of people and vehicles through designated entranceways in a manner that permits the efficient operation of the personnel identification and control system

TYPES OF BARRIERS

There are two major types of physical barriers:

- Natural barriers, such as mountains, swamps, thick vegetation, rivers, bays, and cliffs
- Structural barriers, such as fences, walls, doors, gates, roadblocks, and vehicle barriers

GENERAL CONSIDERATIONS

Physical barriers delay but can rarely be depended on to stop a determined intruder. Therefore, to be effective such barriers, when necessary, must be augmented by security force personnel or other means of protection.

In determining the type of barrier required, the following guidelines will be considered:

1. Physical barriers will be established around all appropriate areas, where practical. The type of barrier to be used will be determined after a study of local conditions.

The barrier or combination of barriers used must afford an adequate degree of continuous protection along the entire perimeter of the area. When a section or sections of natural or structural barriers (or the lack thereof) provide a lesser degree of protection, other supplementary means must be used to detect and assess intrusion attempts.

2. When there is a high degree of relative criticality and vulnerability, it may be necessary to establish two lines of physical barriers at the area perimeter. Such barriers should be separated by no less than 38 feet (9.14 meters) for optimum protection and control. Two lines of barriers should be used only when necessary and in conjunction with an intrusion-detection system between the fences or on the inside fence or with some other form of alarm system and a security force capable of immediate or timely response. The use of two barriers alone provides little extra protection against a determined intruder beyond a few seconds of delay and may actually be counterproductive in that it identifies the location of high-risk items.

3. The perimeter boundaries of all facilities will be either fenced or posted, as appropriate, to establish a legal boundary. This defines the perimeter, provides a buffer zone, facilitates control, denotes private from public areas, and makes accidental intrusion unlikely. It is important to consult with the school board attorney to ensure that the posting of barriers in areas of concurrent or proprietary jurisdiction complies with local or state trespass laws. In addition, designated areas will be posted as specified in Chapter 3.

4. Whenever fencing is impractical, compensatory security measures (for example, increased patrols) will be implemented.

5. In establishing any perimeter or barrier, consideration must be given to providing emergency entrances and exits in case of fire as well as to any necessary controlled pedestrian points. However, openings will be kept to a minimum, consistent with the efficient and safe operation of the facility and without degradation of reasonable security standards.

6. Water boundaries, if present, present special security problems. Such areas, if deemed to be a concern, should be protected by structural barriers and posted. In inclement weather patrols may be increased or supplemented by closed-circuit television, and other methods of assessment of the area.

7. Construction of new security barriers, removal of existing barriers, and related work must be approved by the administrative officer and the office of security. This work must be scheduled in order that security for the activity will not be interrupted.

FENCES

Fencing serves a useful purpose by defining legal boundaries, reducing or eliminating the general public from wandering onto the property and interfering with school activities, impeding a thief or criminal's retreat off the property after committing a criminal or violent act, and in the case of schools in particular, separating "safe" school activities from encroachment onto adjoining general public activity (i.e., cars passing on a busy street, large number of pedestrians taking short cuts, etc.). Certain standards and criteria should be established and considered when dealing with fencing and associated barriers.

Chain-Link Fencing

Chain-link fencing, which is relatively inexpensive, is the type of structural barrier most commonly used and recommended for security purposes. Mesh openings normally should not be covered, blocked, or laced with material that would prevent a clear view of people, vehicles, or material in the outer perimeter areas. Ornamental fencing may be considered and is encouraged due to appearance.

Fabric and Ties

The standard fence fabric will be nine-gauge (3.8 mm) zinc or aluminum-coated steel wire chain link with mesh openings no larger than 2 inches (50 mm) per side and a twisted and barbed selvage at top and bottom. Only nine-gauge (3.8 mm) steel ties will be used. If the ties are coated or plated, the coating or plating will be electrolytically compatible with the fence fabric to inhibit corrosion.

Height

The standard height of a security fence is 8 feet (2.4 meters). This includes a fabric height of 7 feet (2.1 meters), plus a top guard. Building connections may need to be higher. Fencing 12 feet (3.6 meters) high from the connection point with a building to a point 12 feet (3.6 meters) away from the building is suggested. Lesser heights may be used as appropriate in consideration of surrounding neighborhoods.

Fencing Posts, Supports, and Hardware

All posts, supports, and hardware for security fencing will meet the security requirements. All fastening and hinge hardware will be secured in place by peening or welding to allow proper operation of components but to prevent disassembly of fencing or removal of gates. All posts and structural supports will be located on the inner side of the fencing. Posts will be positively secured into the soil to prevent shifting, sagging, or collapse.

Reinforcement

Taut reinforcing wires will be installed and interwoven or affixed with fabric ties along the top and bottom of the fence for stabilization of the fence fabric.

Ground Clearance

The bottom of the fence fabric must be within 2 inches (50 mm) of firm soil or buried sufficiently in soft soil to compensate for shifting soil. Concrete footings or gravel may be used.

Culverts and Openings

Culverts under or through a fence shall be of 10-inch (254 mm) pipe or of clusters of such pipe or the equivalent. Openings under or through a fence will be secured with material equal to or greater in strength than the overall barrier.

Placement

No fence will be located so that the features of the land (its topography) or structures on the land (buildings, utility tunnels, light and telephone poles, fire escapes, trees, vines, ladders, and so on) allow passage over, around, or under the fence.

Top Guards

If appropriate, a top guard may be constructed on perimeter fences and may be added on interior enclosures for additional protection. A top guard is an overhang of barbed wire or barbed tape along the top of a fence, facing outward (away from the protected site) and upward at approximately a 45-degree angle. The top guard supporting arms will be permanently affixed to the top of the fence posts to increase the overall height of the fence at least 1 foot (0.3 meter). Three strands of twelve-gauge (2.7 mm) barbed wire, equally spaced, must be installed on the supporting arms. The top guard of fencing adjoining gates may range from a vertical height of 18 inches (0.45 meters) to the normal 45-degree outward protection, but only for sufficient distance along the fence to open the gates adequately.

Barriers

Buildings, structures, waterfronts, and other barriers used instead of or as part of a fence line must provide protection equivalent to the fencing required for that area. All windows, doors, and other openings or means of access must be guarded or properly secured.

Alternative Fencing

Where a boundary passes through an isolated area (for example, a heavily wooded area or swamp) that is unpatrolled and through which vehicular passage is impossible, the boundary may be defined with a two- to four-strand twelve-gauge (2.7 mm) wire fence approximately 4 feet (1.2 meters) high. It will be posted as specified in Chapter 3.

WALLS

Walls may be used as barriers in lieu of fences. The protection afforded by walls will be equivalent to that provided by chain-link fencing. Walls, floors, and roofs of buildings may also serve as perimeter barriers.

TEMPORARY BARRIERS

The temporary nature of an area sometimes does not justify the construction of permanent perimeter barriers. In such cases, additional security forces, patrols, and other temporary security measures during the period of use will compensate for the resulting lack of security.

VEHICLE BARRIERS

The use of vehicle barriers, such as crash barriers, obstacles, or reinforcement systems for chain-link or other gates at uncontrolled avenues of approach, can impede or prevent the access of unauthorized vehicles. The administrative officer can obtain information from the office of security when barriers of this nature are deemed necessary. Other types of vehicle barriers used for controlling or denying access at various times during the school day (breakaway or hinged barriers, removable poles, swinging arms, and so on), should be put in place where appropriate to control vehicle access to parking or other areas.

INSPECTION OF BARRIERS

Security force personnel will check security barriers at least weekly for defects that would facilitate unauthorized entry and show neglect. They will report such defects to their supervisor. Security personnel must be alert to the following:

• Damaged areas (cuts in fabric, broken posts)
• Deterioration (corrosion)
• Erosion of soil beneath the barrier
• Loose fittings in the barbed wire, outriggers, fabric fasteners
• Growth in the clear zones that would afford cover for intruders
• Obstructions that would afford concealment or aid entry or exit for an intruder
• Evidence of illegal or improper intrusion or attempted intrusion

CLEAR ZONES

An unobstructed area, or clear zone, will be maintained on both sides of and between permanent physical barriers. Vegetation in such areas will not exceed 8 inches in height.

The inside clear zone will be at least 30 feet (9.14 meters) deep. Where possible, a larger clear zone should be provided to preclude or minimize damage from thrown objects such as incendiaries or rocks.

The outside clear zone will be 20 feet (6.09 meters) deep or more between the perimeter barrier and any exterior structures, vegetation, or any obstruction to visibility. Any new fence enclosing an area with a smaller clear zone must be constructed with these considerations in mind.

In activities where the fence does not meet clear-zone requirements in its present location, relocating the fence to obtain a clear zone may not be feasible or cost effective. Alternatives to extending the clear zone include increasing the height of the perimeter fence, extending outriggers, and installing double outriggers to compensate for the close proximity of aids to concealment or access. Where property owners do not object, the area just outside the fence should be cleared to preclude concealment of a person and enhance natural surveillance. All fencing will be kept clear of visual obstructions such as vines, shrubs, or tree limbs that could provide concealment for an intruder.

The inspection of clear zones should be incorporated with inspections of perimeter barriers to ensure an unrestricted view of the barrier and the adjacent ground.

In addition to security, clear zones also provide the safety feature of a 50-foot- (15.2-meter-) wide firebreak between the activity's areas, structures, or storage facilities and adjoining areas. It is especially important to maintain clear zones during periods of high fire risk and if there are other routine activities adjoining school property.

PATROL ROADS

When the perimeter barrier encloses a large area, an interior perimeter road, trail, or footpath, must be considered for use of security patrols in all areas that are not affected by impassable terrain.

PERIMETER OPENINGS

Openings in the perimeter barrier will be kept to the minimum necessary for the safe and efficient operation of the activity. They will be constantly locked or otherwise secured, if appropriate, to prevent unauthorized entry or exit. When locked and not under surveillance, the locking device used will provide the same level of security as the perimeter barrier.

Gates

Gates facilitate the entrance and exit of authorized traffic and control its flow.

Number and Location. Gates will be limited to the number consistent with efficient operations. Such factors as the centers of activity and personnel and vehicular traffic flow inside and outside the area should be considered when locating gates. Alternative gates, which are closed except during peak movement hours, may be provided so that heavy traffic flow can be expedited. When open or operating, all gates will be under limited control, if appropriate. When not in use, they will provide protection equivalent to the fences or barriers of which they are a part. These gates will be locked to form an integral part of the fence.

Inspection. When not in active use and controlled by a guard or receptionist, gates, turnstiles, and doors in the perimeter barrier will be locked and frequently inspected by security patrols. Locks will be rotated at least annually or as necessary. Security for the keys and combinations to the locks on these gates is the responsibility of the administrative officer or designee.

Pedestrian Gates. Pedestrian gates and turnstiles will be designated so that only a minimum number of persons may approach at a time. Some gates may be closed between high-use hours. Where possible, pedestrian and vehicular gates should be clearly separated.

Vehicular Gates. When possible, vehicular gates will be set well back from any public highway so that temporary delays caused by identification control checks or other delays at the gate will not cause traffic hazards. There will also be sufficient space at the gate to allow for spot checks, inspections, searches, and temporary parking of vehicles without impeding the flow of traffic.

Doors, Windows, Skylights, and Other Openings

Exterior building doors on the activity or area perimeter will provide protection commensurate with the value of the assets accessible through those doors. Windows, skylights, and other openings that penetrate the perimeter barrier and have an area of 96 square inches (619.4 square cm) or greater will be protected by securely fastened steel bar grilles or nine-gauge (3.8 mm) wire mesh, framed and permanently bolted to the structure. Such openings are considered inaccessible to personnel when they are 18 feet (5.4 meters) or more above ground level and 14 feet (4.2 meters) or more distant from buildings, structures, and so on, outside the perimeter. Protective screens have the additional value of preventing projectiles such as rocks, bombs, and incendiaries from being hurled through the windows from outside the perimeter. Classroom doors and windows will be free of posters and other materials that obstruct a clear view of the classroom from hallways or of the grounds from the classroom.

Sewers, Culverts, and Other Utility Openings

Sewers, air intakes, exhaust tunnels, and other utility openings that penetrate the perimeter or area barrier and have a cross-sectional area of 96 square inches (619.4

square cm) or greater will be protected by securely fastened bars, grilles, locked utility-access covers, or other equivalent means that provide security commensurate with that of the perimeter or special area barrier. Bars and grilles across culverts, sewers, storm sewers, and so on, are a hazard when susceptible to clogging. This hazard must be considered during construction planning. All drains and sewers will be designed to permit rapid clearing or removal of grating when required. Removable grates will normally be locked in place.

UTILITY POLES, SIGNBOARDS, AND TREES

Utility poles, signboards, trees, and so on, located outside of and within 14 feet (4.2 meters) of the perimeter barrier of the activity, present a possible aid to unauthorized entry. To reduce this possibility, the perimeter barrier should be staggered to increase the distance to more than 14 feet (4.2 meters) and may be heightened to the extent necessary to prevent entry. Otherwise, the hazard should be removed or relocated at least 20 feet (6.09 meters) outside the perimeter barriers in order not to obstruct good visibility of the area.

Chapter 7

Protective Lighting

GENERAL

Protective, or security, lighting provides a means of maintaining a level of security similar to that of the daylight hours. It increases the effectiveness of the security forces in performing their duties, has considerable value as a deterrent to thieves and vandals, and may make the job of planning criminal activity more difficult. Requirements for protective lighting at an activity will depend on the situation and the areas to be protected. Each situation must be carefully studied to find the best possible mix between energy conservation and effective security. The overall goal is to provide the proper environment in which to perform security duties like identifying badges and personnel, enable detection of unusual or suspicious circumstances and activities, and create a psychological deterrent to intrusion and crime. Where lighting is impractical, additional security measures must be instituted to compensate.

GENERAL PRINCIPLES AND GUIDELINES

Good security lighting influences the effective control of crime not only against property but also against people. Schools in many parts of the country are open during times of darkness, and more and more school districts are increasing the community use of schools at night. With the increased use of school facilities during times of darkness comes the need and responsibility for not only deterring the usual incidents of vandalism and burglary, but also addressing the potential increase in exposure to crime against community members who use the school for sanctioned activities. Following are some principles to keep in mind with regards to lighting:

1. Provide adequate illumination or compensating measures to discourage or detect attempts to enter the area and to reveal the presence of unauthorized persons within the area.
2. Avoid glare, which handicaps security personnel and may be objectionable to air, rail, highway, or other traffic or occupants of adjacent properties.
3. Locate light sources so that the illumination is directed toward likely avenues of approach and provides relative darkness for patrol roads, paths, and posts. To minimize exposure of security force personnel, lighting at entry points will be

directed at the gate or entry point and the guard will be in the shadows. This type of lighting technique is often called glare projection. (This subject is discussed in more detail in the following section.)

4. Illuminate shadowed areas caused by structures within or adjacent to high-value areas.

5. Design the lighting system to provide overlapping light distribution. Equipment selection should be designed to resist the effects of environmental conditions, and all components of the system should be located to provide maximum protection against intentional damage.

6. Meet the requirements of any blackout areas.

7. Avoid drawing unwanted attention to specific areas.

8. During planning stages, consideration should be given to the future requirements of closed-circuit television systems and the recognition factors involved in selecting the type of lighting to be installed. Where recognition of colors will be a factor, full-spectrum (high-pressure sodium vapor) lighting vice single color should be used.

9. Choose lights that illuminate the ground but not the air above. These lights must penetrate fog and rain.

10. There should be a lights-out policy for interior lights after all events have concluded and the activity is closed. This deters vandalism and thefts. Assuming that the building interior is alarmed, a limited and flexible exterior lights-out policy should be considered and used as appropriate. However, exterior lighting should be used in support of crime-prevention strategies when circumstances warrant.

TYPES OF PROTECTIVE LIGHTING SYSTEMS

There are some basic types of lighting systems to be aware of when considering or deciding on security lighting:

Continuous Lighting

The most common protective lighting system is a series of fixed lights arranged to flood a given area continuously with overlapping cones of light. The two primary methods of employing continuous lighting are glare projection and controlled lighting.

Glare Projection.   Glare projection uses lights slightly inside a security perimeter and directed outward. This method is useful where the glare of lights directed across surrounding territory will neither annoy nor interfere with adjacent operations. It is a deterrent to potential intruders because it makes it difficult to see inside the area being protected. It also protects security personnel by keeping them in comparative darkness and enabling them to observe intruders or suspicious activity at a distance.

Controlled Lighting.   Controlled lighting is best used when it is necessary to limit the width of the lighted strip outside the area of concern. The width of the lighted strip can be controlled and adjusted to fit a particular need, such as the illumination of a wide strip inside a fence. Care should be taken to minimize or eliminate the silhouetting or illuminating of security personnel on patrol. If, however, there are no security patrols, this silhouetting affect can be used to enhance the presence or activity of vandals or other perpetrators of criminal acts.

Standby Lighting

A standby system differs from a continuous lighting system in so far as its intent is to create an impression of activity. The lights are not on continuously but are automatically or manually turned on randomly or when suspicious activity is detected or suspected by security personnel or the intrusion-detection system. Lamps with short restart times are essential if this technique is chosen. Standby lighting may offer significant deterrent value while also offering economy in power consumption.

Movable Lighting

Movable lighting is a stationary or portable system consisting of manually operated lights that may be lighted during hours of darkness or as needed. This system is normally used to supplement continuous or standby lighting (searchlights, as an example).

Emergency Lighting

Emergency lighting may duplicate any or all of the systems previously described. Its use is limited to times of power failure or other emergencies that render the normal system inoperative. Emergency lighting depends on alternative power sources, such as installed or portable generators or batteries.

PROTECTIVE LIGHTING REQUIREMENTS

It is not the intent of this manual to prescribe specific protective lighting requirements. Except for the minimum standards described in the next section, the administrative officer of the activity and the director of security must decide what other areas or assets to illuminate and how to do it. This decision must be based on the following considerations:

- Relative value of the items being protected
- Significance of the items being protected in relation to the activity mission and its role in the overall mission structure
- Availability of security forces to patrol and observe the illuminated areas
- Availability of fiscal resources (procurement, installation, and maintenance costs)
- Energy conservation

MINIMUM STANDARDS

Lighting in school districts is a frequently debated security measure. Most studies indicate that sufficient lighting prevents or reduces criminal activity. Lighting requirements at schools, however, are often influenced by aesthetic considerations and budgetary constraints. There is also a school of thought that promotes that crime is significantly reduced if a "lights-out" policy is adopted in schools. If this policy is given serious consideration by a school district, other compensatory and supporting measures should be used in order for the intended effects to be realized (such as alarms, having a school police department which responds to calls from the community to a dispatcher, good community relations and response education program between the school police department and residents surrounding school properties). The following are some minimum standards to keep in mind when considering security lighting:

1. Unpatrollable fence lines, water boundaries, and similar areas need not be illuminated. When similar areas are patrolled, sufficient illumination will be provided to assist the security force in recognizing and preventing intrusion.
2. Vehicular and pedestrian gates used for routine ingress and egress will be sufficiently illuminated to facilitate personnel identification and access control.
3. Exterior building doors will be provided with lighting to enable the security force to observe an intruder seeking access.
4. Industrial areas, loading docks, petroleum storage areas, and other critical areas will be provided with sufficient illumination for the security force to detect, observe, and apprehend intruders.
5. There should be a lights-out policy for interior lights after all events have concluded and the activity is closed. This is particularly the case when the inside of the building is alarmed.
6. Protective lighting will be checked daily, if appropriate, by the security force to ensure that all light fixtures are operational. Inoperative lights will be recorded and referred to the administrative officer or other appropriate departments. High impact plastic shields or other similar purpose device should be installed over lights to prevent destruction or vandalism.
7. The administrative officer and other appropriate departments will ensure that all reports of inoperative protective lights are given immediate attention and that corrective actions are taken. If appropriate, a log will be maintained identifying the date of the report, the name of the reporter, and the date of the repair.

EMERGENCY POWER

Priority areas provided with protective lighting should, as appropriate, have an emergency power source located within the area. The emergency power source will be adequate to sustain security lighting and communications requirements and other essential services required within the area. Provisions must be made to ensure the immediate availability of emergency power when the primary power source fails. Emergency power sources should start automatically, if possible. Battery-powered lights and essential communications should be available at all times at key locations within the area in the event of complete failure of primary and emergency sources of power. Emergency power systems will be tested monthly, and the results will be recorded and maintained for a minimum of three years.

TECHNICAL CONSIDERATIONS

General

The differences in building arrangements, terrain, atmospheric conditions, and other factors require that each protective lighting system be designed to meet the conditions peculiar to each activity.

Design

Protective illumination must not be maintained below the minimum required for security. Lack of sufficient illumination contributes to increases in loss and vandalism, which can far exceed savings in energy costs. In designing a lighting system, consideration will be given to local conditions at the activity. Effort will be devoted to reducing the amount of energy used to deliver the illumination required by taking advantage of all lighting energy conservation opportunities (LECO).

Some consideration factors to keep in mind when dealing with LECO concerns are:

- Evaluate LECO in terms of existing systems in the area and future requirements.
- Conduct a lighting energy audit to learn what is installed, its condition, the energy being consumed, the light produced, the amount of light needed, and so on, to determine which types of lamp (incandescent, fluorescent, mercury-vapor, metal halide, high-pressure sodium, or low-pressure sodium) would be best.
- Evaluate new system interactions with existing systems in adjacent areas to determine impact (other light levels, electrical transmission systems, heating and cooling systems, and so on).

Wiring System

Multiple circuits may be used to an advantage in protective lighting systems. The circuits should be so arranged that the failure of any one lamp will not darken a long section of a critical or vulnerable area. The protective lighting system will be independent of other lighting systems and will be protected so that a fire or disaster will not interrupt the entire system.

Controls and Switches

Controls and switches for protective lighting systems will be inside a protected area and will be locked or guarded in an appropriate manner. An alternative is to locate the controls in a central station similar to or as a part of the system used in intrusion-detection alarm central monitoring stations.

Chapter 8

Intrusion-Detection Systems

GENERAL

An intrusion-detection system (IDS) is an essential element of any in-depth physical security program. An IDS consists of sensors capable of detecting one or more types of phenomena, signal media, annunciators, and energy sources for signaling the entry or attempted entry into the area protected by the system. The design, implementation, and operation of the IDS must contribute to the overall physical security posture and the attainment of security objectives. The IDS is designed to detect, not prevent, actual or attempted penetrations. Therefore, the IDS is useless unless it is supported by near-real-time assessment systems and prompt security force response when the system is activated.

PURPOSE

The IDS is used to accomplish the following:

- Permit the more economical and efficient use of security personnel by employing mobile security forces instead of fixed guard posts or patrols
- Provide additional controls at critical areas or points
- Substitute for other physical security measures that cannot be used because of safety regulations, operational requirements, building layout, cost, or some other reason
- Provide insurance against degrees of human error or negligence
- Enhance security force capability to detect and defeat intruders
- Provide the earliest practical warning to security forces of any attempted penetration of protected areas

CONSIDERATIONS

The following factors must be considered to determine the feasibility and necessity of installing IDS equipment:

- Mission
- Criticality

- Threat
- Geographic location of the facility and location of areas and assets to be protected within the facility
- Accessibility to intruders
- Availability of other forms of protection
- Life-cycle cost of the system
- Construction of the building or facility
- Hours of operation
- Availability of a security force and expected alarm response time

TYPES OF SYSTEMS

There are basically four types of IDS: local alarm, central station, police connection, and proprietary IDS station.

Local Alarm

In a local alarm system, the protection circuits and alarm devices actuate a visible or audible signal in the immediate vicinity, usually on the exterior of the building. The alarm transmission/communication lines do not leave the building. Response is handled by any local security forces that are in the area when the alarm is sounded. Otherwise, the security force will only know of the alarm if it is reported by a passerby or found during routine checks. The disadvantage of this system is that intruders know exactly when the alarm is activated and can easily elude capture. This system should be used only when security personnel can respond quickly.

Central Station

In a central station system, the operation of alarm devices and electrical circuits is automatically signaled to, recorded in, maintained by, and supervised from a central station that is owned and managed by a commercial firm. The central station has guards and operators in attendance at all times. They monitor the signals and either respond to or call for response to any unauthorized entry into the protected area. The alarm equipment is usually connected to the central station through leased telephone company lines.

Police Connection

In a police connection system, the alarm devices and electrical circuits are connected via leased telephone company lines to a monitoring unit located in a nearby police station. An agreement with the local or other police department must be arranged prior to establishing this type of system.

Proprietary IDS Station

A proprietary IDS station system is quite similar to a central station system except that the IDS monitoring and recording equipment for all intrusion-detection systems on school district property is located within a constantly staffed security/police force communications center maintained and owned by the district. The district's security/police force responds to all IDS activations. The alarm sensor equipment is usually connected to the security/police force central monitoring station through leased telephone company lines or through cable that is owned and installed by the district. If a computerized IDS is used, it must be safeguarded against tampering.

SUBSYSTEMS

Each IDS comprises various types of equipment that operate in unison. Data generated by the sensing devices installed at protected locations must be transmitted by electrical impulse to control annunciator display equipment in a central alarm annunciating station. Electrical power, including backup power, must be supplied to all equipment. Each equipment category constitutes a subsystem and is described below.

Sensor Subsystem

Sensors are divided into two categories, depending on where and how they are used: exterior sensors and interior sensors.

Exterior Sensors. Exterior IDS sensors should be selected for the best performance under prevailing environmental conditions, such as soil, topography, weather, and other factors that could adversely affect performance or increase the rate of false alarms. Exterior sensors will be an approved commercial type as appropriate. Currently installed sensors that do not meet the standards of this manual may continue to be used until replacement or upgrade becomes necessary.

Interior Sensors. Interior IDS sensors will be an approved commercial type, as appropriate. Presently installed sensors that do not meet the standards of this manual may continue to be used until replacement or upgrade becomes necessary.

Data/Signal Transmission Subsystem

This subsystem links the sensors with the control and monitoring consoles. The transmission medium is used to send data and control signals to and from all sensors, control points, and annunciator panels. It may be hard-wired land lines, radio-frequency links, fiber-optic cables, or a combination. This vital subsystem is the weakest and most vulnerable part of the IDS and requires protection.

Annunciator, Control, and Display Subsystem

The annunciator, control, and display subsystem provides the equipment for the control and monitoring of the IDS. Through this equipment, security force personnel are instantly alerted to the status of a protected area. This subsystem will be located in a restricted area and closed off from public view. Alarmed spaces will be designated by zones.

Operating Power Subsystem

Normal.   The power to operate an IDS is usually 115-volt AC electrical power available in each protected area and the security force headquarters, except where safety requirements prohibit its use (for example, hazardous storage areas).

Emergency Backup Power.   It is vital to ensure that the IDS will operate continuously. Each IDS will have an emergency power source to ensure the system's continuous operation in the event of a power failure. Emergency backup power sources usually consist of rechargeable batteries, an emergency generator, or both. (Refer to the detailed discussion on emergency power later in this chapter.)

INTRUSION-DETECTION SYSTEM POLICY

For the intrusion-detection system, standard equipment with formally evaluated capabilities will be used. No IDS will be procured that cannot be supported for the life span of the equipment, normally considered to be ten years. System design will consider the delay time of associated barriers, the location of responding security forces, and the threat to the protected asset.

Proprietary Intrusion-Detection Systems

All systems within _____ will ideally be the proprietary type, except where approved otherwise or already in existence.   Where no response force is available, the system may be the police connection type (formal arrangements must be negotiated with the local police to ensure that they will monitor and respond to the system) or the central station type (this will require lease or purchase of the equipment and a contract with a commercial company that monitors the system and will respond twenty-four hours a day). Telephone answering services will not be used.

Command, control, and display units will be located at the security force or central station headquarters. The headquarters will be monitored twenty-four hours a day, and security personnel will respond to all alarms. These units will provide an audible alarm and a specific identifying visual alarm for each protected area. Ballistic protection requirements for security force headquarters and dispatching centers should be considered, as appropriate.

Alarm transmission lines between the protected area and the monitoring units may be protected by standard or high-security electronic line supervision systems. These systems are used to detect any signal cutting, shorting, tampering, splicing, or substitution on the sensor signal data-transmission network.

All sensors, transmitters, transponders, control units, and other IDS components associated with a protected zone will be physically located within the protected area. If this is not practical because of design or safety constraints, they will be located within enclosures that are resistant to physical attack and are protected by sensors that detect unauthorized efforts to open or tamper with the enclosure.

Shunt locks (key switches, controllers, or other mechanisms used to activate and deactivate the entire IDS) will be installed inside the protected area. Alarm activation delay devices are available that will allow sufficient time for personnel to exit the protected area after the system is activated.

All IDS equipment whose housing can be opened will be fitted with antitampering devices that will initiate an alarm signal. The antitampering system will be in continuous operation regardless of the IDS's mode of operation (access, secure, day, night).

Emergency Power

An emergency backup (secondary) power source will be provided to ensure the continuous operation of the IDS. This secondary power source will be provided by an uninterrupted emergency generator, if available, or batteries. Batteries will have adequate capacity to maintain proper operation of the system under normal operating conditions for a minimum of four consecutive hours in the event of an AC power failure. To calculate the size of batteries, 105 percent of the capacity necessary must be provided, and it must be assumed that during the period of operation on backup power, 5 percent of the detection circuits will be in the alarm mode. If a computerized IDS is used, the computer must be provided with a continuous-type uninterruptible power supply (UPS).

Power supply units will include automatic constant-potential, solid-state battery chargers of adequate capacity for the purpose required. The charge rate will be constantly tapered. Manually controlled, step-type charging is not acceptable.

Power supplies will be arranged so that batteries are maintained fully charged at all times when AC power is available; batteries are recharged to 85 percent capacity within forty-eight hours from an almost fully discharged state; the system automatically transfers from AC to battery power whenever the former fails, and it returns to AC power upon restoration of the power; alarms are not initiated on detection circuits upon transfer from one power source to the other; and batteries are prevented from discharging into the chargers during any interruption of normal AC power. Supervisory circuits will be installed so that audible and visual signals are created on the monitor, annunciator, or display panel upon failure, and restoration of normal AC power and all power supplies will be protected against overload by fuses or circuit breakers. A positive indicator will be provided for a blown fuse or a tripped circuit breaker indicating which specific fuse or circuit breaker has blown or tripped.

All safety hazards will be identified by caution labels as near as practical to the actual point of hazard.

Contractor Qualifications

Any commercial firms used to install, service, or maintain intrusion-detection equipment or security alarm systems must be listed by Underwriters Laboratories (UL) in a commercial burglar alarm category for the appropriate level of protection required by the facility. In addition, the IDS equipment installed by a commercial firm must be listed by Underwriters Laboratories.

The commercial firm must be staffed and equipped to provide maintenance on the system on a twenty-four-hour, seven-day-a-week basis. They must have a response time of no more than four hours between notification and arrival at the point of maintenance. Telephone answering services will not be used.

UL listings can be verified by calling the group leader of the Burglary Protection and Signaling Department Certificate Service at one of the following numbers:

(847) 272-8800 (Northbrook, Illinois)

(516) 271-6200 (Melville, New York)

(408) 985-2400 (Santa Clara, California)

(919) 549-1400 (Research Triangle Park, North Carolina)

INSTALLATION

The following installation procedures apply:

1. The preferred installation method for all UL-listed IDS equipment is by qualified personnel from school plant facilities or other approved UL listed and licensed sources.
2. Knowledge of the details of a specific IDS may afford an individual the means to effectively bypass the installation. Usually, the original installation of an IDS is accomplished under a construction or installation contract, and various elements are involved, such as the contract document, specifications, detailed drawings, and the actual physical labor necessary to install the device. Sensitive documents, such as the as-built drawings that show both specific design details and locations of components, should be considered confidential. Because most intrusion-detection systems in current use are available on the open market, classification of the system is not appropriate.
3. The general location of the system is not confidential, although its presence should not be publicized. The contract document itself may reveal only sensor

locations and administrative specifications involved in the contract. However, to ensure that trustworthy personnel are used to install, inspect, and maintain the IDS used to protect locations and material, contractors should be chosen from those with the proper clearance and licenses, and only cleared personnel should be used to install, inspect, and maintain the IDS.

4. All as-built drawings, operator instructions, and copies of the maintenance, engineering, and schematic drawings will be provided to the office of security and school plant facilities before installation, testing, and acceptance of the system.

MAINTENANCE

Proper maintenance of an IDS is imperative. Systems that are not properly maintained may fail to detect intruders or may yield a high number of false alarms, thereby losing credibility and irritating the security force to the point where alarm activations are often ignored. As a result, security may be less than it would be without the IDS. The more complex an IDS, the more highly skilled and trained its maintenance technicians must be. The number of technicians required to maintain an IDS depends on the system's complexity and reliability. Vacations, sick leave, coverage of more than one malfunction at a time, and similar factors must also be considered. Maintenance can be provided by trained personnel or by contract licensed workers. An activity that hires contract workers should develop procedures to ensure that only cleared and properly identified personnel inspect and maintain the IDS. Scheduled preventive maintenance will be performed quarterly or more frequently, as recommended by the equipment manufacturer.

Testing Frequency

All intrusion-detection systems will be tested at least monthly to ensure that they are functional. All individual sensors will be tested to determine the continued adequacy of their intended application in the selected location. All transmission devices will be validated to ensure proper operation. Testing will be conducted in concert with guidelines promulgated by the administrative officer of the activity and the director of security. Tests will include the temporary interruption of AC power to ensure AC/DC transfer and that batteries or other alternative power sources are functional. Test results will be recorded and will be retained for a minimum of three years.

For perimeter (exterior) intrusion-detection systems, randomly selected sections (zones) should be tested daily, if appropriate, by causing an actual alarm. Depending on the type of sensor, such alarm activations could include opening doors or windows, walking or running over protected areas, or passing through a sensor beam. The sections to be tested will be selected in such a manner that the entire perimeter IDS is tested at least monthly.

Training

Maintenance training on the IDS installed should be made available. Maintenance problems that result in an ineffective system are frequently caused by one or more of the following situations:

- Maintenance personnel are not adequately trained or equipped (test equipment, tools, publications).
- System maintenance is not assigned a sufficiently high priority.
- There is an insufficient number of trained maintenance technicians.
- Routine preventive maintenance is not performed.
- There is a lack of proper instructions or written procedures for security personnel or others who are responsible for operating and monitoring the system.
- No record is maintained of system tests, maintenance, false alarms, and similar elements for review of performance trends and potential problems.

Availability of Parts

The availability of replacement parts will also directly affect the maintenance of an IDS. When purchasing a system, consideration should be given to the availability of replacement parts as well as maintenance manuals. A school district can best ensure this by requiring vendors who bid on the contract to be factory authorized dealers for the products they offer.

Alarms

All alarms or false alarms to which school or activity personnel respond will be documented on Form _____.

Chapter 9

Security Education and Training

EMPLOYEE SECURITY EDUCATION

General

Every member of _____ has a security responsibility during and after school hours. The employee security education program is a multifaceted program that includes indoctrination training supported by publications, memorandums, and briefings. This chapter provides guidance designed to educate, involve, and solicit the aid of all activity personnel in the security and loss prevention programs. A security program will prove ineffective unless it is supported by a comprehensive security education program. Security personnel cannot effectively accomplish their mission without the active interest and support of all employees. Security consciousness and awareness must be stressed through a continuous, vigorous, and forceful security education program.

Requirement

An employee security education program will be developed and established at each activity to ensure that all assigned personnel recognize, understand, and carry out their responsibilities. The program will include all pertinent aspects of the physical security, law enforcement, and loss prevention programs. Many aspects of these programs have a direct impact on activity personnel.

Initial Security Indoctrination

All personnel will receive the appropriate security indoctrination training within ninety days of employment. All personnel currently assigned who have not attended a security indoctrination training course in the past will do so within one year of the date of this regulation.

Security reindoctrination training, as appropriate, will be given annually (or as appropriate) to all personnel after the initial training. Activities may participate in a single employee security education program under the cognizance of the office of security or may get appropriate training briefings.

The requirement for this type of training may be met by giving each employee a copy of this plan, by having each employee view security related videotapes or attend briefings provided by the office of security, or by other approved means. Reindoctrination training requirements may also be met by being a member of the Security Advisory and Awareness Council, by receiving formal presentations from security/police personnel or pass-down training from SAAC members, or by other approved means.

Objectives

The following are the objectives of the employee security education program:

- To involve all personnel, individually and collectively, in security and in the protection of assets
- To indoctrinate all personnel and keep them focused in applying security interests and procedures in the performance of their primary or collateral duty
- To ensure that all personnel understand the need for security as well as the dangers of neglect or carelessness in performing security procedures or duties
- To ensure that all personnel fully understand the general security measures in effect, such as the pass and badge system, the vehicle/personnel inspection and control system, and administrative inspections

Development

In developing the employee security education program, the following should be taken into consideration:

1. The security education program must approach security as a total package: a comprehensive 360-degree viewpoint. It must be concerned with physical security measures designed to prevent criminal acts as well as measures designed to provide security for information and records, materials, and personnel.
2. The security education program is essential to the successful implementation of a physical security program.
3. The security education program should encourage the prompt reporting of security violations and should attempt to do the following:
    a. Reduce security related infractions and violations
    b. Receive feedback on ways to improve security protection
    c. Reduce loss of property
    d. Reduce vulnerability
    e. Instill security consciousness and solicit information about potential threats

4. The security education program must include a study of vulnerabilities and criminal statistical data for the activity (for example, crime statistics, security incident or complaint reports).
5. The security education program must overcome the assumption by activity personnel that they should not be concerned with security unless they work on security matters directly. The plan must impress on them that a locked door or file cabinet does not constitute an end in itself but is merely an element in the overall security plan.
6. Security consciousness is not an inherent state of mind; it must be acquired. Many people are naive and trusting and are inclined to accept things at face value. These characteristics are not conducive to vigilance or security consciousness.

Visual Aids

The security education program can be reinforced through the use of visual aids, such as posters, placards, and leaflets.

Posters. Posters are an effective means of disseminating the security message. They should be large in size, and the message should be brief. Posters should be displayed in locations where many people pass or congregate.

Placards. Placards are effective where people tend to congregate and have time to read, such as at bulletin boards, telephone booths, vending machines, cafeterias, and recreational areas.

Leaflets. Leaflets are economical and provide broad coverage. The distribution of leaflets should be approved by the administration and the office of security.

Publications

Many professional security publications on specific crimes and security problems are available and can be obtained from the office of security. Materials have been developed by the office of security that identify recent incidents, security deficiencies or violations, and trends that have become apparent in the security posture of the activity or the district.

Program of Instruction

The office of security and the administrative officer of the activity are responsible for planning and administering an effective program of instruction. Coordination with other departments is essential. To make profitable use of the limited time normally available for such instruction, a competent instructor is essential. The office of security should handle the most important portions of the instruction. Other competent instructors may be used for less important topics or for topics that concern their areas of responsibility, training, and experience. This instruction should be coordinated with the office of security. Each of the following people can assist in the formulation of the education program by contributing material from his or her own area of expertise and by presenting security briefings on those topics:

- State/city/commonwealth attorney/school board attorney
- Local, state, and federal law enforcement personnel
- Fire official
- Information services professional
- Medical representative
- Others, as required or appropriate

The program should be based on an evaluation of the total security posture of the activity. It should begin with an explanation of the program and its aims and objectives—the "why." Next, it should seek to develop the necessary tools to reach those aims and objectives. Finally, it should delineate methods of instruction by which the program will be conducted. Each program must provide for initial and refresher training. The education program must, above all, stress the necessity of support from every individual, regardless of work assignment. At a minimum, the program should include material on any recent incidents of security deficiency or violation and any areas of laxity or trends in the security posture of the activity.

Crime Prevention

All security education programs should include material on programs that are designed to reduce crime, including loss of property through pilferage. Crime prevention operates by eliminating or neutralizing factors that cause individuals to commit criminal acts. A security education program provides an excellent means of disseminating crime and loss prevention information and encouraging the active participation of all employees in observing and reporting security deficiencies, violations, or hazards of any nature. Video programs on this topic are available from the office of security.

Training Records and Documentation

Individual security training and indoctrination records will be maintained and documented in personnel training folders, as appropriate. Security/police personnel will have individual training folders maintained by the office of security. These folders will document all training for the individual officer.

SECURITY FORCE TRAINING

The effectiveness of a security force is influenced by the quality of its training program. Effective training depends on leadership, proper organization, and the efficient use of resources. Minimum training standards are essential to enable security force personnel to perform their duties in a professional manner according to professional standards and procedures.

Duties and Responsibilities

Director of Security.   The director of security is responsible for security and law enforcement matters for the district. He or she will:

- Be responsible for the overall security and law enforcement training programs
- Provide technical assistance and guidance to individual activities with the capability to provide portable training and information
- Provide all security personnel assigned to different facilities for security in-service training, and for roll-call training, including current physical security and law enforcement trends, developments, and court decisions
- Review physical security and law enforcement course curricula or changes to course curricula before implementation to ensure uniformity and understanding of material
- Audit physical security and law enforcement programs annually
- Ensure that adequate physical security and law enforcement training is conducted for all security force personnel in accordance with this manual and other applicable directives, instructions, regulations and professional standards
- Ensure that adequate funding is budgeted to enable the security force to attend annual security officer/investigator training institute courses and in-service security training seminars
- Provide broad mission guidance and policy based on federal, state, school board or departmental requirements
- Allocate sufficient training resources based on training needs and priorities
- Be responsible for the overall activity-level supervision and training of the security force and the security education program, with the support of the administrative officer of the activity and other training resources and programs
- Identify the resources needed to support the security force training program
- Monitor all activity-level security force training, evaluations, fitness programs, records, and so on, for compliance with prescribed standards
- Ensure that activity-level security force training documentation and aids are available
- Ensure that adequate time is made available to conduct all necessary security force in-service and annual training with the support of the administrative officer of the activity and other resources

Security Training Coordinator.   The security training coordinator will:

- Be responsible for developing and administering the security force training and employee security education programs for all activities and the district
- Develop lesson plans, visual aids, performance checklists, tests, and so on, for all security force training required by this instruction and any other appropriate training
- Prepare long-range, quarterly, and monthly training plans, as appropriate

- Train all security force personnel, including auxiliary security force personnel assigned to the activity and other activity personnel, as prescribed
- Note in individual security officer training records all security force training received

Field Training Officer.   A field training officer (FTO) function will be established on a collateral duty basis in each activity where security personnel are assigned and additionally where determined appropriate. The FTO's functions include, not only the primary job of security supervisor, but also evaluating the performance of all recent security officer graduates of the physical security and law enforcement training courses when they are first assigned to a facility. The FTO will work closely with the training coordinator to ensure quality training is received by all security officers under their supervision.

The FTO will further:

1. Be a qualified member of the security force.
2. Complete a weekly evaluation of recently graduated security officer trainees and discuss the evaluation with the trainee.
3. Rate the various physical security and law enforcement tasks performed by the trainee on a scale ranging from "not acceptable" to "superior." Evaluations will be conducted for a period of thirty to sixty days after graduation.
4. Evaluate the effectiveness of the security force training program in general and discuss the program with the training coordinator.

Training Requirements

All personnel assigned to full-time security or law enforcement functions must successfully complete Phase I (basic) training (Basic Security Officer Training) as stipulated in Appendix 9.

The Training Program.   Phases I and II (in-service training seminars) are discussed in Appendix 9.

Graduation Requirements.   Students must successfully complete each segment of the training course by passing a written test for classroom work and obtaining an acceptable grade from the instructor for practical exercises or by achieving at least minimum scores, as applicable. For each written examination, students must achieve at least a minimum score of 70 percent.

Students must attain a satisfactory or better rating on each graded or practical exercise. If a student cannot demonstrate at least minimal standards of performance in all graded or practical exercises, graduation and certification will be denied.

Certificates of Training.   Upon satisfactory completion of training, students will be issued a certificate of training for inclusion in their training record. Security and law enforcement certifications of training, citations, diplomas, and so on, issued by other departments or agencies (military and civilian), should also be included in the individual's training record.

In-service Training Program

The in-service training program encompasses three areas: in-service, roll-call, and field training.

Phase II (In-service) Training Course.   The office of security will conduct a minimum twenty-eight-hour (or as determined) Phase II training course annually for all security force personnel. The course of instruction is outlined in Appendix 9.

Evaluation of In-service Training Course.   Periodic review of instructional material and instructors' presentations will be conducted to determine how effectively they meet the security force training requirements specified herein. This assessment is accomplished by internal and external evaluation.

Internal evaluation is a continuous process of assessing the trainee's performance and evaluating the effectiveness of instructional material and presentation methods. Internal evaluation will take the form of written and graded practical examinations and students' appraisals of instructors at the completion of instruction segments.

External evaluation determines whether graduate trainees can perform the security or law enforcement tasks they were trained to perform and whether the tasks being trained are, in fact, required on the job. External evaluations usually take the form of on-the-job critiques of recently graduated trainees by supervisors and field training officers.

Phase II Portable/Mobile Training Package.   Phase II training is available from the office of security as a portable package. The package covers all subjects to be taught with the exception of special equipment, first aid, cardiopulmonary resuscitation (CPR), physical fitness, and local directives. Each activity having security officers assigned may provide input about additional instructions addressing local policies and directives to be incorporated into the training material.

Deficiencies noted in training materials should be brought to the attention of a security supervisor, field training officer, or the training coordinator.

Roll-Call Training.   As needed, roll-call training takes place before each shift and provides training on subjects that all security force personnel need or need reinforced. Roll-call training can be used to convey the following:

- Familiarity with departmental or facility programs and operations
- Knowledge of regulations and departmental guidelines
- Information about new programs or recent incidents
- Knowledge of recent legislation and judicial decisions that may affect security or law enforcement programs
- Familiarity with various agency services and other operations in the community

Records of the subjects covered in roll-call training and attendance will be retained a minimum of three years in the security officer's training folder.

Scheduling

The scheduling of training sessions requires the careful attention of the director of security, the administrative officer of the activity, and the training coordinator to ensure that the allotted time is used to the best advantage. The activity and security support requirements will, to a degree, dictate scheduling. However, when possible preference should be given to routinely scheduling all instruction during the normal hours of duty as additional employee contract days, on teacher record days, or on parent-teacher conference days.

The office of security will prepare long-range plans for scheduling and budgeting of all training activities for security personnel.

Specialized and Advanced Training

The specialized and advanced training that is required for the efficient operation of a modern security force should be provided. This training includes advanced investigative training, the application of intrusion-detection systems, loss prevention, crime prevention, and advanced physical security and law enforcement training. It will normally be provided in normal training sessions or during site visits. Information and availability of funds for attending other professional and technical schools may be sought through the office of security.

Correspondence Courses

Security force personnel should keep abreast of professional developments and new techniques through the publications, periodicals, and specialized security and law enforcement courses offered by various government, private, and professional organizations. These resources offer excellent opportunities for job and career enhancement.

Recording Security or Law Enforcement Training

A detailed record of all security or law enforcement training will be maintained in the individual security officer's training records by the security training coordinator.

Records should document, at a minimum, subjects and courses of instruction, instructors' names, dates of completion, hours of instruction, examination results, and expiration dates of pertinent certifications, licenses, and permits (CPR, first aid, equipment, and so on). All training documents will be retained in individual training records for as long as the individual is employed. The same forms used to schedule planned training are recommended for recording completed training.

CONTRACT GUARD TRAINING

A formal training program will be provided at contractor expense before a contractor employee is assigned to perform duties as a security guard. In addition to other training that may be required, each contract guard will receive training equal to the basic security officer course as outlined in Appendix 9 of this instruction.

If armed contract guards are required at school activities, the contract will so stipulate and prescribe the minimum training standards equivalent to those contained in Appendix 9. No contract guard will bear firearms at an activity until written certification of qualification is provided by the contractor and the guard has successfully completed training in the use of force and the rules of engagement. In addition, contractors must comply with provisions prescribed by the state in which the contract is administered, including current licensing and permit requirements.

Duly sworn law enforcement officers, special police, or other sanctioned peace officers are exempt from this requirement.

Chapter 10

Security Force Communications

GENERAL

At most activities, the general-purpose communications system is not adequate for security purposes. Therefore, the security force must, when applicable, have its own communications system. This system must have direct lines between security headquarters and security personnel, an auxiliary power supply, and sufficient equipment to maintain continuous two-way voice communications among all members of the security force. Alternate communications systems are required for use in emergencies to meet increased communications needs and to maintain sure and rapid communications throughout the emergency.

For the purposes of this manual, security communications include (1) all telephone and radio systems that can be used by security personnel to provide rapid and reliable two-way voice communications and (2) key-operated electric call-box systems strategically dispersed throughout an activity that can be used by security personnel for routine tour reports or by other authorized personnel to summon emergency assistance.

PURPOSE

The purpose of security communications is to provide the following:

- Expeditious transmission of routine and emergency instructions between security headquarters, posts, and patrols and other designated offices
- Integration and coordination of security functions
- Efficient and economical use of security forces
- Expeditious transmission of requests for assistance to outside sources in the event of an emergency that the security force cannot control

The complete ten-code uniform radio voice communications system will not be used. "Plain-voice" communications will be used where possible to avoid misunderstandings.

TYPES OF COMMUNICATIONS SYSTEMS

Although there may be a variety of communication systems available in the market today, two general types are most appropriate when operating in a school environment.

Interior Communications

Interior communications are defined as two-way communications for the exchange of information between two or more points within an identified or planned area.

Exterior Communications

Exterior communications are defined as two-way communications between an identified area and an exterior point or points from which emergency assistance or mission critical information may reasonably be expected and for which contingency plans have been formulated.

GENERAL REQUIREMENTS FOR SECURITY COMMUNICATIONS

A reliable communications system in a school district is necessary for perpetuating an effective security or policing program which concentrates on crime prevention and intervention. If people cannot effectively communicate in a timely manner, security related incidents will probably increase in numbers and duration.

General Communications Requirements

To be effective, a communications system must be tailored to the requirements and needs of the security programs and network in place. Considerations include flexibility, criticality, time sensitivity of information, vulnerability to interception, size of the activity, natural terrain obstructions, and need for responsive reaction. The communications system is largely subject to local determination, but the following are general requirements:

- At least two systems of exterior communications, one of which will be a radio system with either an independent or emergency power source
- At least two systems of interior communications that cover all important fixed areas, one of which must have either an independent or emergency power source
- A system of radio communications that reaches all motor patrols, fixed posts, and portable ground stations and is provided with either an independent or emergency power source. Radio communications equipment must be capable of being switched to an alternate frequency in the event that the primary frequency is jammed or inoperable.

- Self-contained, multiple-frequency capability for portable communications equipment procured for security purposes. Voice encryption, scrambling, and frequency-agile radio systems should be considered to prevent media or other monitoring.
- One dedicated (tactical) frequency and one dedicated backup frequency for security forces only
- A system that provides continuous, or capability of (i.e., digital key pad on radio, cell phone, etc.), reliable voice communications with local, state, and federal agencies during crisis or serious situations
- A duress code (changed immediately when compromised and at least annually) to alert all security forces of an emergency
- A central communications and dispatch center for all security forces
- Adequate physical security protection for the communications center
- Provides easy carrying (not bulky)

Tests and Inspections

All communications circuits will be tested daily to ensure that they are operating properly. All communications equipment will be inspected at least quarterly by qualified personnel under simulated emergency conditions. A record of all tests and inspections, including results and action taken to correct any detected problems, will be maintained for at least three years.

Requests for Radios

All requests for new or replacement radios will be made to the director of security.

Chapter 11

Security Devices and Equipment

GENERAL

This chapter contains information that will be helpful in determining the need for some specific security equipment. It explains general and specific policies on certain devices and equipment not covered in the preceding chapters and describes their basic characteristics, purposes, and limitations.

SECURITY VEHICLES

Federal, state, and local law enforcement agencies throughout the United States routinely use sedans equipped with heavy-duty components and equipment for safety and operational reasons. These sedans are designed for the special demands of law enforcement. Years of testing and actual use have proven them to be safer and to require less maintenance than the standard commercially procured sedan.

Various operational endeavors place security vehicles and security force personnel in a hazardous position in which they require immediate identification and visibility. Therefore, security vehicles must be distinctly marked. Statistics reveal that distinctly marked security or law enforcement vehicles on patrol through parking lots or roadways contribute significantly to reducing and deterring crime.

Patrol Vehicle Requirements

The security force will be furnished with enough vehicles to conduct investigations, maintain required patrol standards, respond to emergencies, and maintain supervision of security force personnel and responsibilities. Each security force vehicle will be well maintained, identified as a security vehicle, and equipped with emergency equipment as appropriate and a mobile security force radio.

Local and State Vehicle Requirements

Security force vehicles that will be used in or will transit jurisdiction areas on or off activities should conform to local and state requirements for the equipping and certification of security and emergency vehicles.

Vehicle Markings

Vehicles will be painted the manufacturer's standard gloss white. A security department logo of either magnetic or decal manufacture will be applied to the front doors of the vehicle, if warranted.

Leased Vehicles

The preceding acquisition specifications and marking requirements also apply to leased vehicles.

Vehicle Replacement Standard

The standard for replacement of security vehicles will be six years or 72,000 miles, whichever comes first, or as dictated by school board policy. A compact or full-size sedan will be used. Leases for security vehicles should include two one-year renewal options because of high mileage.

Use of Security Vehicles

These vehicles will be used solely by security force personnel in the performance of their assigned duties.

CLOSED-CIRCUIT TELEVISION

Closed-circuit television (CCTV) is not an alarm device, but it is very useful in physical security operations and is frequently used to complement an intrusion-detection system. This purpose may be accomplished by placing cameras at critical locations to provide direct visual monitoring from a remote vantage point. Closed-circuit television may be used on gates, halls, stairwells, entrances, parking lots, and so on, that are not staffed continuously or on entrances to vaults or other places where there is a security interest.

The system normally consists of a television camera, a monitor, and electrical circuitry. The camera may be remotely controlled by monitoring personnel.

Closed-circuit television can also be useful in assessing alarms. It can be triggered automatically when an alarm sounds or by personnel at the alarm control center to determine whether response forces should be dispatched.

The effectiveness of CCTV is limited. Constantly monitoring a television screen tends to have a hypnotic effect on the viewer. Other distractions include gaps in attention and periods when an individual is otherwise occupied, such as when answering the telephone or writing. The effectiveness of a CCTV system can be improved with the addition of motion detectors that will activate an audio or visual alarm at the control center when movement is detected within the camera's area of vision. In addition, a time-lapse videotape recorder can be added at the control center. It can be installed so that it will be activated automatically by the camera's motion detector or by personnel in the control center.

The normal use of CCTV on gates or other access points must incorporate the use of a two-way communication system between the monitor panel and the gate or access point in conjunction with an electronically operated lock. With this configuration, the person at the monitor panel can be alerted by a person desiring entry, can converse with the person using the speaker system, can observe the individual on the monitor to determine his or her authority to enter, and then, if appropriate, can release the lock. The equipment can be adapted to enable security personnel to make a side-by-side comparison of a person's face with the picture on his or her identification badge. Closed-circuit television can minimize the number of security personnel normally needed for checking identification at gates or other designated areas.

Closed-circuit television controls should be enclosed in metal housings and properly secured to preclude tampering by unauthorized personnel. The delay caused as the camera warms up and is adjusted can be eliminated by keeping the camera in continuous operation.

The following are some features that should be considered for inclusion in a CCTV system:

- Pan/tilt/zoom capability if appropriate
- Closed circuit (non-tube)
- Fixed varifocal or wide-angle lens as appropriate
- Low lux
- VHS time-lapse recorder or multiplexer as necessary
- Color (most cameras for school applications should be color vice black and white particularly where there is a security officer response; this also facilitates identification of persons involved in incidents; black and white cameras may be appropriate in other applications).
- Emergency backup power
- Fast warm-up capability
- Remote adjustment
- Special environmental enclosures or covers that are vandal-resistance
- Moving image sensor

A common problem with CCTV systems is the light intensity required for available cameras. This requirement must be determined and the availability of sufficient light verified before the system is purchased and installed. Other factors that must be considered are the initial cost of the system, the cost of maintaining it, weather conditions that may hamper visibility, and proper installation requirements.

Closed-circuit television maintenance contracts will include wording similar to the following: "When removal of a system component is necessary, the contractor will be fully responsible for any loss or damage. A loan of the same type of component, operable within the CCTV system, will be furnished by the contractor within four working hours after removal of the system component to be repaired, without additional cost. Also, without additional cost, the contractor will be responsible for maintaining this replacement component in a totally functional condition until the repaired component is returned and made to operate in a totally functional manner within the system." CCTV by itself should not be considered as security, but as a piece of equipment to improve your ability to assess situations and determine the appropriate response. CCTV does not replace security personnel but allows them to be more efficient without hiring additional personnel.

SPECIALIZED SECURITY EQUIPMENT

Specialized equipment is available to enhance the efficiency of the security force. The director of security will obtain or seek funding for any equipment required to improve the security program. Items in this category include cameras, binoculars, portable lights, night-vision devices, surveillance cameras, listening devices, flashlights, portable radios, first-aid kits, traffic-control devices, and special clothing for the health, comfort, or safety of security personnel. The office of security must keep abreast of new equipment that may improve the effectiveness of the security program. All items of security equipment for the use of security personnel or other individuals (appropriate clothing, self-protection devices, radios, handcuffs, and so on) will be procured by the office of security and issued to approved members of the security force.

DRUG AND ALCOHOL TESTING EQUIPMENT

The use or possession of alcohol and illegal or controlled substances by students is not unfamiliar to school administrators or security and law enforcement personnel. Along with traditional education and drug-resistance programs in the schools and the community, proactive prevention and deterrence measures must be in place and publicized to all students.

Recent court decisions have ruled in favor of school districts that conduct the random drug testing of student athletes, but the testing of other students is still conditioned on "reasonable suspicion" by school administrators. Should administrators suspect a student to be under the influence of alcohol or drugs, they should have available in the school a "breathalyzer" and presumptive drug-testing kits. These tests can consist of a simple change in color used as prescribed to test for the presence of alcohol or specific suspect drugs.

Another effective deterrence measure is to use drug-detection dogs to randomly inspect lockers and cars. Dogs can also be used to inspect student belongings. In this case, as an example, students are asked to leave their belongings (book bags, coats, purses, etc.) at their desks and to leave the classroom with the teacher as a class before the dog and handler enter the room. Drug-detection dogs and their handlers are usually available from local law enforcement agencies and can usually be requested with advanced planning and scheduling. Explosive-detection dogs (trained to detect traces of gun powder and other explosives) may also be available from local or state law enforcement agencies to seek out guns, bullets, and explosive related material. Some school districts have their own drug detection dog and handler as part of the school security/police department.

Appendix 1

Sample Security and Loss Prevention Plan

Every facility and "the district" should develop and publish a written security and loss prevention plan either in coordination with other emergency or improvement plans or, ideally, as a separate document. The plan should address and contain standard operating procedures or desired practices pertaining to security and loss prevention related matters and crisis management actions. The plan should have separate annexes for fires, explosions, bomb threats, hostage situations, or any other serious security related situation or potential crises. This appendix is intended to provide the reader with a sample format that can be used for developing the above described plan. Figure A1.1 is a sample of an implementation memorandum which a school district could use when a "district" plan is written. A similar type memorandum to all facility employees by the administrative officer would be appropriate when implementing an individual facility plan. An individual facility plan should also be included in the "district" plan as an appendix.

SAMPLE PLAN

School/Location: _____   Date: _____

Purpose

State the purpose of the plan.

Area of Security

Define the areas, buildings, and other structures that are considered critical, and establish priorities for their protection.

Control Measures

Define and establish restrictions on access and movement into critical areas. These restrictions can be categorized as related to personnel, vehicles, and materials.

85

MEMORANDUM

TO: All School Employees
FROM:
SUBJECT: _____ Security and Loss Prevention Manual

Purpose. To establish regulation, provide guidance, and set forth uniform standards for security, physical security, and loss prevention measures to safeguard personnel, property, and material on property.

Scope. Enclosure (1) addresses security and loss prevention responsibilities, physical security measures, and minimum criteria for physical security.

Discussion. To be effective, a security, physical security, and loss prevention program must receive attention and direction from all echelons, and security functions must be carried out by properly trained and equipped personnel. It is the responsibility of all principals, directors, supervisors, and department heads to ensure that their security posture is accurately assessed and that security resources are appropriate to execute these programs.

Responsibilities. Security is the direct, immediate, and moral responsibility of all employees of _____ . Security should be viewed as a requisite component of education and an integral part of the school infrastructure.

a. Principals, directors, department heads, and supervisors are responsible for physical security and loss prevention within their areas of responsibility.

b. The director of security is the designated representative of the superintendent of schools responsible for planning, implementing, enforcing, and supervising the security, physical security, and loss prevention program with the support of all assistant superintendents, principals, directors, department heads, and supervisors.

c. Assistant superintendents, principals, department heads, and supervisors at all echelons will evaluate the physical security, loss prevention, and security response program of subordinates and will ensure compliance with enclosure 1.

Intent. Enclosure 1 is intended to give a long-range plan and direction for security goals. It is understood that it will take time to implement and meet the intent of some programs; however, many other security measures and programs can be realized early on with the proper attitude and attention to security objectives.

Enclosure

Figure A1.1   Sample Memo to School Employees

Personnel Access.   Establish controls that are pertinent to each area or structure. Address each in terms of authority and criteria for personnel access.

Authority for access
Access criteria for the following:
> Assigned personnel (school staff, students, employees)
> Visitors (parents and others)
> Vendors and tradespeople
> Contractor personnel

Identification and Control.   Describe the system to be used in each area. If a badge system is used, provide a complete description of the system, including the requirements for identifying and controlling those who are visiting or conducting business at the activity.

Application of the system. The badging system used should be identified for the following:
> Assigned personnel (school staff, students, employees)
> Visitors (parents and others)
> Vendors and tradespeople
> Contractor personnel

Material Control.   Describe procedures and prevention or deterrence programs or measures in operation at the facility as they pertain to the following:

Incoming materials
> Requirements for admission of materials and supplies
> Search and inspection of materials
> Special controls on delivery of supplies or shipments

Outgoing materials
> Required documentation
> Controls, as outlined above

Hazardous materials
> Controls on movement of hazardous materials at the facility
> Controls on shipment or movement of hazardous materials leaving the facility or moving between facilities

Vehicle control
> Policy on administrative or other inspection of vehicles
> Parking regulations
> Controls for entrance and exit of the following:
> > Privately owned vehicles (students and staff)
> > Government vehicles
> > Emergency vehicles
> Vehicle registration and decals

Aids to Security

Describe how the following aids to security are being implemented at the activity:

Protective barriers
    Definition
    Clear zones
        Criteria
        Maintenance
    Signs
        Types
        Posting
    Gates
        Types
        Posting
        Lock security
Protective lighting systems
    Use and control
    Inspection
    Action to be taken in the event of a failure of commercial power
    Action to be taken in the event of a failure of an alternate source of power
    Emergency lighting systems
        Stationary
        Portable
Intrusion-detection systems
    Security
    Inspection
    Use and monitoring
    Action to be taken in response to an alarm
    Maintenance
    Alarm logs or registers
    Sensitivity settings
    Fail-safe and tamperproof provisions
    Location of monitor panel
Communications
    Location of communications equipment
    Use
    Tests
    Authentication

Security Forces

Include general instructions that apply to all security force personnel (fixed and mobile) on site or who respond to serious incidents. Cross-reference any pertinent detailed instructions, such as special orders or a district departmental Standard Operating Procedures (SOP) Manual.

The security force or security force personnel assigned should also be addressed with regards to the following factors and operating criteria:

Composition and organization
Tour of duty
Essential posts and routes
Equipment
Training
Use of drug- and explosive-detection dogs and metal detectors
Method of challenging
Auxiliary security force
    Composition
    Mission
    Equipment
    Location
    Deployment

Crisis Management

Describe the actions required in response to various emergency or serious situations.

Coordinating Instructions

Indicate matters that require coordination with other security, law enforcement, or service agencies.

Integration with plans of other organizations
Liaison and coordination
    Local authorities
    Federal agencies
    Military organizations

Signed: _____
Administrative Officer
Appendixes (as appropriate):
A: Map of Facility

Appendix 2

Bomb Threats and Loudspeaker Messages

APPENDIX 2A: BOMB THREAT PLANNING

General

Bomb threat planning is an important facet of any physical security program, whether for a single building, a facility, or an activity. This appendix provides a basic outline from which an effective bomb threat plan and training program can be developed.

Definitions

Bomb. A bomb is a device that is capable of causing injury or death and damage to buildings and materials when detonated or ignited. Bombs are classified as explosive or incendiary. An explosive bomb causes damage by fragmentation, heat, and blast wave. The heat produced often causes a secondary incendiary effect. An incendiary bomb generates fire-producing heat without a substantial explosion when ignited. Bombing occurs when an explosive bomb detonates or an incendiary bomb ignites.

Bomb Threat. A bomb threat is a message delivered by any means. It may (1) specify the location of the bomb, (2) include the time planned for detonation or ignition of the bomb, or (3) contain an ultimatum related to the detonation, ignition, or concealment of the bomb.

Bomb Incident. A bomb incident is any occurrence of the detonation or ignition of a bomb, the discovery of a bomb, or the receipt of a bomb threat.

Countermeasures

Countermeasures are measures that can be taken to minimize the placement of bombs, including their disruptive effects. Preplanning is an essential prerequisite for developing a workable bomb threat plan. In the preplanning phase, provisions must be made for the following:

- Communication channels
- Support organizations
  - Primary
  - Alternate
- Command and control
- Standard security and access control measures

Communications Equipment

Do not operate radio transmitters in the vicinity of the device; they could detonate it. The following elements should have communications capabilities:

- Emergency operations center
- Facility/area inspection
- Reporting system
- Search teams
- Security teams

Preparing the Bomb Threat Plan

An effective bomb threat plan must address at least the following considerations:

- Control of the operation
- Evacuation
- Search
- Finding the bomb or suspected bomb
- Disposal (explosive ordinance disposal/state police, local police)
- Detonation and damage control (barricade material around the device to guide device fragments upward)
- Control of publicity
- Erection of barriers
- Fire and medical service standby
- Disconnection of utilities
- Removal of flammable and explosive materials
- Follow-up report

Evaluating the Threat

The very first thing that takes place after a telephone bomb threat is received is that management has to evaluate the threat. The person who received the call must be interviewed, the bomb threat checklist or other notes must be reviewed, and prior calls, similar threats, and other characteristics must be considered in order to determine credibility.

Activating the Plan

Once the threat has been evaluated and a determination has been made to evacuate, the next step for management is to activate the plan. Hopefully, management is prepared with a written plan that was developed, implemented, and previously tested by responsible and trained employees. The activation of the plan will provide management with an overall framework to confidently exercise an appropriate and safe response at the outset, during, and after an incident.

Search Techniques

A bomb threat is usually received by any of the following means: telephone message, suspicious package sent through the mail, or written message sent through the mail. The choice of search techniques will depend on whether the threat is overt or covert. The following decisions must be made before the proper technique can be applied:

- Will the search be conducted before, after, or without evacuation?
- Will the search be conducted by supervisors, occupants, or a special search team?
- What percentage of the building will be searched?

If a search team is used, it should be divided as follows:

- Search of outside area: 25 percent
- Search of public areas: 25 percent
- Detailed search of building: 50 percent

Equipment

There is a variety of equipment or devices that may be used when dealing with the detection of bombs. The inspection is made by trained law enforcement or special trained personnel who use an arsenal of tools such as metal detectors, x-ray viewers, mobile robots, and explosive detection dogs. Other pieces of specialized equipment include bomb barrels, bomb blankets, and specially reinforced vaults and rooms. Often, depending on the geographic location and other demands, the availability of this specialized equipment in a timely manner, can be a factor.

Evacuation Procedures

In the event that a threat has been received and a bomb found, the following evacuation procedures will be put into effect:

- Predesignated routes of evacuation
- Priorities for removal of people
- Predesignated guides

- Other considerations
  - Authority to order evacuation
  - Decision to permit reentry into building
  - Signal to evacuate
  - Members of the evacuation team
  - Evacuation procedures
  - Destination of evacuating occupants
  - Responsibilities of occupants during evacuation

Telephonic Bomb Threats and Loudspeaker Messages

Figure A2.1 is an approved form for recording a bomb threat received by telephone. This form is available through the office of security. It can also be used to record information relating to any other type of threat received by telephone or in person. Appendix 2C contains loudspeaker messages that can be used to alert staff to bomb threats and other dangers, such as hostage situations or armed intruders on campus.

Trace of Telephone Number. According to _____ Telephone Company's office of security, if a bomb threat is received on a telephone, which is on the _____ CENTREX System, the telephone number from which the call is being made can be traced by pushing _____ on the telephone handset (_____ on a rotary phone). The traced telephone number can be identified and the number can be released to a law enforcement agency upon request.

BOMB THREAT CHECKLIST AND TELEPHONE PROCEDURES
SAMPLE

INSTRUCTIONS: BE CALM. BE COURTEOUS. LISTEN. DO NOT INTERRUPT THE CALLER. NOTIFY THE SUPERVISOR, SECURITY, POLICE, AND FIRE BY PREARRANGED PLAN WHILE CALLER IS ON THE LINE. Initiate recording number by dialing_____ or_____ (Rotary Phone).

Notification Checklist:

      Police and Fire (911)_____   Director of Informations Services _____
      Superintendent _____   Department of Pupil Services _____

Caller's identity:
      ____ Male ____ Female ____ Adult ____ Juvenile ____ Approximate Age

Origin of Call:
      ____ Local ____ Long Distance ____ Booth ____ Internal (If call is within building)

VOICE CHARACTERISTICS:
  ___ Loud ___ High pitch ___ Raspy ___ Intoxicated ___ Soft ___ Deep ___ Pleasant ___ Other

LANGUAGE:
      ____ Excellent ____ Good ____ Fair ____ Poor ____ Foul ____ Other

MANNER:
  ___ Calm   Rational ___ Coherent ___ Deliberate ___ Righteous ___ Angry ___ Irrational
                       Incoherent ___ Emotional ___ Laughing

SPEECH: ___ Fast ___ Distinct ___ Stutter ___ Slurred ___ Slow ___ Distorted ___ Nasal
Lisp

ACCENT: ___ Local ___ Not Local ___ Foreign ___ Race ___ Religion

BACKGROUND NOISES:
  ___ Factory Machines ___ Bedlam ___ Music ___ Office Machines ___ Mixed ___ Street Traffic
           ___ Trains ___ Animals ___ Quiet ___ Voices ___ Airplanes ___ Party

Pretend difficulty hearing—KEEP CALLER TALKING.
If building is occupied, inform caller that detonation could cause injury or death.

WHEN WILL IT GO OFF? Certain hour_____
QUESTIONS WHERE IT IS LOCATED? Building_____ Area_____
ASK: WHAT KIND OF BOMB? Incendiary_____ Explosives _____
WHERE ARE YOU NOW? WHAT IS YOUR NAME AND ADDRESS?

HOW DO YOU KNOW SO MUCH ABOUT THE BOMB?

ACTION TO TAKE IMMEDIATELY AFTER CALL: Notify your supervisor as instructed. Talk to no one other than instructed by your supervisor or security.

Figure A2.1   Sample Bomb Threat Checklist and Telephone Procedures

APPENDIX 2B: SAMPLE BOMB THREAT PROCEDURES

Purpose

This appendix provides guidance and procedures for incidents involving the receipt of bomb threats to _____ property.

Background

_____ has not received a significant number of bomb threats in the recent past. However, this can foster an attitude of complacency that can add to the disruption and cause delays in reestablishing normal operations when such a threat is received. Every community, city, and school, regardless of its size, is confronted with the potential problem of bomb threats. Bomb threats account for more actual disruption of activities than do bombs, and they represent a major economic loss. The time has come for every educational facility to formulate a plan of action for the safety of individuals and property and to develop a comprehensive plan to deal with bomb threats. The absence of a prepared plan and coordination with public safety agencies could place the unprepared facility in an undesirable position. A hasty overreaction to a bomb threat may result in panic, which could further endanger the safety of those involved.

Planning

Bomb threats to public schools are a frequent occurrence in most cities. A bomb threat is a fearful situation for an unprepared individual. What should be done if a receptionist is suddenly confronted with a telephone caller who announces, "A bomb is going to explode in your building in forty-five minutes"? Preparations for this call should be made well in advance by training the personnel who are most likely to answer incoming calls.

Instruct all personnel to follow established procedures when a bomb threat is received. The individual receiving the threat should stay as calm as possible and should attempt to secure as much information as possible from the caller, including the following:

- The actual building involved. The target could be a school complex with many similar structures.
- The exact location of the bomb. The caller may supply the location to reduce the chances of injury to innocent people.
- The type of bomb or device. Again, the bomber may be interested only in the destruction or disruption of a building and not the loss of lives.
- A description of the device. The caller may provide a complete description of the bomb to indicate that the call is not a hoax.
- The time the bomb is expected to detonate. This information is often furnished by the caller.
- The reason for the bombing. This information could add to the validity of the threat and assist the authorities in developing a suspect in the offense.

The recipient of the threat should ask the caller to repeat the message. If the caller complies, the recipient should record every word of the message. The recipient should note the time of the call, the tone of the voice, the caller's sex and race, if possible, any speech variations, and any background noise that may indicate the location where the call was made. The recipient should ask the caller his or her name as the last question (he or she may give it without thinking). Most of the time, the recipient of a bomb threat will not be able to get any information beyond the threat, but a genuine effort should be made to obtain the aforementioned information. The bomb threat checklist (Figure A2.1) will be completed immediately after the call, by the recipient of the call. The recipient of the call (usually the school office) can also record the telephone number from which the call is being made by dialing _____ (_____ on a rotary phone) on the telephone the call is received on. The telephone company will release the number only to a law enforcement agency. A standard tape recorder with telephone adapter can also be used to record the conversation between the caller and the person receiving the call.

Once a threat has been received, the designated individuals responsible for initiating the bomb threat plan should be notified immediately. A list of key personnel, compiled by management during the planning phase, should be kept at the most likely locations where a threat would be received.

The purpose of planning for a bomb threat situation is to ensure the continuation or re-establishment of operations should such an event occur. Coordination, command, and control are key elements to be considered in this area, and these elements are designed to ensure mutual planning approaches and objectives.

Coordination should be maintained with police and fire departments. Direct contact and discussion with these agencies will determine in what manner and to what extent they will assist in the emergency situation. Some public safety agencies will assist in the physical search of the premises, whereas others will only stand by until a device is located. For this reason, contact should be made in advance to ensure cooperation with all parties concerned. In _____, dialing 911 is the established procedure for calling the police. The fire department will stay on standby until called by police when an actual device is found. It is the responsibility of the school or other facility to actually look for and identify a suspect device.

The assignment of command clearly designates the levels of responsibility and authority. In most facilities, the chain of command has already been established. The list should provide for alternates or successors for the important positions in case of absence. The ones who occupy the key assignments must have the accompanying authority to make the necessary decisions at various levels of the emergency. At some point in every bomb threat incident, someone in authority will have to make decisions on such particulars as searching, evacuation, and reentry. Major disruptions to normal operations are not desired, but each threat must be treated seriously and not assumed to be a hoax. In _____, the administrative head (principal, department head, director, and so on) of an activity or a designated representative is the only person authorized to declare a bomb threat a hoax.

A control center must be clearly designated. In the control center, management decides on actions to be taken during various phases of the bomb situation. The primary control center (emergency operations center—EOC) should ideally be located at the communications center of the facility or other designated location. A secondary location should also be selected in the event that the communications center is the focal point of the attack. The control center should contain adequate personnel, equipment, and supplies to ensure its efficient operation. A personnel roster should be maintained in the center that lists the names, duties, and responsibilities of each person in the facility. Only a test can determine what is necessary in each particular control center.

Evacuation Procedures

In the past, it was common practice to evacuate the entire facility, regardless of its size, upon receipt of a bomb threat. Today, the decision to evacuate may be made during the process of devising the comprehensive bomb response plan. Some plans adopted by management call for immediate evacuation. Under this policy, if the threat is a hoax, the loss of production time could be costly. The alternative is to evaluate each threat and make the decision based on common sense, reasoning, and merit.

The decision to evacuate the premises is a managerial decision. In determining whether to evacuate, the following questions should be considered:

- What is the source of information about the threat?
- Is this the first threat, or have there been repeated threats, evacuations, and searches?
- Are the students or employees excused from school or work because of the threats?
- How large is the building?
- How many occupants does the building have, and what is the type of occupancy?
- Can the facility withstand a complete evacuation of the premises?
- What kind of standard security procedures or measures are routinely in place?

It is a mistake to evacuate a large number of people unless complete control of the situation is maintained. Panic caused by the fear of an unknown bomb may increase the potential for personal injury or property damage. This could be an underlying cause for the threat. When the panic stage is reached during the evacuation, it may become difficult for management to regain control of the group. Panic-stricken employees and students may lose confidence in management decisions if threats are received in the future. An effective program of informing employees and students of what is expected of them in an emergency, along with competent leadership, will go far toward preventing panic.

There should be a prearranged plan for evacuation. The following actions are suggested:

1. Determine who will evaluate the threat and decide whether to evacuate.
2. Establish a signal for evacuation. This may be accomplished in a variety of ways, but the fire drill approach is not recommended. During a fire, all windows and doors should be closed, but the opposite is advisable in an explosion situation to reduce structure damage in case of detonation.
3. Post a list of priority and alternate routes (same as fire drill routes) of evacuation within the building, and emphasize the importance of using the selected routes.

4. Individuals should be selected and trained to assist in the evacuation to ensure control and to reduce the chance of panic if an explosive device is located.
5. Before an evacuation order, the primary and secondary routes should be searched for clear passage and explosive devices.
6. Occupants should be instructed to leave office spaces open, unlock all desks, lockers, and file cabinets, turn off machinery, and remove all personal belongings, such as purses, lunch boxes, book bags, packages, and attaché cases.
7. Select evacuation holding areas where building occupants can be held and controlled pending completion of the search. The areas should be far enough away from the building to protect individuals against debris and other hazards in the event of an explosion. A minimum of 300 feet is recommended. The selected areas should also offer protection from the weather, if possible.
8. Determine points of utility line cutoffs. It may sometimes become necessary to shut off gas and fuel lines to reduce additional explosive hazards.
9. Provide a good means of communication for coordinating the total evacuation, search, security, and reentry of the building.
10. Determine who controls entry into the building during the search and who permits reentry into the building following a search in which no bomb was found.

There may be times when the total evacuation of a building is not necessary. This can depend on the type and size of the structure and the location of personnel in relation to the area where the bomb is located. In a partial evacuation, school officials must consider the legal liabilities that would arise if a bomb explodes, resulting in injuries or death to personnel, customers, or visitors. A partial evacuation requires much more preparation and coordination than a total evacuation.

A well-established and proven procedure recommended when a school receives a bomb threat is for the administrative head to give a pre-established code word over the public-address system. Upon hearing this code, all teachers, custodial staff, and food-service personnel will casually (and without causing disruption or alarm) check their spaces for any unusual item that might be an explosive device. When all spaces have been searched and no suspicious item is found, the office will be notified. Based upon this information, the administrative head can determine whether the threat appears to require further investigative attention, warrants evacuation, or is a hoax.

Search Techniques

The purpose of a bomb search is to locate any device, whether explosive or incendiary, that could have been placed by a bomber. Bombs may or may not look like bombs, and they may or may not be concealed. Therefore, the success of the search depends on the skill of the searchers and the imagination of the bomber. Searches must be well planned, coordinated, and tested. Searchers must be orderly, complete, and thorough. The number of searchers should be limited; they should include employees and others who are familiar with the facility and would more than likely recognize any object that is out of place.

There are basically three categories of people in an organization who would conduct the searches: (1) supervisors, (2) occupants, and (3) team search personnel. Any or a combination of these people could be employed in a search. There are advantages and disadvantages to each of these categories, and each should be weighed by management.

Custodians and maintenance personnel should be solicited to search because they have access to all locked rooms. Supervisors are usually asked to search when the building's occupants will not be notified of the search. If building occupants are asked to search, they must be trained; such a search is extremely hazardous if training is not received. The most efficient search is conducted by a specially trained team. One of the main disadvantages of the team search is that it requires a considerable amount of time.

Searchers should familiarize themselves with the normal building sights and sounds in order to detect unusual noises and objects more quickly. Should management decide on the use of a search team, all members should have with them certain tools and items to assist in the search: a flashlight, knife, standard and Phillips screwdrivers, crescent wrench, pliers, mirror, and tape.

Once it is decided who will conduct the search, how should it be conducted? The answer to this question is different for every type of building and circumstance. Many methods and techniques have been employed and used successfully. As a general rule, searching operations should start on the outside and work inward. Once inside, the search starts from the lowest level and works up. Some suggested techniques are discussed in the following paragraphs.

The organizers of the search should use their personnel wisely. The division should ideally employ 25 percent of the complete unit in an exterior search, 25 percent in a search of public areas, and the remaining 50 percent in detailed room searches. When the exterior unit completes its search, it should join the unit conducting the detailed room search.

The search of the exterior area should be thorough. The exterior is the most accessible area for would-be bombers, especially at night when the building is closed. Exterior searching should begin at ground level, systematically checking shrubbery, entrances, trash cans, window wells, and crawl spaces. The area should be checked from the building out to about 25 to 50 feet. After the search has been completed at ground level, it should be continued to the height reached by a person, with particular attention to window ledges, signs, fire escapes, and exterior window air conditioners. If the roof is accessible from the exterior, it must also be searched.

The unit searching the public areas should start as soon as possible, searching the areas that would be most accessible to a bomber. The unit should start in the lobbies and then search waiting rooms, halls, rest rooms, empty rooms, staircases, and elevators. Searchers should start on the ground level and work upward toward the top level as quickly and thoroughly as possible. Searchers should mark each area that they check so that no time is wasted in duplicated effort. Rooms may be marked with a piece of tape across the entrance of a room or where it may be readily seen after the search.

The final unit is responsible for conducting detail searches from room to room in the areas that are not searched by the public area searchers. This unit should begin its search in the basement and work systematically upward to the top level, marking each room upon completion of the search. Maintenance and custodial personnel should work in these units because they are familiar with furnace rooms, telephone switch rooms, air conditioning units, and other utility rooms.

Upon entering a room for a detailed search, searchers should make a visual check without turning on or off existing lights. Next, the searchers should go to various sections of the room and listen to all noises that are natural to the surroundings. Few rooms are completely soundproof, and it is surprising how many different background noises can be heard that may be of value in the search. A ticking device may be heard during this brief search period.

The actual detailed search of a room should be made in two, three, or possibly four sweeps. Each sweep should start at the room entrance. Half of the search detail unit should go clockwise; the other half counterclockwise around the walls and into the center of the room until they return to the entrance for another sweep.

The first sweep should cover the floor and wall up to approximately waist high. This will usually take in all of the furniture in the room and the rugs. The first sweep is the most time consuming and tedious, and utmost care must be taken not to move objects unnecessarily to avoid detonating an antidisturbance type device.

The second sweep should cover the room from about waist high up to the head area, starting at the entrance and working in the same manner as the first sweep. The third sweep should cover the room from head high to the ceiling. The fourth sweep involves searching the ceiling (if the room has a false or suspended ceiling), air conditioning ducts, speaker systems, and light fixtures.

Not all rooms will require all four sweeps. The third and fourth sweeps can often be combined. Once the room search has been completed and the team leader is satisfied that no device was located, the room should be marked, and the team should continue to another room to repeat the procedure. As the search progresses, team members should contact the control center via pre-established means to keep management abreast of their progress.

Different types of structures and facilities present unique problems to search units. For this reason, management should train and test search personnel to locate the peculiarities of a location and develop methods to overcome problem areas. The same basic searching technique can be used to search small school buildings to large convention centers.

The person in control of a search should never risk his or her life or that of others to protect against possible property damage. If the caller of the threat has given a time for detonation, evacuation plans should be implemented fifteen minutes before the designated time, if possible. Reentry should not occur until thirty minutes after the designated time.

Responding to a Suspicious Device

If, at any time during the search, a suspicious device is located that is thought to be a bomb, the search unit should notify the management official in charge of the search. In no case should a searcher touch, move, jar, or attach anything to a suspicious object. Searchers should be instructed that their assignment is only to search for, locate, and notify management of a suspicious device. It is then up to the search coordinator or the police to notify designated officials that a suspicious device has been located and to request the assistance of bomb technicians to disarm or dispose of the device.

The management coordinator should direct the execution of the following actions once a suspected device is located:

1. Contact the local police, the fire department, and the office of security, giving as much information as possible as to the location, description, and facts surrounding the suspicious device.
2. Barricade the device using sandbags, mattresses, bomb blankets, or other improvised materials that will not add to fragmentation if the device detonates. The barricade items should in no way touch or cover the device.
3. Open all windows and doors in the immediate area to minimize property damage from a blast or fragmentation.
4. The danger area should be barricaded and identified.
5. Evacuate the building in a prearranged plan, moving personnel at least 300 feet from the building to an area that will be protected from blast fragmentation and flying debris.
6. Do not permit reentry into the building until the device has been rendered safe or has been removed.
7. Stand by to direct a bomb technician to the suspicious device.

The location of one suspicious device should not be considered the completion of the search. It is not unusual that multiple bombs are planted in a building. Therefore, the searching must be continued. The continuation of a search, under these conditions, is dangerous and will affect the morale of the search units, but the search must be completed.

Letter and Package Bombs

Letter and package bombs are favorite tools of some individuals who are intent on harming others. Just as these bombs can be made for any number of motives, their size, shape, components, and methods of delivery can also be varied.

The following are some of the indicators pointing to a letter or package bomb:

- The unexpected delivery of an item, either through the mail or by a delivery service, or the unexpected discovery of an item at an office, at home, or near a car
- An address that includes a title only (for example, Superintendent, Principal, Supervisor)—no name
- A restrictive address (for example, "Personal")
- No return address
- Postmark from an unfamiliar area
- Excessive postage
- Rigid, bulky, or heavy package
- Misspelling

- Bad typing or handwriting
- Strange odors
- Stained wrapping

A letter or package bomb may have all, some, or none of these indicators.

If a suspicious letter or package is received, these safety precautions should be followed:

1. Do not take chances.
2. Do not attempt to open or move the item. Leave it alone.
3. If so noted on the letter or package, check with the person who is listed as the sender.
4. Evacuate everyone in the vicinity of the item to a safe, protected distance.
5. Notify the police, the fire department, and the office of security of the situation.
6. Await the arrival of a bomb technician, and provide all pertinent information about the suspicious item.

Detonation

Even when buildings are completely and thoroughly searched, a detonation may still occur. When this happens, plans for casualties, fires, crowd control, and protection of the postblast crime scene must be implemented.

The casualties must be given medical help, the contents of the building must be protected, and the crime scene must not be allowed to become contaminated to the point of jeopardizing the criminal investigation. To prepare for these eventualities, every bomb threat plan should include these contingencies. In the event of a detonation, administrative heads will use security and other appropriate personnel to cordon off and protect the crime scene until investigators arrive.

Summary of Action to Be Taken by Threatened Activity

The administrative head (principal, department head, director, and so on) of the threatened activity will become the on-scene commander and will accomplish the following:

1. Ensure that the individual who received the bomb threat completes the Telephonic Threat Checklist. The data recorded on the checklist is extremely valuable to bomb threat investigators. Note the telephone number for recording the number from which a call was made: _____ for touch-tone phones; _____ for rotary-dial phones.
2. Ensure that the individual receiving the bomb threat has immediately notified the following:
   a. Police and fire (911)
   b. Superintendent's office
   c. Deputy superintendent's office
   d. Director of information services

    e.   Department of pupil personnel services

    f.   Any other appropriate department or agency

3. Initiate increased security precautions; for example, increase the number of guards posted. Divert all vehicles around the area with the exception of police, fire, and official vehicles transporting personnel on business associated with the threat. Deny access to personnel not connected with the incident.

4. If the caller identified the threatened area, evacuate the immediate vicinity.

5. Conduct a search of the threatened area for explosive devices or suspicious-looking objects. If explosives or a suspicious object is found, the object must be considered dangerous. Do not touch or move the object unless instructed otherwise by the on-scene explosive ordnance disposal (EOD) team, which the police or fire department will call to the scene.

6. Prepare all required reports.

Once the fire department, the police, or the bomb disposal team have arrived on the scene, the building will not be reentered until they have granted approval.

Policy

Many bomb threats are unfounded. This can foster complacency on the part of those who receive the threats. To avoid any possibility that loss of life or property damage may occur, it must not be assumed that any bomb threat is a hoax. Major disruptions to normal operations are not desired, but all threats must be taken seriously. The only person authorized to declare a bomb threat a hoax is the administrative head of the facility receiving the threat.

Action

All bomb threats will receive immediate attention, and positive action will be taken as outlined in this procedure. To make the most effective and timely use of this procedure, it is imperative that all personnel be familiar with its contents. All personnel will periodically review and practice internal procedures to enhance their ability to respond to a bomb threat.

These procedures may be practiced in conjunction with fire drills or other procedures. Copies of the Bomb Threat Checklist and Telephone Procedures will be readily available in all schools' main offices and where incoming calls are received at other offices (immediately adjacent to all telephones, in sealed envelopes). The recipient of the call will complete this form while the caller is on the line or immediately thereafter.

APPENDIX 2C: SAMPLE LOUDSPEAKER MESSAGES TO ALERT STAFF TO A DANGER

This appendix provides for a sample procedure that can be implemented at a school to alert all staff to a dangerous situation taking place, or having the potential to take place, in the school. Often, announcing an incident in progress over the loudspeaker leads to greater disruption and fear, whereas having a plan to deal with unexpected but foreseeable emergencies can influence order, prevent or reduce incorrect reactions that may increase the potential for exposure to greater danger, and ultimately allow for greater staff confidence in their response to unexpected crisis situations because of prior training and planning.

Fire Drill

In the event of a fire drill, the regular fire bells will be sounded.

Bomb Threat

In the event of bomb threat, you will hear, "We are having a fire inspection. Please check your area now." You will check your areas or room and report to the team leader, who will report to the office. If you see anything out of place, try to describe it in detail when you come to the office. Do not pick up any unusual objects or packages.

Evacuation Due to Bomb Threat

If the school must be evacuated due to a bomb threat, someone will come on the loudspeaker and ask the teachers to take their students outside. Get at least one block or no less than 300 feet away from the building. Go out in the same manner as you would for a fire drill.

Hostage Situation or Armed Intruder on Campus

Someone will announce on the loudspeaker, "Greta Doorcheck, the _____ aides will meet with you now." The location stated in the announcement will be the current location of the danger. For example, "Greta Doorcheck, the fourth grade aides will meet with you now" means that the dangerous situation is in the fourth grade area. "Greta Doorcheck, the office aides will meet with you now" means that the dangerous situation is in the office. When you hear this announcement, lock your door, get your students quiet, position them so that they cannot be seen from the window in the door, and turn out the light. Wait for further information.

Evacuation Due to Hostage Situation or Armed Intruder

If we need to evacuate the building because of a hostage situation or armed intruder on campus, one of the following statements will be announced over the loudspeaker:

1. "Teachers, please hand out the bus area information now." When you hear this announcement, evacuate by the nearest safe exit, and go quickly and quietly to the bus area.
2. "Teachers, please hand out the _____ information now." When you hear this announcement, evacuate by the nearest safe exit, and go quickly and quietly to the location specified in the announcement.

Appendix 3

Administrative Random Inspection Program and Use of Metal Detectors

APPENDIX 3A: QUICK REFERENCE GUIDELINES FOR ADMINISTRATIVE RANDOM INSPECTIONS

Required Paperwork

Request for Use of Metal Detector (Figure A3.1).   This form will be submitted in advance. If a problem develops that requires the use of metal detectors (for example, a weekend incident carries over to the school), the form can be faxed to the director of security before conducting operations. See Figure A3.1.

Report of Search of Student or Student's Possessions (Figure A3.2).   This report must be completed only when a student does not voluntarily submit to a search or inspection. See Figure A3.2.

Administrative Random Inspection Report (Figure A3.3).   This report must be filled out after completion of every inspection for the day and forwarded or faxed to the director of security. It is also required after inspections by drug- and explosive-detection dogs. The departments of _____ must also be notified by telephone when a gun or other weapon is found. Information should be entered on the report form according to the explanations in the "Note" block. See Figure A3.3.

Inspection Procedures

Selection of Random Number.   Random numbers will be selected by the director of security once a month for each week of the month and will be posted on e-mail to building principals and security personnel. All metal detector operations will be conducted using the appropriate randomly selected number for that week. Metal detector inspections will be conducted at least three days per week, and classrooms must be included at least one of those three days. More inspections may be conducted as deemed appropriate for effective deterrence; additional inspections are encouraged. The more visible these measures are to students, the more deterrence will be experienced.

Applying the Number to the Operation.   The approved randomly selected number will be applied to the site situation as indicated in the following example:

PUBLIC SCHOOLS
Request for Use of Metal Detector

TO: _____   DATE OF REQUEST: _____

FROM: _____
        (Name of School)

        _____
        (Name/Position of Requester)

WEEK OF: _____ thru _____
          (month/day)   (month/day)

Day of Week	* M	* T	* W	* THR	* FRI
Period of Day					
0 (Before School)					
1 (Home Room)					
2 (1st Period)					
3 (2nd Period)					
4 (3rd Period)					
5 (4th Period)					
6 (5th Period)					
7 (6th Period)					
8 (7th Period)					
9 (Other)					

* A Buses   D Halls   G Library   K Other (Explain):
  B School Entrances E Stairs   H Rest Rooms
  C Classrooms   F Cafeteria   J Parking Lots

CENTRAL ADMINISTRATION APPROVAL:

Approved:_____ Date: _____
Not Approved: _____ Date: _____

WHITE COPY: SECURITY · YELLOW COPY: DEPUTY SUPERINTENDENT· PINK COPY: SCHOOL

Figure A3.1   Request for Use of Metal Detector

- Classroom: Beginning from a chosen starting point classroom (which should vary), every (x) classroom will be administratively inspected for a specific number of class-rooms or time frame. Every student in the selected classrooms will be inspected, or every (x) student will be inspected. The number of classrooms chosen can vary depending on the amount of disruption you choose to deal with.

REPORT OF SEARCH OF STUDENT OR STUDENT'S POSSESSIONS

Name of individual conducting search: _____

Date, place, and time of search: _____

Name, age, and sex of individual searched:
_____
_____

Items searched:
_____

Events that formed the basis for search:
_____
_____
_____

How search was performed:
_____
_____
_____

Duration of search:
_____
_____
_____

Contraband items confiscated during search:
_____
_____
_____

Signature: _____   Date: _____

Signature: _____   Date: _____
                (Student)

Figure A3.2   Report of Search of Student or Student's Possessions

- Bus: The (x) bus that pulls up in the morning will be inspected, and every student or every (x) student getting off the bus will be inspected.
- Hallway: Every (x) student traversing the chosen hallway during the selected time frame and in the selected direction of travel will be inspected.
- Other: Other selected sites, such as students coming into or from the cafeteria, gymnasium, bathrooms, library, and parking lot, will be inspected using the above guidelines. Students must not be inspected in areas where there is an expectation of privacy (such as in bathrooms, locker rooms, etc.).

ADMINISTRATIVE RANDOM INSPECTION REPORT

DATE: _____   SCHOOL:_____

DATE OF USE	LOCATION*	SIGNATURE ADMINISTRATOR:_____
TYPE*		SIGNATURE SECURITY:_____

FINDINGS *(Indicate the number of each item found. If more space is needed, please use disposition section):*

_____	Radio	_____	Razor
_____	Beeper	_____	Box Cutter
_____	Portable Phones	_____	Live Ammunition
_____	Alcohol	_____	Fireworks/Explosives
_____	Drugs	_____	Cigarettes
_____	Drug Paraphernalia	_____	Tobacco Products
_____	School Property	_____	Lighter
_____	Staff Property	_____	Matches
_____	Gun	_____	MACE/Pepper Gas
_____	Gun (toy or look-alike)	_____	Other (Describe):
_____	Knife		
☐	Nothing Found		

* *DISPOSITION OR OTHER INFORMATION AS NECESSARY:*

* *NOTE:*

TYPE:	Drug Dog (DD); Explosive Dog (ED); Metal-Detector (MD)
LOCATIONS:	Room No.; Hallway; Bus No.; Cafeteria; Library; etc.
FINDINGS:	Check or describe contraband found
DISPOSITION:	Note any additional information necessary and if Evidence/Property Custody Receipt (Form A-49) was completed.

Figure A3.3   Administrative Random Inspection Report

Posting of Signs.   Any time an administrative random inspection is in operation (other than by drug-or explosive-detections dogs), the vicinity will be posted with a sign (see Figure A3.4) that reads, "Administrative Inspection in Progress." Posting of all the building ingress/egress points with the sign/decal noted in Figure 3.1 will also meet this requirement for notice.

Refusal of Student to Submit.   If a student refuses to submit to an administrative random inspection, the student should be considered as if there was a weapon in his or her possession and will be given a ten-day suspension with a hearing that could lead to expulsion. If a student runs from an inspection, verbally advise the student to return; however,

NOTICE

ADMINISTRATIVE

INSPECTION

IN

PROGRESS

Figure A3.4

do not make any extraordinary efforts to go after the student to force him or her to return. If, after being asked to return, the student does not return voluntarily, the student will be given a ten-day suspension with a hearing when the student returns to school.

Additional Notes

To avoid the random number being considered arbitrary and capricious, it must be chosen by a central office administrator, not a school administrator or staff member in the school.

The number of students or locations inspected according to the random number selection may be determined as appropriate, keeping the value of deterrence in mind. This program is designed to be as least disruptive as possible to the learning environment as well as serve as a deterrence program.

When students apply for a parking decal, both the student and the parent or guardian or registered owner of the vehicle students drive must sign a statement added in the application granting permission for the vehicle to be inspected under the guidelines of the program to include searching under the seats, in the glove compartment, and in the trunk.

All property removed from an individual, during and incidental to an inspection or search, that is not prohibited by law or school rules and regulations must be returned to that individual upon completion of the search or at the end of the school day.

Nothing in these procedures will limit or take away from the authority of a school administrator to search an individual when there is a reasonable suspicion that he or she is in possession of a weapon or any other contraband. This program is a separate program designed to deter weapons and other items.

APPENDIX 3B: ORGANIZATION AND COMMAND STRUCTURE OF ADMINISTRATIVE RANDOM INSPECTION PROGRAM

Structure of School Inspection Team

Each school inspection team will, if possible, consist of one male and one female staff member, drawn from school administrators, security officers, or both, who are certified in the use of a hand-held metal detector. Each team should include, *if possible*, a facilitator in addition to the two metal detector operators. The facilitator's role is to serve as team supervisor and to direct students when they are selected for inspection. One facilitator may be used to supervise more than one team, when necessary.

Other staff will be assigned as needed to maintain control and cause as little disruption as possible to the normal flow of student traffic.

Staff Responsibilities

Principal, Assistant Principal, or Supervisory Security Officer.   The principal, assistant principal, or supervisory security officer assigned to the facility will:

- Submit the Request for Use of Metal Detector (Figure A3.1) for approval by the director of security.
- Organize, schedule, and supervise the site setup (metal detectors, tables, desks, signs, logs, personnel, and so on, as appropriate).
- Issue the orders of the day, including site locations, times, assignments, and the randomly selected number, in cooperation with the director of security.
- Serve as liaison with the director of security with respect to special conditions, arrests, contraband, searches, and continuation or termination of screening due to emergencies, weather, or other considerations.
- Ensure that the school maintains an Administrative Random Inspection Report file (Figure A3.3) indicating the dates, times, and locations of inspections, the contraband found, the names of students on which contraband was found, if appropriate, and other necessary information.

The principal or other administrator is encouraged to occasionally be present, if appropriate, to observe the scanning procedures.

Inspections with metal detectors will be conducted a minimum of three days per week, and classrooms will be included at least one of those three days. Additional inspections may be conducted and are encouraged in order to have high visibility of the program.

Director of Security.   The director of security will do the following:

- Coordinate scheduling changes, equipment, or any need for additional security officers at the facility, with the police if necessary, and with the school making the request after a Request for Use of Metal Detector has been received.

- Manage, supervise on site, and monitor the school inspection team program with the support of each school principal.
- Coordinate with each school principal, issue on-site changes and assignments, and institute changes in the number and ratio of individuals to be randomly selected for scanning.
- Ensure that the police are appropriately notified of any situations that require their assistance or attention.

Team Supervisor.   The team supervisor will do the following:

- Serve as team facilitator.
- Supervise the overall operation of the team in compliance with standard operating procedures, as set forth by the principal, director of security, and approved program guidelines.
- Oversee maintenance of the record book and submission of operation reports, as necessary and required.

Team Responsibilities

Team members will arrive at the site before the scheduled time of the inspection, as designated by the office of security and the principal. Each team, supported by the school custodian if so directed by the principal, will be responsible for setting up the following equipment, as appropriate, at the chosen inspection site:

- Signs
- Desks, tables, and trays
- Stanchions, ropes, and chains
- Evidence/Property Custody Receipts

Each team member will be responsible for calibrating the hand-held metal detector before using it each day. Extra nine-volt batteries should be kept on hand at the school or in the office of security for replacements.

Purpose

The purpose of the metal detector inspection is to prevent and deter students from bringing weapons to school. The degree and nature of the inspection will never exceed what is necessary to allow the staff to discharge its responsibility. The number of forbidden objects that are discovered will never be used as the measure of the inspection program's success. A program that discourages students from testing the detection efforts should be the goal. Random screening is an ideal solution because students can never be certain who will be inspected or when or where.

A Request for Use of Metal Detector (Figure A3.1) may include the request for randomly selected screening of students throughout the school day in the halls, entering or leaving a classroom or the cafeteria, exiting or boarding a bus, or any other selected school building or grounds site. The random-selection method acts as a deterrent because students can never be certain just when or where they may be inspected for weapons. The selection for screening of just certain classes of individuals based on racial, ethnic, or similar characteristics is strictly prohibited, and the selection of individuals screened will always be truly based on random selection and not on any particular characteristic or condition.

The random-selection technique has another deterrent value in that it helps combat the "pack-mule" technique in which known violators of security regulations coerce another student to transport weapons and forbidden objects into and around the school for them. These other students are usually docile, nonaggressive individuals who are easily manipulated by threats and intimidation. Female students are particularly susceptible to this tactic when threatened with physical or character attack or when friendly with the other student.

Notification

When a metal detector inspection is being conducted in a hallway, classroom, cafeteria, bus, or elsewhere, a sign will be posted in the vicinity. In addition, the screening area will be set up in such a way that the subjects of the inspection are screened in view of the general student population. When students see the inspection taking place, it reinforces the program and adds to its deterrent value. On the day when a metal detector scan is being conducted at a particular school on *everyone* entering the school, all entrance doors will be locked on that morning before the start of classes. Signs will be posted outside the building at normal or designated entrances to notify those entering the school that they will be required to enter at a designated entrance door and submit to a screening for weapons as a condition of entry.

Procedure

Principals or their designees should, if possible, be present to observe the inspection of students. When there is more than one scanning site, designees may be assigned at the direction of the principal to ensure proper coordination of the inspection procedure and follow-up activities. This presence will further enable the principal to get an accurate feel for the results and to provide an evaluation of the inspection procedures. In addition, the presence of the principal or designee will have a calming effect on students who are the subject of the scan. Generally, either randomly selected students or all students will be inspected. However, when necessary because of inclement weather, an emergency, or a backlog, the director of security, principal, or designee may elect not to screen every person, may change the ratio of students randomly selected, or may cancel the screening for that day. In such cases, the principal and the director of security will determine the number of students to be screened using one or both of the following alternatives:

- Screen every (x) student seeking entry, exit, or traversing
- Allow a number of students to enter without being screened; then resume screening all students or a specific ratio of students

Under no circumstances may school officials select a particular individual to be searched unless there is reasonable suspicion that he or she is in possession of a weapon or other unlawful item.

Use of Hand-Held Metal Detectors

When possible, weapons scanning will be conducted by a school inspection team member of the same sex as the subject who is certified in the use of a hand-held metal detector. Efforts will be made to ensure that the team members assigned to the particular school are allowed to become familiar with the students and school activities. If, however, a same-sex team member is not available, the inspection should not be canceled. Effort should be made during the initial scanning to avoid having the scanning officer or the scanning equipment come in physical contact with the subject.

The facilitator or scanning officer will greet the student, explain the process, and give directions. Before scanning, he or she will ask student to place their bags or parcels on a table and to remove any metal objects from their pockets and to lay these items on a tray or other appropriate fixture.

Students who refuse to cooperate with the inspection will be referred to the principal for appropriate action. See Figure A3.5 for a suggested procedure for use of the metal detector.

Response to Activation of the Metal Detector

If the metal detector activates while scanning a bag or parcel, the inspector will ask the student to open the bag or parcel. The team member will then examine the contents for weapons. If items in the bag or parcel must be shifted to provide a better view, the team member will do so, not the student.

If the metal detector activates while scanning a student and the source of the alarm is not apparent (for example, jewelry), the team member conducting the scan will direct the student to remove any remaining metal objects from his or her person and will conduct a second scan. If the detector activates again, the individual will be escorted to a stage II station (a separate or private area), if appropriate, and a further inspection will be conducted in accordance with the procedures outlined in the next section.

Pat-down Search Procedures

The search must be conducted by a staff member of the same sex as the subject. The search must be conducted in the presence of another staff member.

Security Inspection Procedure

The following procedure is only suggested. Security directions will establish specific inspection methods. However, this technique gives good coverage of the inspected subject.

With the metal detector turned on and tested for correct sensitivity (by passing the probe near a metal object), approach the subject from the front. Start with the probe held alongside the neck, lightly touching the collar of the clothing, moving down to the shoulder and down the arm to the hand. The outline of the body is then traced up the inside of the arm to the armpit, down to the waist, and along the outside of the leg to the feet. Be sure to bring the probe fully to the floor (level alongside the feet) to detect metal objects hidden in shoes or heels. Each foot may have to be raised/picked up off the floor a foot or two if metal in the floor causes the metal detector to go off routinely in this area.

Move the probe to the inside edge of the same shoe sole and follow up one leg and down the other. Move around the shoe on this other side, scan up the outside of the leg to the armpit, down the inside of the arms, and up the outside to the shoulder, ending at the collar.

Step to the side of the subject (the side first searched). Hold the probe parallel to the ground at the top of the chest. Make one pass down the front of the subject to below knee level, then move the probe behind the person. Make a final pass over the back surface of the body, starting below the knees and moving upward.

Check all headgear (hats, turbans, and so on) and unusual hairstyles <u>carefully</u> with the probe, as well as visually.

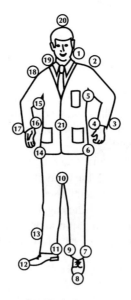

Figure A3.5   Sample Security Inspection Technique

Before conducting the search, the staff member will once again ask the student to remove any remaining metal objects from his or her person. If the student declines, he or she will be searched in accordance with these procedures.

The search will be conducted around the area of the body that activated the metal detector. The search will commence with the patting of the individual's external clothing in the vicinity of pockets, belts, shoulders, or other specific areas, for the limited purpose of discovering items that may have activated the metal detector.

If the staff member feels an object that may have activated the metal detector, the member will ask the student to remove the object. If the student refuses, the staff member will remove the object.

If an object voluntarily provided by or removed from the student could have activated the metal detector, the staff member must cease performing the search. He or she will then scan the individual again, and the search will continue only if the metal detector again activates.

The staff member will complete a Report of Search of Student or Student's Possessions, which will be noted in the Administration Random Inspection Report.

Discovery of Contraband

If an individual is in possession of contraband (weapons, controlled substances, prohibited objects like beepers), it will be seized, and the school inspection team facilitator will notify the appropriate school official, who in turn, will summon the police, as appropriate. If an arrest is made, the police will take custody of the contraband after the school has completed an Evidence/Property Custody Receipt (Form _____). An entry will also be made in the Administrative Random Inspection Report.

If the police do not arrest the subject, an administrator or security officer will take custody of the seized contraband and confiscate it. He or she will complete an Evidence/Property Custody Receipt and will note the incident in the Administrative Random Inspection Report.

Return of Property

All property removed from a student that is not prohibited by law or school rules and regulations must be returned to the student upon completion of the search.

Sweep of School Grounds or Areas Inside School

Following an inspection, the school inspection team will conduct a perimeter sweep around the scanning area for weapons or other contraband that students may have thrown aside when they became aware that a search was in progress.

Nothing in these procedures limits the existing authority of a school administrator to search an individual when there is a reasonable suspicion that he or she is in possession of a weapon or any other contraband.

Contingency Plans

The following procedures will be used as guidelines when approval is granted to screen every student entering selected schools when school opens and before the start of classes.

Metal Detector Procedures and Stages.   Figure A3.6 is organized to show the different stages students go through and the different roles and junctions staff members perform when an individual school is chosen to undergo a metal detector inspection for all students who enter the school before classes begin on a selected date. This is a manpower intensive operation which requires prior planning and confidentiality concerning the date of the inspection. This is not intended to be a routine procedure at a school but is intended to be used when there is prior information to indicate a serious incident that is likely to take place at school, or the administration desires to make a statement to the student body about the seriousness of bringing weapons and other unlawful items to school. An operation of this nature can be expected to take about two hours depending on the size of the staff and physical layout of the school.

Teams.   Figure A3.7 is organized to show how a school district with proprietary security/police force personnel assigned to a number of schools can utilize these personnel effectively to build metal detector teams to provide coverage when the operation in Figure A3.6 is implemented at a school. This type of pre-planning will not only allow for easy implementation, but also give consideration for all other schools not undergoing such an inspection, to have as equal security presence as possible under the circumstances.

TEAM STRUCTURE
Each team should include at least one group leader (the supervisory security officer of the selected site) and eight security officers. The principal of each site selected for screening under the administrative random inspection program will ensure that a minimum of thirty-six administrators and teachers are on site early enough to help set up and operate the inspection program according to Figure A3.6. They must be knowledgeable about their required duties.

Staff Responsibilities
PRINCIPAL OR DESIGNEE
The principal or his or her designee will do the following:

- Submit a Request for Use of Metal Detector (See Figure A3.1).
- Organize, schedule, and supervise the site setup (including signs, tables, stanchions, ropes, trays, and having bags, tape, forms, etc. available) and the school administrators and teachers in their support role.
- Issue the orders of the day, including changes of location or assignment, changes in the number or ratio of individuals to be scanned, and patrol assignments of team numbers and support staff, in cooperation with the director of security.
- Serve as liaison with the director of security with respect to special conditions, arrests, contraband, searches, and continuation or termination of screening due to emergencies, weather, or other considerations.

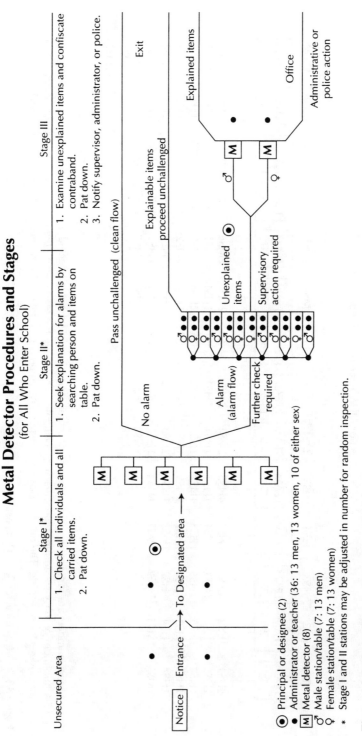

Figure A3.6   Metal Detector Procedures and Stages

Metal-Detector Team Composition*
(for All Who Enter the School)

(School Name)

School	Team	Composition
HS1	TEAM 1	4HS1, 1HS5, 1HS2, 1HS3, 1HS4, 1MS5
HS2	TEAM 2	4HS2, 1HS1, 1HS5, 1HS3, 1HS4, 1MS5
HS3	TEAM 3	4HS3, 1HS1, 1HS5, 1HS4, 1HS2, 1MS2
HS4	TEAM 4	4HS4, 1HS1, 1HS5, 1HS2, 1HS3, 1MS7
HS5	TEAM 5	4HS5, 1HS1, 1HS2, 1HS3, 1HS4, 1MS4
MS1	TEAM 6	2MS1, 1HS1, 1HS5, 1HS4, 2HS3, 1HS2, 1MS3
MS2	TEAM 7	2MS2, 1HS1, 1HS5, 1HS4, 1HS2, 1MS1, 2HS3
MS3	TEAM 8	3MS3, 2HS1, 1HS5, 1HS4, 1HS3, 1HS2
MS4	TEAM 9	2MS4, 1HS1, 2HS5, 1HS4, 1HS3, 1HS2, 1MS1
MS5	TEAM 10	2MS5, 1HS1, 1HS5, 2HS2, 1HS4, 1HS3, 1MS7
MS6	TEAM 11	3MS6, 1HS1, 1HS5, 1HS4, 1HS2, 1HS3, 1MS7
MS7	TEAM 12	2MS7, 1HS1, 1HS5, 1HS2, 1HS3, 2HS4, 1MS1
MS8	TEAM 13	2MS8, 1HS1, 1HS5, 1HS2, 2HS3, 1HS4, 1MS3
ELEM	TEAM 14	0, 1HS1, 1HS2, 1HS3, 1HS4, 1HS5, 1MS8, 1MS5, 1MS2, 1MS6

*Team numbers are for security officer team composition when named school is selected. Each school will be required to have a minimum of thirty-six administrators/teachers available to complete the teams when their school is selected for or requests a metal-detector screening. The number may vary, depending on prior planning and variables at each individual school.

Figure A3.7   Metal Detector Team Composition

- Ensure that the school maintains an Administrative Random Inspection Report file (See Figure A3.3) indicating the dates, times, and locations of inspections, the contraband found, the names of students on which contraband was found, if appropriate, and other necessary information.

DIRECTOR OF SECURITY
The director of security will do the following:

- Establish a schedule for site coverage and communicate that schedule, after the request has been approved, to the site principal, other necessary school administrators, and supporting school team composition members.
- Manage, supervise on site, and monitor the school inspection team program with the support of each school principal.
- Coordinate with each school principal, issue on-site changes and assignments, and institute changes in the number and ratio of individuals to be randomly selected for scanning.
- Ensure that the police are notified of any situations that require their assistance or attention.

TEAM SUPERVISOR
The team supervisor (supervisory security officer) will do the following:

- Work with the director of security to set up the security officer teams on site with the supervisory security officer and any other person designated by the principal of the selected school.
- Ensure that the metal detectors used by team members are properly calibrated.
- Ensure that the school maintains, at all times, extra nine-volt replacement batteries for the metal detectors.
- Oversee maintenance of reports and submission of reports in conjunction with the principal or his or her designee.
- Coordinate site post assignments:

The weapon scanning teams will be stationed inside the school entrance doors or in another designated area, such as the cafeteria, in full view of entering students and employees. The location should be selected to avoid disrupting the flow of traffic.

Post assignments will depend on the number of entrances used and other unique conditions at each site. Men and women will be assigned as appropriate or as available at the stage stations after the initial screening.

Team Responsibilities.   Security officer teams and selected school administrator and teacher support teams will arrive at the site, set up, and be ready for operation 30 minutes before the Breakfast Program (usually 6:45 A.M. for high schools and 7:15 A.M. for middle schools), or as directed by the principal.

A site will be assigned to each security officer team as noted in Figure A3.7. Each team member will bring a metal detector to the assigned site. The security officers will first calibrate their metal detectors and then will aid the school in setting up the necessary equipment.

Search Procedures
PURPOSE
The purpose of the metal detector inspection is to prevent and deter students from bringing weapons to school. The degree and nature of the inspection will never exceed what is necessary to allow the staff to discharge its responsibility.

NOTIFICATION
On the day that a metal detector scan is being conducted, all entrance doors will be locked or appropriately controlled. Signs and appropriate personnel will be posted outside the building at normal or designated entrances to notify those entering the school that they will be required to enter at a designated entrance and submit to an inspection as a condition of entry. (See Figures A3.4 and A3.6.)

PROCEDURE
Principals or their designees should, if possible, be present to observe the inspection of students. When there is more than one scanning site, designees will be assigned at the direction of the principal to ensure proper coordination of the inspection procedure and follow-up activities. This presence will further enable the principal to report accurately on the results and to provide an evaluation of the inspection procedures. In addition, the presence of the principal or designee will have a calming effect on students who are the subject of the scan.

Everyone entering the school building will be searched. However, when necessary because of inclement weather, an emergency, or a backlog, the principal or director of security may elect not to screen every person or may cancel the screening for that day. In such cases, the principal and the director of security will determine the number of students to be screened using one or both of the following alternatives:

- Screen every (x) student seeking entry
- Allow a number of students to enter without being screened; then resume screening all students or a specific ratio of students

Under no circumstances may school officials select a particular individual to be searched unless there is reasonable suspicion that he or she is in possession of a weapon or other unlawful item.

USE OF HAND-HELD METAL DETECTORS
Weapon scanning will be conducted by a school inspection team member certified in the use of a hand-held metal detector. Effort should be made during the initial scanning to avoid having the scanning officer or the scanning equipment come in physical contact with the subject being inspected.

During the initial scanning, team members will attempt to identify all items to which the metal detector is alerting. If an item is not apparent (for example, jewelry), the security officer conducting the scan will ask the individual to voluntarily produce the item. If the metal detector again alerts on the individual or his or her hand-carried parcels and the security officer conducting the scan is not satisfied as to what is causing the alert, the student will be escorted to the appropriate stage II examining table and further inspected in accordance with the procedures outlined below. The area on the student's person to which the detector was alerting will be identified to the staff escort. Students who can produce the object that activated the metal detector and thus satisfy the scanning officer may proceed to class via the "clean flow" route.

Students who refuse to cooperate with the inspection will be referred to the principal for appropriate action.

INSPECTION PROCEDURES

Before conducting any further inspection, a staff member at the stage II table will ask the student to remove all metal objects from the identified alert area, as well as all other metal objects, and to empty any hand-carried articles or parcels onto the examination table for an examination of contents. The contents of all hand-carried parcels will be examined for weapons.

An inspection will also be conducted (by members of the same sex) only in the area of the body that activated the metal detector. The inspection will commence with the patting of the individual's external clothing in the vicinity of pockets, belts, shoulders, or other specifically identified areas for the limited purpose of discovering items that may have activated the metal detector.

If the staff member conducting the inspection feels an object that may have activated the metal detector, he or she will ask the student to remove the object. If the student refuses, the staff member will escort the individual to the stage III area and will explain the circumstances and point out the item in question to a staff member in that area. If the student removes the object and it is identified to the satisfaction of the staff member, the student may proceed to class via the "clean flow" route. If the student voluntarily removes the object and it is contraband, he or she will be escorted to a stage III area, and the circumstances will be explained to a staff member there.

If a student is referred to stage III because he or she refused to remove an object in question, the scanning officer will scan the student again. If the metal detector alerts, the student will again be asked to remove any object from the location on the body to which the scanner alerted. If the student refuses, the scanning officer will remove the object. A Report of Search of Student or Student's Possessions will be completed.

If the object voluntarily provided by or removed from the student could have activated the metal detector, the staff member or security officer will cease performing the search. He or she will scan the individual again, and the search will be continued only if the metal detector is again activated.

DISCOVERY OF CONTRABAND

If a student is in possession of contraband (weapons, controlled substances, prohibited objects like beepers), the security officer or staff member will escort the student to the stage III station for appropriate administrative action and notification of the police, if warranted. The contraband will be confiscated when it is found. A staff member at the stage III station will complete an Evidence/Property Custody Receipt.

If the police make an arrest, they will take custody of the contraband only after signing for it on the Evidence/Property Custody Receipt.

If the police do not make an arrest, a school administrator will confiscate the objects seized. An Evidence/Property Custody Receipt will be completed, and the incident will be noted in the school's Administrative Random Inspection Report.

RETURN OF PROPERTY

All property removed from a student that is not prohibited by law or school rules and regulations must be returned to the student upon completion of the search. Other contraband items may be returned later only after the owner has signed the Evidence/Property Custody Receipt.

SWEEP OF SCHOOL GROUNDS

Following the morning search, the school inspection teams, supervised by the team supervisor, will conduct a perimeter sweep of the school grounds for weapons or other items that may have been deposited there.

Nothing in these procedures limits the authority of a school administrator or security officer to search an individual when there is a reasonable suspicion that he or she is in possession of a weapon or any other contraband.

Improvements

Feedback from everyone involved in this proactive security program is encouraged. Contact the principal or the director of security with suggestions for improving the metal detector program and its procedures.

It is suggested that before a district implements an administrative random metal detector program that parents be given proper notice. Figure A3.8 is a sample letter.

Dear Parents:

Among the six national goals for improving the nation's educational system is the following:

"By the year 2000, every school in America will be free of drugs and violence and offer a

 disciplined environment conducive to learning."

As superintendent of _____ , I am charged with the responsibility of undertaking

any and all reasonable, necessary, and proper measures provided by law, rules, and regulations

to safeguard our students, employees, and property. In that regard, administrative searches,

using metal detectors will be implemented and conducted by certified school personnel. Persons

who enter onto the property may be searched, as may the property under their control. The search

may include the use of metal detectors, patdowns, and removal of suspected contraband.

I take this opportunity to inform you of this new procedure and to ask for your

continued support and cooperation as we work together to keep _____ safe, secure, and

conducive to the teaching and learning process.

Sincerely,

Superintendent of Schools

Figure A3.8   Administrative Inspection Notice

Appendix 4

Sample "No Trespassing" Signs

One of the most frequent safety and security problems confronting school building administrators is that of trespassing. Trespassers are often unauthorized transients with criminal intent, but a large number are students who leave his or her home school to visit another school or students who are on suspension, expulsion, or just simply playing basketball on a lower school court while the lower grade level school is still in session.

Response to trespassing range from student identification cards (a difficult program to maintain), using hall passes (inherent control problems), hall sweeps (good for controlling unwanted activities of students), employee and visitor badging, to securing doors against outside entry, up to and including elaborate access control systems. All of these measures have a prevention or deterrent role with regards to trespassing. Along with the above measures, no matter which you choose, there must also be the necessary response measure of prosecuting trespassers when necessary. In order to prosecute successfully, however, the building and grounds must be posted with the proper notice signs. Figure A4.1 is a sample of a sign/decal which can be placed at all ingress/egress points to the building. This sign also has wording which reinforces the notice required in the administrative random inspection program (Figure A3.4) or other loss prevention measures requiring notice. Figures A4.2 and A4.3 are samples of notice signs that can be placed on the building, grounds, and fences (reference Chapter 3). Usually a combination of a district-wide reinforced employee and visitor identification badging program, good building access control measures which control or allow access only through the least number of doors necessary to operate, along with roving security or police patrols, reduces trespassing and contributes to a psychological deterrent because there is an appearance of attention to security.

Notice
Only authorized persons and students
permitted. All visitors must obtain
authorization at school office upon
entering grounds.
**TRESPASSERS WILL BE
PROSECUTED.**
Authorized entry into area constitutes
consent to inspection of persons and
the property under their control

Figure A4.1

_____ PUBLIC SCHOOLS
PROPERTY
NO TRESPASSING.
VISITORS REPORT TO OFFICE.
VIOLATORS WILL BE PROSECUTED

Figure A4.2

_____ PUBLIC SCHOOLS
PROPERTY
NO TRESPASSING.
VISITORS REPORT TO OFFICE.
VIOLATORS WILL BE PROSECUTED

Figure A4.3

Appendix 5

Pilferage and Its Prevention

PILFERAGE

Pilferage, the theft of property, is probably the most common and annoying hazard with which security personnel are concerned. It can become such a financial burden and detriment to operations that a large portion of the security force's efforts must be devoted to its control. Pilferage is frequently difficult to detect, hard to prove, and dangerous to ignore.

Larceny involves the wrongful appropriation of any property or funds owned in whole or part by _____. The possession or illegal sale of such property is also considered larceny.

The citywide loss of _____ property would increase by millions of dollars each year if pilferage were undeterred. However, losses and risks cannot be measured in terms of dollars alone. Loss of critical supplies could result in the unnecessary endangering of life and the loss of the ability to efficiently or effectively perform responsibilities. All facilities can anticipate loss from pilferage. Actual losses will depend on such variable factors as the type and amount of materials, equipment, and supplies produced, processed, and stored at the facility; the number of people employed; the social and economic condition of the surrounding communities; the attitudes of administrators and other leaders toward accountability (this is an important consideration); and the physical security measures employed and enforced. Because these factors differ greatly in the various types of facilities and in different geographical locations, each influencing factor must be considered separately.

It is not always easy to determine the amount of loss that is occurring at a specific activity, because accounting methods are not always designed to pinpoint thefts. Such losses remain undisclosed or are grouped with other shrinkages; thus, effectively camouflaging them.

One of the most common inventory methods is conducting periodic inventories of property and assuming that unaccounted-for inventory loss is due to theft. This is a convenient but deceptive procedure because theft is only one of many causes of inventory shrinkage. The failure to detect shortages in incoming shipments, improper usage, poor accounting, poor warehousing, improper handling and recording of defective and damaged stock, and inaccurate or "pencil-whipped" inventories cause inventory losses that may be inaccurately labeled as pilferage.

In some cases, inventory losses may be impossible to detect because of the nature and quantities of material involved. Stock inventory records may not be locally maintained, or there may be no method for conducting spot checks or running inventories frequently enough to discover shortages. This undesirable situation should be corrected when possible, and running inventories should be maintained.

Established estimates of the level of pilferage and larceny may have to be revised because of anticipated changes in the economic or social condition of nearby communities, increases in the number of employees, introduction of new materials into the facility, or any of the other factors on which estimates of expected losses are based.

The degree of risk that a facility faces can be determined only by analyzing the relative vulnerability of each area of the facility to the hazard of pilferage. To do this, it is necessary to consider the problem of who is likely to steal and what items they are most likely to take.

PROFILES

Security personnel must be prepared to counteract, or at least recognize, two types of pilferers so proper physical security measures may be taken to afford the best protection against them: casual pilferers and systematic pilferers.

Casual Pilferers

Casual pilferers are normally employees of the facility, and they are usually the most difficult to detect and apprehend. They steal primarily because they are unable to resist the temptation of an unexpected opportunity and because they have little fear of detection. There is usually little or no planning involved in casual pilferage, and the thief normally acts alone. Casual pilferers may take items for which they have no immediate need, or they may take or borrow small quantifies of supplies for use at home and just not return it. Casual pilferage occurs whenever the individual feels the need or desire for a certain article and the opportunity to take it is provided by poor security or accountability measures. The degree of risk involved in casual pilferage is also normally slight.

Although it involves the unsystematic theft of small and usually easily concealed articles, casual pilferage is nevertheless very serious and may have a great cumulative effect if it is permitted to become widespread—especially if the stolen items have a high value. In addition, there is always the possibility that casual pilferers, encouraged by their successful past track record, may turn to systematic pilferage.

Systematic Pilferers

Systematic pilferers steal according to preconceived plans. They steal any and all types of supplies to sell for cash or to barter for other valuable or desirable commodities. The pilferer may work with another person or with a well-organized group of people (for example, members of a cleaning team). The thief may be in a position to locate or administratively control desired items or to remove them from storage areas or transit facilities. Systematic pilferers may be employees of the facility. When they are not, they frequently operate in conspiracy with employees.

Acts of pilferage may extend over a period of months or even years. Large quantifies of supplies with great value may be lost to groups of people engaged in elaborately planned and carefully executed systematic pilferage activities.

MOTIVATION OF PILFERERS

The factors that drive pilferers to steal are varied. No pattern can be detected from the uses that thieves make of stolen items or the money that they derive from them. In fact, a modus operandi is difficult to detect due to changing motivations.

Pilferers can by anyone. They may not be profit oriented. They may operate alone or with others. Common danger signs include an increase in personal spending and a refusal to accept or reinforce material control procedures.

Among the elements that induce dishonesty are a target of opportunity, a strong personal need or desire, and a rationalization of personal actions. Pilferers rationalize their dishonesty in a variety of ways:

- "Why not? Others are doing it."
- "It's morally right to me."
- "It's not stealing, only borrowing."

OBSTACLES TO PILFERAGE

Both casual and systematic pilferers must overcome certain obstacles in order to steal. The following are among those obstacles:

- Locating the item to steal
- Determining how to gain access to and possession of the desired item
- Moving the stolen item to a safe place without drawing attention

Finally, to derive any benefit from the act, pilferers must use the item themselves or must dispose of it in some way. Casual pilferers steal supplies primarily to satisfy their own needs or desires. Systematic pilferers usually attempt to sell the stolen goods through fences, pawnbrokers, or black-market operations.

METHODS OF PILFERAGE

There are many ways in which thieves can remove pilfered items from a facility, because the motives and targets of casual and systematic pilferers are likely to be very different, the methods of operation for each are also different.

Casual pilferers steal whatever is available. They generally remove it from the facility by concealing it on their person, in a carry bag, or in their vehicle.

The methods of systematic pilferers are much more varied and complex. Shipping and receiving operations are extremely vulnerable to systematic pilferage. It is here that facility personnel and drivers of vehicles have direct contact with one another and have a readily available means of conveyance. For example, tanker trucks used to ship petroleum products can be altered to permit pilferage of the product. As a security precaution, one individual must not have control of all shipping and receiving transactions. The opportunities for monetary kickbacks increase without a sound system of checks and balances.

Trash disposal and salvage disposal activities also offer excellent opportunities for systematic pilferers to move valuable material off a facility. Property can be hidden in waste material to be recovered by a co-conspirator who removes the trash from the facility.

DETERRING PILFERAGE

The specific measures implemented to prevent pilferage must be based on a careful analysis of conditions at the facility. The most practical and effective method is to establish psychological deterrents. This may be accomplished in a number of ways.

The most common means of discouraging casual pilferage is to inspect individuals and vehicles leaving the activity at unannounced times and places. Administrative inspection procedures involve legal restrictions emanating from the Fourth Amendment to the U.S. Constitution. These procedures must comport with judicially acceptable standards, including a bona fide method of random selection of vehicles and individuals stopped for inspection. Liaison with the school board attorney is required before instituting such procedures.

An aggressive security education program is an effective means of convincing employees that they have much more to lose than to gain by engaging in acts of theft. All employees must be informed that they have a responsibility to report all losses to the administrative officer of the facility and to the office of security. It is particularly important for supervisory personnel to set a proper example and maintain a desirable moral climate for all employees.

Adequate inventory and control measures should be instituted to account for all material, supplies, and equipment. The identification of tools and equipment by some mark or code, where feasible, helps ensure that property is identifiable. In addition, individuals should be required to sign for all tools and equipment used. This control method reduces the temptation for employees to fail to return the item.

Small items of equipment, tools, and supplies that are easily pilferable must be stored in a caged area or adequately secured. Access must be limited to employees whose position authorizes their entrance. A running inventory should be maintained and periodically checked by supervisory or other designated and accountable personnel.

The following measures will also help prevent losses attributed to systematic pilferage:

- Establish security surveillance of all exits from the facility.
- Establish an effective package and material control system.
- Locate parking areas for private vehicles outside the perimeter fencing of the facility or as far away as practical (minimum 15 feet from the building).
- Eliminate potential thieves during the hiring procedure through careful screening and interviewing.
- Investigate losses quickly and efficiently.
- Establish an effective key or other access control system.
- Install mechanical and electrical intrusion-detection devices.
- Coordinate with supply and school personnel to establish customer identification and authenticate supply release documents at warehouses and exit gates or other egress points.
- Establish appropriate perimeter fencing, lighting, and parking facilities and effective pedestrian and vehicle gate security controls.

In establishing deterrents to pilferage, security personnel must not lose sight of the fact that most employees are honest and disapprove of theft. Any security measure that infringes on human rights or dignity will jeopardize, rather than enhance, the overall protection of the facility and reduce employee support and participation toward desired goals.

EMPLOYEE THEFT

No matter what it is called—internal theft, pilferage, inventory shrinkage, stealing, embezzlement, or defalcation—thefts committed by employees are responsible for at least 60 percent of all crime-related losses. So many employees are stealing that employee theft is the most critical crime problem facing business today. Although employee theft results in part from factors beyond control, the extent of employee theft in any business is a reflection of its management: The more mismanagement, the more theft.

An effective policy to stop employee thefts must include the following:

- Preemployment screening
- Analysis of opportunities for theft
- Analysis of how employees steal
- Management-employee communication
- Management support for security measures
- Prosecution of employees caught stealing

Employers must strive to reduce losses as much as possible without creating a police state or spending large sums of money. Too many opportunities exist for dishonest employees to exploit. Employers must reduce these opportunities through a comprehensive and viable loss prevention program.

Appendix 6

Programming for Safe and Secure Schools

APPENDIX 6A: KEY CONSIDERATIONS IN CONDUCTING SCHOOL SECURITY SURVEYS/ASSESSMENTS

True and effective security surveys (assessments) of safety and security vulnerabilities and measures in schools should, ideally, be conducted by professional security consultants or security professionals with the security *and* law enforcement education, training, experience, and certification to conduct such assessments. Security professionals are professionals because of their years of training and experience in security and law enforcement and not because of attending a number of recent conferences to learn the buzz-words and peripheral knowledge promoted sometimes by self-proclaimed or overnight school security experts or by reading collections of articles and statistics relating to school safety issues.

Many districts respond to school safety and security issues by addressing only one part (such as prevention curriculum only) of the security picture instead of conducting a comprehensive review and assessment prior to a crisis taking place. However, it is often difficult for some school districts to afford to hire their own security professional or the services of a competent security professional. The following list, therefore, is provided as a general guideline on which to focus broad key considerations when taking proactive steps to self-assess existing or planned security measures. These by no means replace the knowledge and experience of a professional security consultant or practitioner.

Survey of Physical Security and Environmental Influences Affecting Security

Zone 1: Immediate Neighborhood
Type of facilities and sites

Vehicular and pedestrian traffic patterns

Surveillance

Community organizations, such as neighborhood watch

Zone 2: Property Boundaries
First line of defense

Access control

Separation of public and semipublic space

Identification of space with notices

Zone 3: Open Space and Clear Zones
Movement control (vehicles and personnel)

Surveillance

Perception of territoriality

Design conflicts

Unassigned spaces

Lighting

Zone 4: Building Exterior
Access control

Notices and signs

Doors

Windows

Alarms

Lighting

Zone 5: Building Interior
Movement control, clear direction, signs and notices

Use of space

Secure areas

Monitoring, surveillance, assessment (halls, classrooms, stairwells, vending areas, and so on)

Means of identification (visitor badges, employee badges, hall passes, and so on)

Report of Findings and Recommendations

Report of Findings (Analysis of Security)
Collection and analysis of data

Identification of risks

Discussion of existing conditions

Determination of degree of vulnerability

Identification of real or perceived problems

Specific Recommendations to Improve Security

Data collection and analysis

Security management

Physical and environmental security

Cost

APPENDIX 6B: PROCEDURAL CONSIDERATIONS FOR CONDUCTING SCHOOL SECURITY SURVEYS

Overview of Security

Crime, violence, and related problems can be managed, prevented, or reduced through a process that systematically attempts to reduce, remove, and deter the opportunity for crime. In law enforcement, this process is known as crime prevention. In most other sectors of the society, including education, it is known as security.

Improving security does not necessarily require a large expenditure of funds. The desired outcome can sometimes be realized through the development and consistent management of well-constructed policies and procedures. It is usually preferable to hire a director of security for the school district or, less so, to assign a specific person to be responsible for security and to provide that person with the necessary training, staff, resources, and authority to meet his or her responsibilities.

Regardless of the strategy chosen, there is no absolute guarantee that there will be no future crimes. The intent of these security measures is to help reduce, deter, and in some cases remove the opportunity for crime, violence, and related problems, and reduce a district's exposure to security litigation.

The obligation to provide a safe environment is often complicated by the wide range of during-school, after-school, and public events that occur in schools. It would be relatively easy to develop tightly controlled environments; it is more difficult to balance the need for a secure environment against the need for an accepting educational environment. At times, these competing goals will require difficult choices and changes in the way educators traditionally think about security's role in the schools, and how security is organized, operated, and supervised.

The process of security involves the following:

- Anticipation, expectation, and intuition ("what-ifing")
- Recognition and acknowledgment through data collection or experience
- Appraisal, evaluation, and estimation through data or incident analysis
- Initiation of some action (tactical and strategic planning using professional security methodologies)
- Removal or reduction of opportunity (implementation of programs, initiatives, and deterrents)

Reducing Opportunities for Crime

Opportunities for crime and related problems can be reduced through the use of organized methods and procedures and by "hardening the target." The built environment should be designed to provide the following:

- Territoriality and legal boundaries
- Surveillance of grounds and facility

- Control of access and vehicle and personnel movement
- Unnecessary design conflicts (does the intended design support the intended function?)
- Limits on unassigned spaces (are all spaces or areas assigned a use and function?)

Organized Methods.   Although the built environment can have the effect of reducing the opportunity for crime and associated problems, it is usually necessary to employ other means to ensure the security of property and assets and to enhance the personal safety of those who use the facility. Organized methods provide the best avenues for change. The following are examples of organized methods:

- Security forces (best method)
- Training and security awareness
- Development of policies, procedures, post orders, crisis and emergency plans, and so on
- Educational material
- Notice and warning signs
- Data collection and crime analysis

Target Hardening.   It is often necessary to install or upgrade security applications in order to project an image of control and to reduce, deter, or remove opportunities for crime. This "target hardening" is the most expensive way to reduce opportunities for crime. The specific application of security hardware depends on identified or surveyed risks. The following are some common applications:

- Lighting (consider crime prevention versus energy conservation)
- Improved locks (simplex mechanical push-button combination-type locks have affordable access-control applications in schools)
- Doors and windows
- Alarms (fire, intrusion, burglar)
- Closed-circuit television
- Portable video cameras in buildings and buses (new to school applications)
- Access-control systems and identification badging programs
- Fences and other barriers

APPENDIX 6C: MECHANICS OF CONDUCTING A SCHOOL SECURITY SURVEY/ASSESSMENT

Purpose

The purpose of conducting a security survey of a site is to identify crime risks, vulnerabilities, and associated problems in order to determine the extent to which the site and its users are vulnerable and to take the appropriate measures to improve security or to plan for changes or upgrades in security-related programs, procedures, and equipment.

Collection and Analysis of Data

An in-depth analysis of policies and practices along with information from surrounding sources can help school officials to clarify responsibilities and plan for measures that affect drugs, crime, discipline, student/faculty safety, and morale. A list of some areas to give attention to when developing information follows:

1. Review reported crimes in the area, considering police "calls for service" in the immediate and surrounding vicinity. Having knowledge of the types of crime occurring not only in the school but in areas adjacent to the school can provide for a much broader picture regarding crime and allow for more proactive prevention planning and appropriate communications with the community and public service agencies.
2. Analyze data specific to the school site. Examine crime reports by type, time, location, day of week, victim, offender, and particular circumstances.
3. Interview students, faculty, and staff to determine their perceptions about the school climate, problems, causes, and solutions. Interviews should be conducted by security or law enforcement officials in addition to school administrators. Other random interviews should also take place.
4. Examine existing security practices.
   a. Review written policies and procedures (update, consolidate, form committees).
   b. Inquire about unwritten security practices. (These practices, particularly if they are not approved, are viewed as being approved practices by the administration if they are allowed and not changed via good supervision.)
   c. Determine who has responsibility for security, including extracurricular activities.
   d. Examine the relationship between the school and the police.
   e. Review disciplinary reports.
5. Review related information.
   a. Hours of operation (consider staggering working hours of security, if staff is limited, to provide coverage).
   b. Organizational structure (a centrally district-managed and operated security force reduces liability exposure because of professional training, operating standards, and supervision of security personnel).
   c. Class schedules
   d. Extracurricular activities
   e. Disaster, emergency, and crisis plans

APPENDIX 6D: SCHOOL SECURITY CHECKLIST

Zone 1: Immediate Neighborhood

Are adjoining properties compatible with the school, or are they in conflict?

Are there crime generators (i.e., drug activity, vacant housing, "homeless," etc.) in the immediate neighborhood?

Can the school property be observed from surrounding facilities and streets?

Are neighborhood property values increasing or decreasing?

Does the community have a neighborhood watch program? (If so, make contact.)

Do residents use school property for recreational purposes? If so, does this occur during school hours?

Zone 2: Property Boundaries

If the function or design of adjoining properties is adverse to that of the school, is school property separated by screening or other barriers?

Are property boundaries clearly identified, and is there a clear zone, or separation, between public space and school property?

Are entrances to the property limited so that they can be seen from the school?

Zone 3: Open Spaces

Do open spaces provide for vehicle access around buildings to permit night surveillance and access by police patrols, emergency vehicles, and fire equipment?

Are blind spots minimized through the use of crime-prevention landscaping?

Are trees kept at least ten feet from buildings to prevent access to windows and roofs?

Are trees trimmed to increase visibility, keeping lower limbs no less than seven feet above the ground?

Are shrubs limited to low ground cover or below windows (no higher than 3 feet)? Hedging along walks or other desired areas helps to channel pedestrian traffic to controlled entrances. Benches provide areas to congregate in plain view.

When fencing is required, are chain-link, decorative aluminum, or wrought iron fences used to maintain visibility and natural surveillance?

Are common keys or access devices used for gate or building locks throughout the district to allow security, fire, police, and maintenance personnel to enter with minimal delay?

Are school grounds free of gravel or loose rock surfaces?

Are directional signs painted on curbs or streets, if appropriate, instead of using signs on poles?

Are trash receptacles placed far enough away from school buildings so that they do not provide access to upper floors or roofs, or provide convenient storage for thieves?

Are meters, transformers, valves, and other mechanical or electrical devices put inside buildings or in locked, fenced areas?

If access to the roof by an intruder is not too difficult, are flagpoles mounted on the roof provided with nylon-covered wire halyards and locked covered boxes for the halyard cleats?

Is roof access limited by securing exposed drains, window frames, stored items, decorative ledges, vehicles, vegetation, and other things onto which a person can climb or grasp?

Are walkway covers limited near second-floor windows?

Do exterior lights illuminate the exterior of buildings and surrounding grounds?

Are exterior lights fitted with break-resistant lenses or mesh covers?

Are light standards made of galvanized steel or concrete?

Are grounds posted with "no trespassing" signs?

Parking Lots

Does the design of the parking lots discourage cruising?

Are speed bumps or other obstacles used to reduce traffic speed?

Do faculty and students park in the same lots, providing adult supervision of the lots?

Are there designated secured areas for motorcycle and bicycle parking?

Do students have access to the cars during school hours?

Is lighting sufficient to deter crime? (Lighting for crime prevention and energy conservation are often in conflict.)

Are designated entries and exits secured with lockable gates or other barriers? (These should be constructed of heavy-duty material, with the main crossbar above bumper height to discourage forced entry.)

Zone 4: Building Exteriors

Carefully evaluate access requirements. Allow ingress through as few doors as possible. Remember that good security is often inconvenient.

Is one entrance, or the least possible number, designated for use during school hours?

Are all access instructions and notices in highly visible locations?

Are all doors posted with "no trespassing," inspection, and visitor notice signs or decals?

Can recessed doorways be observed and protected?

Are door hinges welded or equipped with nonremovable pins?

Have locks been installed on all doors leading to high-risk areas?

Have simplex mechanical push-button combination or other similar purpose-type locks been considered for frequently used doors that require exit and reentry by authorized staff but need to be locked and not propped open after exit (elementary schools in particular for classes leaving the building and controlled employee access via a designated door near parking)?

Have surface-mounted locks or locks with knob-mounted key access been replaced?

Is exposed hardware on exterior doors kept to a minimum?

Are door frames made of pry-proof metal?

Is the armored strike plate securely fastened to the door frame in direct alignment to receive the latch easily?

Are fire doors provided in appropriate locations?

Are hard, scratch-resistant, unbreakable coatings used for windows, particularly when vandalism is a recurring problem?

Are wire mesh security screens or grillwork used where repeated window breakage occurs due to vandalism?

Is the use of sliding or casement windows that create significant security risks avoided?

Can emergency exit be made via classroom windows or other means should exit through classroom doors be denied?

Are broken windows repaired immediately (not doing so reflects a lack of feeling of ownership).

Zone 5: Building Interior

Is money never left unattended in cash registers, and are register drawers left open when empty?

Are all cabinets and files locked when not in use?

Are cafeterias, multipurpose areas, administrative offices, safes and vaults, science laboratories, music rooms, shops, arts and crafts rooms, student stores, supply rooms, library and media centers, gyms, locker rooms, and service areas locked and secured when not in use?

Are suspended tile ceilings, which are easily vandalized and often used to hide weapons, drugs, and other items, avoided?

Are the entry and movement of people within school buildings limited and supervised?

Are signs posted in conspicuous places advising visitors that they must report to the office or other designated area upon entering the school?

Are visitor's badges issued to and signed for by all visitors, and is the procedure enforced?

Are closed-circuit television or portable video cameras used in halls, cafeterias, stairwells, or other areas where deterrence or assessment is necessary?

Is a random or other metal detector screening program implemented to deter guns and other weapons?

Are hall passes or late passes required for students who are tardy or in the halls while classes are in session? (A metal detector program can also be designed to help deter this problem.)

Managing Security

Are students, faculty members, and staff given photo identification cards, and are they required to wear them openly?

Has a written description of visitor regulations been provided to students, parents, and community members and posted at all entrances?

Are visitors required to wear a visitor's badge while in the school? (Each school should have serialized badges, and each school's badge should be visibly different in appearance by color or other characteristic and have a return postage guaranteed on the reverse of the badge.)

Are teachers and staff instructed to challenge visitors or other unidentified individuals in the school who are not displaying a visitor's or temporary badge?

Is the maintenance staff required to wear a uniform while working?

Are teachers and staff required to monitor hallways, cafeterias, and other gathering places during the day and between classes? (Teachers can be posted during "planning periods" at desks or in chairs to increase supervision of students).

Are teachers required to stand at their doors while classes are changing?

Are teachers and staff assigned to after-school activities, and are they provided clear instructions with respect to their roles and responsibilities?

Are parking lots monitored during the school day by staff, teachers, or security?

Are parking lots and bus-loading areas monitored before and after school?

Are students allowed to leave school property for lunch?

Has the school developed data collection and analysis systems that include the following?

- Nature of the problem—all violations of the law and of school rules and regulations
- Specific location type, and time of violation
- Process for analysis and strategies to influence change or prevent reoccurrence

APPENDIX 6E: CRIME PREVENTION CHECKLIST

Organization

Yes | No

☐ | ☐ Is there a district policy for dealing with violence and vandalism in your school and during school-sponsored activities?

☐ | ☐ Is there a district incident report system available to all of the staff?

☐ | ☐ Is statistical information available concerning the scope of the problems at your school and in the neighboring community?

☐ | ☐ Has the administration taken any preventive steps to deal with anticipated potential problems?

☐ | ☐ Is there a good working relationship with local law enforcement?

☐ | ☐ Is there a good working relationship with the courts, probation, and human services?

☐ | ☐ Are both students and parents aware of expectations and school discipline codes, and are these in writing?

☐ | ☐ Have any district plans been developed to deal with student disruptions, vandalism, or law violations?

☐ | ☐ Is there a district policy concerned with restitution or prosecution of perpetrators of violence and vandalism?

☐ | ☐ Does the district have written emergency procedures for incidents such as fires, bomb threats, and hostage situations?

☐ | ☐ Does the staff receive crime-prevention awareness training?

☐ | ☐ Is your school actively involved in an antidrug or life skills training program?

☐ | ☐ Does the staff receive conflict mediation training?

Existing Security Measures

Yes | No

☐ | ☐ Is a district administrator, preferably a professional security director, responsible for overall security procedures and practices?

☐ | ☐ Are school employees made aware of security procedures on an annual basis?

☐ | ☐ Are vandalism costs made known to the community?

☐ | ☐ Do local law enforcement officers or district security/police professionals help and advise on crime prevention?

☐ | ☐ Are staff members and students encouraged to cooperate with security/police and report all incidents that are serious in nature or are violations of the law?

☐ | ☐ Are local residents encouraged to report suspicious activity around the school?

Yes | No

☐ ☐ Is the evening and weekend use of school facilities encouraged?

☐ ☐ Are specific individuals designated to secure school buildings following after-hours activity?

☐ ☐ Are the school grounds patrolled after school hours?

☐ ☐ Are students actively involved in security efforts?

☐ ☐ Have there been any serious security problems or incidents in the past year?

☐ ☐ Does the custodial staff work evenings and weekends?

☐ ☐ Is there a visitor badging and sign-in procedure?

☐ ☐ Do students or employees have photo identification badges?

☐ ☐ Are hallways and other gathering places for students supervised during and after school hours?

☐ ☐ Are hall passes or late passes issued to students who are tardy or in the halls while classes are in session?

☐ ☐ Are vandalism and graffiti damage repaired or eliminated immediately?

☐ ☐ Does the school district have an administrative random inspection program that uses metal detectors?

☐ ☐ Are explosive- and drug-detection dogs used to perform random administrative inspections of lockers, parking lots, and classrooms at schools?

Exterior Security

Exterior security is one of the first lines of protection.

Yes | No

☐ ☐ Are high-risk areas fenced?

☐ ☐ Are gates properly secured with weather-resistant locks or other access control devices?

☐ ☐ Is the perimeter free of rocks and gravel?

☐ ☐ Are vandal-proof signs posted concerning security rules and enforcement?

☐ ☐ Is there enough exterior lighting, especially in high-risk areas, and is it an appropriate type?

☐ ☐ Is there good visibility of the parking areas?

☐ ☐ Are all window ledges, roof accesses, and other equipment that could be used for climbing or gaining entry properly secured?

☐ ☐ Is the school designed with vandal-resistant walls?

☐ ☐ Are mobile units and portable classrooms also posted with visitor and "no trespassing" notice signs?

☐ ☐ Is there a key control system?

<u>Yes</u> | <u>No</u>

☐ | ☐   Are first-floor windows properly secured?

☐ | ☐   Are protective screens or window guards used where necessary?

☐ | ☐   Have outside handles been removed from doors used primarily as exits?

☐ | ☐   Are all exit doors secured by either dead bolt or cables/chains and locks after hours, limiting the easy escape of intruders?

☐ | ☐   Can any door locks be reached and manipulated by breaking out glass?

☐ | ☐   Are doors constructed properly, with pry-proof frames?

☐ | ☐   Are locks or other locking devices maintained and replaced when necessary?

☐ | ☐   Is the school sectioned off with portable or roll down gates to limit access by evening users?

☐ | ☐   Are high-risk areas (shops, offices, and so on) sufficiently secured?

Interior Security

<u>Yes</u> | <u>No</u>

☐ | ☐   Is all school property permanently and distinctly marked?

☐ | ☐   Has an inventory of school property been conducted within the last year?

☐ | ☐   Are school files locked in vandal-proof containers?

☐ | ☐   Is valuable equipment (computers, typewriters, audiovisual equipment) securely bolted/locked down or locked up when not in use?

☐ | ☐   Is all money removed from cafeteria and bookstore cash registers after hours and deposited or properly stored and secured?

☐ | ☐   Have additional personal computers recently been purchased, or have computer classes been expanded?

☐ | ☐   Are highly pilferable items, such as computers, television sets, videocassette recorders, and so on, stored away from windows, particularly when on the ground floor?

☐ | ☐   Are portable gates or other means used to limit access to unauthorized areas of the school at night when authorized activities are taking place?

☐ | ☐   Are classrooms provided with two means of egress for emergencies, and do doors or windows in fact operate and open?

☐ | ☐   When highly pilferable equipment is locked up, is it locked in cabinets, files, or rooms with a lock or latch that is not easily manipulated or defeated?

Intrusion and Fire Alarms

<u>Yes</u> | <u>No</u>

☐ | ☐   Does your school have an intrusion-detection system (IDS)?

☐ | ☐   Does the IDS provide for at least two means detection?

Yes | No

☐ | ☐ Does your school have a fire alarm system?

☐ | ☐ Are alarms monitored twenty-four hours a day?

☐ | ☐ Are alarms remote or local? (Local alarms alone are not recommended.)

☐ | ☐ Is there a sprinkler system in your school?

☐ | ☐ Are there smoke detectors in your school?

☐ | ☐ Do you, as an administrator, understand both systems' capabilities and limitations?

☐ | ☐ Do teachers and staff understand the basics of both systems, so as to prevent false alarms?

☐ | ☐ Is the number of false alarms kept to a minimum? (Two or fewer for any six-month period is a good guide.)

☐ | ☐ Is there a standard form for reporting false alarms? Is what's reported on the form actually monitored for scheduling preventive maintenance?

☐ | ☐ Is there a clear procedure for alarm notification and response?

☐ | ☐ Is there a policy for preventive maintenance and testing of both fire and intrusion detection system?

☐ | ☐ Can selected areas of the school be "zoned" by the intrusion-detection system, indicating which area is being entered by an intruder?

☐ | ☐ If a commercial firm is used to install, service, or maintain IDS equipment or security alarm systems, is the firm licensed and listed by Underwriters Laboratories?

APPENDIX 6F: SCHOOL DESIGN CONSIDERATIONS

Proper school design can reduce crime and the fear of its occurrence and can increase the user's and public's perception of the school's attention to security. There is often a relationship between crime and the perception users of space have as to whether the space is "safe" or "unsafe." Physical environments can be constructed or manipulated to produce behavioral effects that reduce the fear of crime and deter criminal behavior. The following is a list of some concepts and strategies to consider when designing schools or when trying to gain control of a school back:

- Install approved fire and intrusion detection systems.
- Establish a physical or clearly recognized boundary separating public from private property. Use transitional zones from the neighborhood to the school.
- Design vehicular and pedestrian traffic patterns to maximize natural surveillance of arrivals and departures and to minimize entrances and exits.
- Consider S-shaped access roads to naturally reduce traffic speed.
- Clearly indicate primary and secondary entrances for employees and a primary entrance for visitors.
- Use clear, understandable signs and directions to indicate visitor and vendor processing points at site entrances.
- Locate playgrounds and other areas where violence could occur in front of the school, creating a buffer zone before visitors reach the building. Provide clear lines of sight from all points.
- Consider ease of perimeter patrol by police and security to encourage patrol.
- Locate reception areas and the security office (clearly marked) to provide an unobstructed view of the main entrance.
- Ensure that visitors must first be processed at the main reception area, signing in and receiving a visitor's badge, before proceeding to secondary areas of the facility.
- Erect physical barriers to separate public reception areas from private office areas.
- Locate meeting and conference rooms toward the outside of the building.
- Establish physical and electronic control over exterior and interior access points.
- Compartmentalize and electronically or mechanically control access to critical areas, such as computer rooms, executive areas, power and telephone closets, and other sensitive areas.
- Limit the number of facility exit doors to the minimum required by fire and loading regulations.
- Control access to inventory storage areas.
- Locate student parking in the rear of the school, and ensure that traffic flows one-way.
- If possible, separate employee and visitor parking.
- Fence grounds as appropriate (decorative fences, living fences, and so on), and post grounds with "no trespassing" notice signs at the appropriate locations.
- Ensure that all landscaping next to the building is no higher than thirty to thirty-six inches.
- Ensure that all windows lower than fourteen feet (if necessary) and all skylights or other openings greater than ninety-six square inches are covered with wire mesh or other covering that is bolted to the structure.
- Provide reception personnel with a silent duress alarm to call for assistance.

- Set the building back from the perimeter to help prevent casual passersby from entering.
- Reduce any building features that provide access to upper windows and roof, including half walls, fences attached to the building, projections or ledges, fixtures that provide hand- or footholds, and landscaping.
- Design windows and openings to provide direct lines of sight to outside play areas or gathering locations.
- Install windows in walls along problem corridors, in exterior stairwells, and in all classroom doors or classroom walls, if necessary, and keep windows clear of all obstructions that restrict view.
- Locate teacher planning spaces or post teachers during their "planning periods" in areas that permit surveillance and supervision of student movement.
- Close dead ends and blind spots, such as areas under open stairs.
- Remove fixed benches or other fixtures from crowded halls.
- Remove lockers in halls or assign lockers by section, and separate each grade level by color of lockers.
- In bathrooms, replace doors with zigzag entrances and install roll-down gates or sliding gates for after hours and consider scream alarms if necessary.
- Where roll-down or sliding gates are installed in halls, eliminate the possibility for circumvention through adjoining rooms or other levels.
- Use straight hallways in the interior of the building to eliminate small spaces and make the hallways easier to monitor.
- Use straight walls, if possible, on the exterior to increase natural surveillance and reduce areas for concealment.
- Situate auditoriums and gyms, which are used after hours, so that they can be isolated from main building with security gates or other barriers.
- Provide adequate lighting for surveillance in accordance with site use:
  - Parking lots: Provide adequate lighting.
  - Grounds: Provide adequate lighting and consider silhouetting on building.
  - Exterior: Lights should not be recessed into the structure.
- Windows and doors: Provide all with positive latching.
- Interior: Provide spaces that allow for uses of the space to have a feeling of ownership.
- Closed-circuit television: Install CCTV in areas for assessment purposes and as a deterrent for unwanted activities.
- Consider interior ceiling heights in relation to the height of doorway openings in halls to allow for closed-circuit television fields of view and to reduce the number of cameras needed for effective observation.
- Simplex-type mechanical push-button combination, or other access control locks where appropriate to secure rooms, perimeter doors, and so on.
- Perimeter Lighting: Provide for adequate exterior lighting using motion sensitive, high pressure sodium or metal halide lights.
- Consider mounting lights on concrete or steel balusters instead of poles or sides of the building.
- Provide a means of emergency communications (call back) between classrooms and the office, including portable units/classrooms.
- Consider installing emergency call stations or "safe zones" at strategic, justifiable locations in the building or on the grounds.

Appendix 7

Security Force Uniforms and Equipment

PURPOSE

The purpose of this appendix is to show that there is a need for a school district to have a written policy for security force members' uniform dress and authorized equipment. The specifics may vary based on what is authorized and assigned or in the case of a school police department, what is required, usual, and customary under state law.

The uniform and equipment described in this appendix will be worn by personnel who are permanently assigned to the security force and by other personnel when authorized by the proper authority. Members of the security force who are required to wear the official uniform at work may wear it to and from their place of employment but will not wear the uniform or any part of it elsewhere. Other equipment and uniform items may be utilized as becomes necessary and when approved by the director of security.

SECURITY UNIFORM

The uniform consists of shirt, tie, and slacks for men and equivalent professional attire for women. Members of the security force will also wear an appropriate dress shirt, shoes, and socks or stockings that they provide themselves. Tennis shoes are not appropriate. No auxiliary clothing, except an issued windbreaker, may be worn unless approved.

Uniform Allowances

The following uniform items are standard apparel for members of the security force who are authorized to wear the uniform:

Description	Number Authorized
[List as appropriate]	[List as appropriate]

Standards for Wearing the Uniform

Security personnel will keep their uniform clean and pressed, and they will wear it when in public places. They will maintain a neat, professional image at all times.

Care and Cleaning

After the initial issue of the prescribed uniform, members of the security force assume responsibility for the care and cleaning of their uniform. Clothing may be tailored to ensure proper fit. Appearance is important!

SECURITY EQUIPMENT

Leather Items

Security personnel may wear the following standard black or brown leather or web items as required:

- Leather or web belt/utility belt
- Key ring holder
- Handcuff case, if authorized

Devices and Equipment

Security personnel will wear the following devices and equipment, as well as other approved items:

- Badge or shield with holder
- Handcuffs, if authorized
- Pepper spray with holder, if approved
- Hand-held radio

Communications Equipment

The office of security will ensure that there is sufficient and adequate two-way voice radio communications equipment available for use by the security force. This includes not only two-way walkie-talkies, but also bullhorns, beepers, cellular telephones, and other appropriate equipment.

Appendix 8

Safety Precautions for Individuals

Every _____ employee is important to the mission of our school system, and considerable training and money have been invested in each of you. The following information is designed to make you more knowledgeable about the measures that you can take to enhance your safety at home, at work, and while traveling, both in the U.S. and abroad. If you develop a security-conscious attitude and become aware of the threat of possible terrorist and criminal acts, you can do a great deal to protect yourself and your family. Some of the precaution measures addressed in this text are more appropriate when living, vacationing, or traveling in a foreign environment.

GENERAL PRECAUTIONS

The following precautionary measures are suggested for day-to-day living as well as travel at home and abroad:

1. Understand the threat and your role in dealing with the threat. Have a protection plan in mind, and know what to do in an emergency.
2. Try to avoid falling into a predictable routine. Vary the routes and times you travel to and from work even avoiding the same restaurant a second time in a row. Consider varying your method of transportation and style of dress (particularly abroad). Past incidents show that attackers keep their victims under surveillance for long periods of time to learn their travel patterns and to arrange a suitable time and place for the assault, kidnapping, or assassination. Keep your workplace and family aware of your comings and goings. Get in the habit of "checking in" before departing and after reaching your destination. Report any unexpected changes. Do not regularly go to work when no one is present.
3. Avoid going out alone when possible. Travel in a group. There is safety in numbers.
4. If possible, travel to and from work or on long distances (particularly abroad) in a convoy. Vary the order of organization and the route used. If a convoy is not possible, consider a small car pool. Traveling alone makes you an easy target.
5. Vary the order, time of pickup, and land route to and from work when in a car pool.
6. Be sensitive to the possibility that you are being watched. Before leaving an area, check the street for suspicious cars or individuals.

7. Be aware of the possibility that you are being followed to and from work or other places. Notify police if you feel that someone might be following you.

8. If you are being followed, move as quickly as possible to a safe place, such as a police station. Always move toward safety, not just away from trouble. Report the incident, identify the vehicle or person if possible, and ask the police to check on it. Inform the local security officer of the incident.

9. Do not carry a concealed gun if it is illegal to do so. If you do carry a gun, get training in its use, and practice safety procedures. Never use a gun unless you are in a life-and-death situation.

10. Use tear gas pens and other protective devices with caution. They may enrage an attacker instead of rendering him or her helpless. You must have training in the use of such special items. Pepper spray is recommended for self-defense instead of Mace™.

11. Stay away from high-risk areas.

12. If you must carry large sums of cash, keep it well concealed. Carry a few additional $5 bills ("throw away") in your pocket to give to a mugger. If a mugger asks for your money, pull the "throw away" out, say that it is all you have, throw it in one direction, and run in the opposite direction yelling "Fire!" instead of "Help!" "Fire" draws more attention and involvement from strangers.

13. Do not routinely attend (particularly abroad) the same nightclubs or restaurants or participate in activities like movies, golf, or tennis on a regular basis and at the same location. Social events should be held in secure areas and with limited invitation.

14. Shun publicity by not reporting social gatherings.

15. Do not permit your photograph to be taken for unofficial dissemination.

16. Safeguard your home address, telephone number, and information about your family.

17. Do not habitually stand by open windows, especially at night with a light in the background.

PERSONAL SECURITY CONSIDERATIONS

The following suggestions can help you avoid becoming a victim of criminal activity. Collectively, these actions will make it more difficult for a criminal to attack. They give attention to an environment for increased personal security.

When Shopping

1. Never leave your purse unattended in a shopping cart or on a counter.

2. When asked for identification, give only the information requested. Never hand the clerk your entire wallet or card case.

3. Do not display large amounts of money, and carry with you only the credit cards that you expect to use.

4. After making a large purchase, check to be sure you are not being followed when you leave the store.
5. Check your credit cards regularly, and immediately report any that are missing. Keep a record of the account numbers for your credit cards, and know the addresses and telephone numbers of the companies that issued them.

When Driving

1. Search the backseat and around your car before getting in. An attacker may be waiting for you.
2. Inspect your car for suspicious objects or unexplained wires or strings inside or underneath. If you find a suspicious item, report it immediately to the proper authorities. Do not attempt to remove it yourself.
3. Keep the gas tank full.
4. When traveling by car, store your purse on the floor under your knees, roll up the windows, and lock the doors.
5. If you believe that you are being followed, blow the horn repeatedly to attract attention, and drive directly to a safe place.
6. If your car breaks down, raise the hood and trunk. Stay inside the vehicle with the doors locked and the windows rolled up until the police arrive. Ask anyone who offers to help to call the police.
7. Insofar as possible, travel only on busy, well-traveled thoroughfares. At night, drive only on well-lighted streets, if possible, even if it means going out of your way. Stay away from isolated country roads. Know and avoid the dangerous areas in a city.
8. When driving on a multiple-lane highway, use the center lane. This makes it difficult for your car to be forced to the curb or to be attacked from the driver's side, which is the most common direction of attack.
9. Do not pick up hitchhikers.
10. Park your car in a well-lighted area near your destination. At night, garage the car or park it on a well-lighted street.
11. Lock your car when you leave it unattended, even for a short time.

When Taking Other Modes of Transportation

1. When riding in a taxi, do not let the driver deviate from known and desired routes. In your conversation with the driver, make it obvious that you know the driver's name and the taxi number. Do not use the same taxi repeatedly. Never take the first available cab.
2. When traveling by bus, vary where you get on and off. Wait for the bus at well-lighted bus stops. On the bus, observe your fellow passengers. If you feel frightened, sit near the driver.

When Walking

1. Walk on well-lighted, heavily traveled streets. The safest place to walk is in a well-populated area during rush hour. Avoid cutting through alleys and walking on isolated or deserted streets. Walk in the middle of the sidewalk.
2. Keep your head up and be alert. Hold your purse under your arm, with the latch on the inside, and use the strap around your body instead of holding it in your hand.
3. Do not routinely walk near your home or workplace on a set schedule. Vary the time and place for your walk. When walking to and from work, use different routes and vary your times of departure and arrival. If possible, use different entrances and exits.
4. If you believe that you are being followed, be prepared to run. Go into a store or police station, and report the incident. Identify the individual.
5. If you are approached by a suspicious person, cross the street or change direction. If threatened from a car, run in the opposite direction to seek help.

At Work

1. Do not risk being attacked in a poorly lighted or soundproof stairwell. Use an elevator when possible, and stand next to the control panel. If threatened, punch all of the floor buttons and the alarm button, not the emergency stop button.
2. Never leave keys or valuables in coat pockets. When working, keep your purse locked in a desk or file cabinet.
3. Use discretion in revealing your personal plans to others.
4. When working late, inform the building security officer, and tell someone at home when to expect you.
5. Report suspicious people or behavior in your building to the security officer or your supervisor.

When Traveling Abroad

Those who travel abroad on business or pleasure are subject to international terrorist threats. The following precautions will help ensure that your trip is a pleasurable one.

1. Do not discuss your travel plans within hearing distance of strangers. Do not leave your itinerary or related papers where others can read them.
2. Always carry identification papers and an emergency medical card stating your blood type and any allergies to medication. The card should be in English and in the language of the host country.
3. Learn enough of the local language to be able to say, "I need a policeman," "Take me to a doctor," "Where is the hospital?," "Where is the police station?," "Fire," and "Help."
4. Know how to use a local commercial telephone, and know the emergency telephone numbers for the police, the fire department, and the American Embassy.

Always carry exact change for a pay telephone in case of an emergency. Telephone booths may offer refuge against some forms of violence while waiting for assistance.

5. Avoid anything that could easily identify you as an American, a wealthy person, or someone of importance. Drive a domestic car of a popular color. Do not wear clothes that identify you as an American.
6. Avoid disputes with local citizens. If you do become involved in a dispute or an accident, call the local police immediately.
7. When abroad, consider the unexplained absences of local citizens as an early warning of possible terrorist actions.

If Attacked

If you are attacked, only you can decide what action, if any is appropriate, to take against the attacker. Remember that your first priority is to get away—not stand and fight.

1. Scream "Help!" or "Fire!" as loudly as possible.
2. Strike back quickly, aiming for the attacker's vital spots: gouge eyes with your thumbs, scratch face with fingernails, keys, or nail file; hack temple, nose, or Adam's apple with purse or book; jab your knee into the groin; stomp down on the instep; kick the shins; grab fingers and bend back sharply; or poke umbrella, comb, fist, or elbow in the midriff.
3. Never allow an attacker to take you to another location where your privacy is denied. Chances are that if you voluntarily go with the attacker to another location, this only increases your chances of being raped or killed and in essence becomes a secondary crime scene.
4. Remember: An attacker lies. Don't believe what they say to you because they can act differently.
5. Report the incident as soon as possible. At work, notify the building security officer or the local police. At home, report the incident to the police. Give a good description of the attacker, including height, weight, build, color of hair and eyes, complexion, and scars or tattoos. It is important to report all incidents to help prevent others from being attacked.

If Kidnapped or Taken Hostage

The following suggestions are for kidnapping victims and hostages *only*. An attacker who intends just to rob you has a different psychology, and your actions should be in accordance with the preceding recommendations.

1. Unless there are clear indications that your efforts stand a good chance of success, do not resist or attempt to flee, or you may become an assassination target.

2. Suppress your initial panic, and remain as calm as possible. Even if you are frightened, try to appear calm. Remember that people are actively working to secure your release.
3. Try to get on a first-name basis with your captors. This will help them think of you as a person rather than an object and should ease the tension.
4. Do not become depressed if negotiations become prolonged. Time is on your side: The more time that passes, the better your chances for a safe release.

Appendix 9

Minimum Training Standards for Security Force Personnel

PHASE I (BASIC) TRAINING

Phase I basic training is required for all security personnel. Approximately twenty-one to thirty-two hours should be allotted for this training. The length of time devoted to individual topics should be based on the mission and level of experience of the employee. The director of security may select additional training subjects based on the mission's overall needs and the needs of the individual security employee. Phase I training requires the new security officer to obtain the Professional Security Television Network (PSTN) certificate or equivalent in basic security officer training, plus any additional training required to meet individual or post needs. At least seven hours of self-defense tactics training will be included. Phase I training will be documented in each security officer's individual training file.

Basic Security Officer Training Certification

The importance of a comprehensive, basic, pre-assignment, and in-service training program for security personnel and supervisors is unquestionably a recognized necessity. Current, relevant, and well-structured training programs are essential to the success of any organization—especially a security department or anyone who performs a designated security function as their primary job. Timely and relevant training is an absolute necessity if security team members are to perform safely and effectively. People need to know what is expected of them and exactly how to do their job. Most security professionals, fortunately, want to do a good job; regrettably, however, management sometimes fails to organize and train them properly—particularly if they are viewed as a support function only—which has serious consequences. Studies show that people who do not receive sufficient and effective initial and continuing in-service training are likely to be: less productive; more cautious; uninformed about their responsibilities; suffering from low morale; unfamiliar with their assigned equipment; less proficient with the skills previously taught; suffering from increased job-related stress; and in need of more supervision. When the security employee experiences these consequences the entire organization suffers. Even more serious can be the liability to which an organization exposes itself. Generally today, the first things to be examined in a lawsuit are personnel and training records as attorneys attempt to prove negligent hiring, retention, supervising, and training practices. Organizations that give attention to establishing a professional security organization with the proper selection, training, and supervision of security personnel can minimize the associated liability and risks and can more successfully defend themselves against security related litigation.

The following are some minimum subjects that must be addressed in a security officer training certification program. Sworn peace officers may have additional subjects as dictated by state peace officer standards of training.

Subjects

Introduction to security

Importance of the security officer

Legal issues I

Legal issues II

Human and public relations

Communications

Patrol

General duties

Report writing

Fire prevention and control

Emergency situations

Safety

Other topics should be included as required and particular to each organization's structure and operating procedures.

PHASE II (IN-SERVICE) TRAINING

All security personnel must complete Phase II training annually. The required training is also available via a Phase II Portable Training Package available in the office of security. It includes all of the material necessary for the annual training except for self-defense tactics and specialized skills.

The subjects listed in this section are required for all members of the security force. Not included are specialized skills that may also be required, such as equipment proficiency, CPR, first-aid, other skills requiring periodic certification, and self-defense tactics.

The overall Phase II training will encompass a minimum of twenty-eight hours of classroom and practical exercises given by means of scheduled in-service training days or as necessary for individual security officer refresher training. The training coordinator and the director of security will determine the length of time to be devoted to each subject based on the mission's overall needs. The director of security and the administrative officer of each facility where security officers are assigned will ensure that adequate time is scheduled to provide security force personnel with sufficient knowledge of each subject.

Documentation of the completion of all annual Phase II training will be maintained in each security officer's individual training file.

Subjects	Suggested Hours
Jurisdiction	1.0
Law, jurisdiction, and authority	1.0
Use of force	1.0
Crime scenes	1.0
Search and seizure	1.0
Interview and interrogation techniques	2.0
Reports and forms	1.0
Crisis intervention	1.0
Juvenile offenses	1.0
Crime-prevention program	1.0
Preliminary investigations	1.0
Public relations, citizen interaction	1.0
Surveys and assessments	1.0
Access control and perimeter security	1.0
Disaster and emergency plans	1.0
Local instructions and procedures	1.0
Court services, intake, magistrate	1.0
CPR and first-aid certification/recertification	7.0
Self-defense tactics	7.0

Additional Subjects for Phase II (In-Service) Training

Phase II in-service training is a continuing annual evolution of training designed to provide up-to-date information and refresher training to security personnel. Due to the ongoing nature of the training, in-service training should be flexible and allow for easy inclusion of new material, subjects, and skills in order to keep the training from becoming too boring. Training should be relevant to the job as well as to the individual as a security professional. In addition to the previously identified Phase II subjects, the following subject elements are examples of the variety of subjects that can be added to the training presentations as deemed appropriate.

Administrative
Overview and orientation

Security department duties and functions

Standards of conduct

Forms and reports, report writing

Area familiarization, on-the-job training

The security/police image

Physical Security
Vehicle and personnel movement control

Loss prevention and the M-L-S-R program

Physical security safeguards

Legal
Jurisdiction and authority

Rules of evidence

Search and seizure

Self-incrimination, admissions, and confessions

Apprehension and arrest

Testifying in court

Court services, intake, magistrate

Traffic
Directing traffic

Patrol
Crime scenes, preservation of evidence, collection of evidence

Crime prevention

Crimes in progress

Juvenile matters

Communications

Patrol procedures

Gathering information from people

Preliminary investigations

Handling disturbance calls, disturbed people, and "special education" students

Improving officer-citizen contacts

Unusual Incidents
Crowd control

Bomb threats and search techniques

Professional Skills
Use of handcuffs and other temporary restraining devices

Weapons proficiency training (if authorized)

Use of force

Self-defense tactics

Metal detector certification (if appropriate)

Pepper spray training and certification (if appropriate)

CROSS-TRAINING

In addition to the standard training received in Phase I and Phase II, security officers will participate, biannually, in scheduled temporary reassignments for a period of one week each to other schools than normally assigned. As part of the professional training and development of security officers, cross-training is a valid training component of each security officer's ongoing professional security development. Cross-training will compliment and reinforce in-service training, and due to the discretionary nature of a security officer's job, increase their ability to deter, detect, respond to, and handle different situations because of increased self-confidence and exposure to different or variable conditions and incidents. Security officers can become complacent, unchallenged, and somewhat of a "fixture" rather than a dynamic pro-active deterrent due to the length of time at one school. It is anticipated that well supervised and planned cross-training will give a security officer greater incentives to perform at a high level as well as an avenue to have exceptional service and abilities recognized.

Appendix 10

Barricaded Captor/Hostage Situation Plan

PURPOSE

This appendix provides guidance on countering barricaded captor/hostage situations on school property. It is highly recommended that a barricaded captor/hostage plan be in writing and be exercised/drilled under simulated conditions with school administrators, staff, and police participation. Drills of this nature are learning experiences for school staff and can go a long way in preventing or reducing mistakes should an actual incident take place in the future. Every full exercise/drill conducted should have a critique session following the drill in order to identify what was done correctly as well as what actions should be avoided.

BACKGROUND

In recent years, there has been an increasing number of incidents in which hostages have been taken and held in an attempt to further the captor's objectives. A number of incidents have occurred in public schools and on school buses across the nation.

DISCUSSION

Because of the complex nature of barricaded captor/hostage situations, a response must be coordinated between schools and police in order to deal effectively with such situations, and contingency plans for such events must be in place. What is particularly troublesome about potential hostage situations in schools is that because schools are public places there are limitations on what can be done to prevent a hostage situation from taking place. A good access-control program and employee and visitor badging program will, however, go a long way in deterring and hardening a school as a potential target of this type of activity. Several variables affect a hostage situation: the number of hostages and captors, the captors' motivation, whether weapons are involved, the location and isolation of the school, the training of police personnel in handling hostage situations, and the school's planned response to crisis situations.

CONCEPT

When school administrators face a barricaded captor/hostage situation, they can expect to encounter one of four basic types of people:

1. A common criminal (robber, burglar, and so on) who is trapped or seeks refuge while or after committing a crime
2. A person being detained who takes hostages in order to escape from confinement or to voice a protest
3. A terrorist whose objective is to draw attention to a particular cause; terrorists are the most dangerous because they are usually well organized, operate in small groups, and are often willing to die for their objectives
4. An emotionally upset or disturbed person, frequently involved in a domestic situation

The hostage situations to which schools are subjected usually fall into the first and last categories, in which a stranger, a parent or relative of an employee or student is involved. What makes these four situations different is the motivation that leads to the event. In types 1 and 2, the motivation is to escape; in type 3, the true motivation may not be known; and in type 4, the motivation is usually the release of a child or a personal disagreement or conflict.

There are two operational considerations in a hostage situation: (1) protecting the lives of everyone involved, including the captors, and (2) protecting property and avoiding disruption. There is no absolutely correct way to handle a hostage situation. At best, all that can be done is to minimize the severity of injuries, protect those who are not involved, and negotiate the situation to a successful conclusion.

It is essential that there be only one administrator in charge of the situation until the police assume responsibility. Because the principal is ultimately responsible for school property, the on-scene command will remain with him or her or their designee until the designated police representative arrives on the scene.

ACTION

Upon notification of a possible hostage situation within an activity or school, the provisions of this instruction will immediately be implemented.

COMMAND AND CONTROL

The principal or administrative head or designee (or, in his or her absence, the next eligible) will exercise command in a barricaded captor/hostage situation until the police assume command and control. He or she will then take on a follow-up position in the critical incident management center (CIMC). The CIMC will be established by the police and may be located in an area away from the incident site. The CIMC will usually be occupied by police command personnel, necessary city officials, and any other designated personnel needed to aid in making effective decisions. The school principal, an information services representative, and other necessary school administration personnel should be available to assist in the CIMC.

SPECIFIC TASKS

The school or activity office will notify the following:

- Police and fire (911)
- School security/police
- Superintendent
- Deputy superintendent
- Director of information services
- Department of pupil services
- Transportation
- School plant facilities

The director of information services will do the following:

- Contact the police department's public information officer to coordinate media information.
- Proceed to the critical incident management center set up by the police near the incident site.
- Have personnel available to answer telephone calls to the superintendent's office and the office of information services.

Transportation will do the following:

- Have an appropriate number of buses and drivers available to proceed to the affected location to transport students or other personnel, if necessary.
- Designate an on-scene coordinator to facilitate bus movements.

OPERATIONAL PLANNING GUIDE

A school administrator's self-confidence in effectively dealing with a barricaded captor/hostage situation can be increased through prior planning and having a greater understanding of the different roles played by police and the school, police procedures and operational objectives, and other concerns in a hostage situation. The following information is provided for consideration and awareness.

Principal Considerations

The goal that must prevail during hostage situations is to effect the safe release of the hostages. Every decision that is made should be predicated on the philosophy that the preservation of human life (hostages, students, employees, law enforcement personnel, and captors) constitutes the first priority. The initial precepts should be containing the barricaded captors within the smallest possible area, establishing a perimeter, and stabilizing the situation with the least amount of disruption.

It is important to ease anxieties and tensions, if possible, to allow the captors to assess their situation rationally. The proper use of time is the key dictate. As a general rule, the more time captors spend with their hostages, the less likely they are to harm them. As they become acquainted, they may develop an affinity for one another. Negotiations should be used to attain the objective of the foregoing precepts.

Buying Time

In addition to the principal consideration of preserving human life, buying time through the use of hostage negotiators generally works to the advantage of law enforcement personnel after they arrive on scene. In addition to allowing the captors time to develop empathy, it also provides law enforcement personnel with the opportunity to prepare for different eventualities and gives the captors the opportunity to make a mistake.

Initial Response and Containment by School Personnel

The first school personnel on the scene of a hostage situation should consider the following actions:

1. Immediately advise _____ police and superiors that a hostage situation is taking place.
2. Assess the situation.
3. Evacuate first the general area and then the entire building of nonessential personnel, moving them to a designated area out of the line of sight from the crisis area initially, and the entire school if possible.
4. Ensure arrangements for the transportation of students and other personnel from the designated area to appropriate safe locations.
5. Refrain from any activity that needlessly endangers the hostages or others or that involves unnecessary, rapid movements of personnel or vehicles within sight of the captors.
6. Seek to confine and isolate the hostage situation to the smallest possible area by establishing a perimeter, preventing the incident from expanding or becoming mobile.
7. Detain all witnesses to the occurrence so that arriving law enforcement personnel can debrief them. These witnesses include anyone who can describe what took place; can identify the hostages, captors, or suspects; can describe any equipment, such as weapons, hand-carried items, radios, and so on, that the captors have; or can identify possible avenues of escape, the location to which additional police units should respond, or any unsafe corridors that the police should avoid.

Upon being relieved by the police, the initial containment and response personnel should report to the police tactical command post or other appropriate area for debriefing.

The principal and school custodian should be available to assist the police throughout the incident. They should offer to the nearest police commander blueprints of the school and any other information that would aid police in bringing the incident to a successful conclusion.

Communication with Captors by Police

In a barricaded hostage situation, an initial consideration should be establishing communication between the captors and the hostage negotiators. Negotiations may be conducted in person, by telephone, or by other available means.

Efforts should be made to identify telephones or other devices that are available in the location where the captors are barricaded so that communications can be established. Telephone lines that are not needed by the hostage negotiators should be deactivated, if possible. Experience has shown that if extra telephone lines are left operational, the captors may contact journalists or other individuals to gain support for their position. Additionally, members of the public may communicate with the captors and provide them with advice and counsel, which would not help bring the situation to a timely and successful conclusion.

If no operational telephone lines are installed, consideration should be given to installing a dedicated line and placing an instrument with adequate cable where the captors can gain reach for communication with negotiators. Another possibility is to provide the captors with a simple two-way radio.

News Media

The director of information services should establish liaison with the news media in conjunction with the police department's public information officer in an attempt to secure the media's cooperation during the course of the operation. Past experience has shown that captors sometimes have access to normal AM-FM radios in the barricaded area and might listen to news accounts of the ongoing operation. On several occasions, members of the news media have jeopardized success of the operation by reporting possible contingency plans or describing the actions of the police or other personnel.

Communications

All communications directly related to or in support of the operation must be conducted over covered radio circuits or via land line. Discipline must be maintained, and everyone must be aware that the captors may be in possession of frequency scanners.

School Bus Hostage Situations

If a hostage incident takes place on a school bus, the following should be considered in addition to other departmental procedures:

1. Evacuate as many students as possible from the bus, if allowed, and notify the transportation dispatcher.
2. Disable the bus or throw the keys away from the bus if possible.
3. Clear the area of as many students and others as is safely possible.
4. Send an on-scene coordinator to the incident site to assist the police.
5. Have a representative from the transportation department go to the police CIMC and be available to provide assistance.

_____ POLICE DEPARTMENT SERVICES

The _____ Police Department's role in barricaded hostage situations will call for the following procedures as well as any other police department procedures in place.

Advice

Police department personnel will provide professional advice to the administrator regarding the operation. They will use discretion in this role so as not to assume the administrator's prerogatives prior to _____ assuming command and control. The administrator will turn the operation over to the police at the appropriate time and will be present in the CIMC to provide assistance.

Investigation

The _____ will have investigative responsibility. In the hostage context, investigation means in-progress investigation and the collection of evidence by all available means as offenses are committed. A part of this investigation should be the immediate interviewing of any hostages who are released, the interviewing of any personnel when relieved from the inner perimeter for both evidential and intelligence purposes, and the appropriate processing of the crime scene after the captors have been apprehended.

Intelligence

The _____ will collect intelligence, with assistance from school personnel, concerning the physical environment in which the hostage situation is taking place (floor plans, building layouts, available means of communication within the locale, and other information of value to the on-scene police commander). Intelligence collection will also be initiated concerning the background of both the captors and the hostages.

Hostage Negotiations

The _____ will provide hostage negotiators and will coordinate their activities. School personnel who negotiated with the captors before the police arrived will cooperate with the police regarding the continuation of their role. If a captor makes requests before the police command arrives, no one will agree to these requests but will concentrate on delaying and buying time until professional negotiators arrive. Giving in to requests could make it more difficult to bring the situation to a successful conclusion.

Returning Responsibility to _____

The _____ administrator who has responsibility for the affected site will resume responsibility of the site when it is turned over by police command personnel.

MESSAGES TO ALERT STAFF TO A DANGER

Appendix 2C contains loudspeaker messages that can be used to alert staff to potentially dangerous situations, including hostage incidents and armed intruders on campus. Prepared alert messages help maintain control and reduce unnecessary exposure to further danger in these situations.

Appendix 11

Security Force Standard Operating Procedures

A complete, well written, up-to-date policies and procedures manual is an extremely important and necessary component of employing and operating a modern, professional security/police agency. A written manual can help protect a district from civil actions for vicarious liability and demonstrate that an organization has shown due regard in directing the actions of security/police personnel. The manual further provides a means by which lines of authority and accountability can be clearly established, the direction of the operations can be set, and the status as an efficient, professional, and responsive organization can be maintained. A manual also informs all personnel who work in security/police roles of their responsibilities, indicates what is expected of them, outlines methods of accomplishing tasks, and provides general performance standards. The manual allows for security managers and supervisors to achieve consistency in decisions and provides for a means to determine if existing policies and procedures are consistent with the intended direction of the organization or require change as needed.

General orders and standard operating procedures are standards well established, today, in a modern and professional security/police operation. School districts who have security/police personnel will be expected to have such written documents. School districts should not convince themselves that they will not, in the future, be held liable and accountable for not organizing, supervising, and operating security/police personnel according to professional standards and practices.

This appendix is provided as an example of what should be included in written standard operating procedures for a security force. This example is not meant to be all inclusive nor address all issues or types of incidents. Variations will be dependent upon each district's policy and laws of the jurisdiction under which security/police operates.

SECTION I: SCHOOL AND DEPARTMENTAL ORGANIZATION OF SECURITY

Organization of the Office of Security

Purpose.   This section explains the organization of the office of security and the mission of each of its divisions and branches. Variations may be applied as appropriate for individual districts.

Staff Division.   The Staff Division consists of the director of security, security secretaries, the division investigators (as assigned), and others as deemed necessary. It is the mission of the Staff Division to coordinate security activities, execute planning, handle financial matters, provide guidance, ensure that administrative requirements are met, and establish regulations and supervision for security force personnel.

Operations Division.   The Operations Division consists of security officers whose mission is to provide security services to the schools, including (1) the preliminary investigation of criminal acts and (2) crime prevention and intervention through patrolling and enforcement of rules, regulations, and laws applicable to everyone on school district property.

Training Division.   The mission of the Training Division is to coordinate and teach basic and in-service security training, maintain individual training records and plans, ensure that in-service training is accomplished, arrange for participation in courses held outside the department, and provide for district employee security awareness training.

Investigations Division.   The mission of the Investigations Division is to investigate criminal acts and prepare cases to aid police and school administrators in prosecuting the alleged perpetrators of those acts, investigate and prepare tort claim rendering opinions as to fault and liability, and carry on a continuing drug and weapon interdiction program, including coordinating the drug- and explosive-detection dog teams and the administrative random inspection program.

Physical Security Division.   The mission of this division is to implement, coordinate, develop, and conduct security surveys/assessments, crime-prevention programs, loss prevention programs, "school-oriented policing" concepts, and to liaison with other divisions to ensure that the programs are included and accepted in overall security operations and training.

All security officers assigned to schools will be supervised by a supervisory security officer who will be responsible to the school principal and director of security who will be the line authority. The divisions of the office of security, when in place, will support the security efforts of the school principal and director of security in providing for a safe school environment and a trained and professional security force. Security personnel *will not* perform nonsecurity duties.

It is the intent of all divisions and operational personnel to work in support of the school principal to ensure that the school's security needs are met within the existing staff and budget constraints.

Jurisdiction, Authority, and Apprehension

Purpose. This section sets forth the authority of members of the security force in detaining and apprehending individuals suspected of criminal acts.

Policy. It is the policy of _____ that individuals committing crimes will be apprehended and turned over to the proper authority for prosecution of the crime or for other administrative action.

General Jurisdiction for Detention or Apprehension. All individuals within the limits of _____ property are subject to federal, state, and local laws. Any person on _____ property may be detained by a security officer to ascertain the seriousness of a violation and to discover pertinent information about the violation. Further, the security officer may detain the individual until the arrival of the appropriate authority. If a person has committed a crime, the security officer will notify the principal, conduct a preliminary investigation, seek prosecution, or refer such information to the police, if appropriate. The police will conduct the investigation or refer the case to the appropriate agency for investigation. Any time a person is detained for a crime, the principal and the office of security will be contacted and advised of the situation.

Line of Authority. The superintendent of schools is ultimately responsible for the security, peace, and tranquillity of all schools. The school principal and the director of security will be held accountable to the superintendent for the proper discharge of their duties. School principals and those in charge of other facilities will support the director of security in carrying out approved security operations according to professional security standards and procedures.

Insubordination. All security officers are subject to disciplinary action, including termination, for insubordination. The failure to carry out a reasonable job assignment or reasonable request by the appropriate line supervisor can result in termination, after being warned that failure to do so will constitute insubordination.

Posts

Purpose. This section establishes the posts for the Operations Division of the office of security and sets forth the duties of each post.

Security Investigator
POST
This post will be filled by an experienced individual who is knowledgeable in security and law enforcement and investigations and who possesses a mature and cooperative attitude in following regulations and guidelines. He or she must have initiative, tact, and skill in dealing with antisocial behavior.

HOURS
The hours of duty for a security investigator assigned to a specific location will be determined by the building administrator and the office of security. Normal duty hours for

investigators not assigned to a specific location (for example, the operations officer or training coordinator) are from 7:30 A.M. to 4:00 P.M. daily or as promulgated by the Investigations Watch Bill, scheduled in the office of security. A designated duty investigator will be on call at times deemed appropriate by the director of security. This position will be shared equally by all investigators, as appropriate.

UNIFORM
Male security investigators will wear civilian clothes of a professional nature, including dress shirt and slacks, sports coat or suit, as appropriate, with a tie and issued security/police badge. Other issued outer garment may also be worn. Female security investigators will wear civilian clothes of a similar professional nature or other provided outer garment. The investigator's appearance will be neat and professional at all times.

EQUIPMENT
Security investigators will carry a field notebook, pen, chemical spray and handcuffs (if authorized), radio, and issued badge. They will have a complete investigation/identification kit and will drive an appropriately equipped vehicle. They must be certified in the use of metal detectors.

USE OF FORCE
The use of force will be restricted to only the minimum force necessary to control and terminate unlawful actions and resistance and to preclude any further physical attack against others.

DUTIES
The following are the duties of the security investigator:

- Investigate incidents and offenses occurring on or against property or personnel (students, employees, visitors, and so on) on _____ property.
- Maintain liaison with _____ and work in cooperation with the police and other law enforcement agencies.
- Render assistance and contribute to the welfare and general well-being of _____ personnel.
- Prepare all required reports.
- Be thoroughly familiar with the contents of all office of security procedures and general orders and all instructions and laws related to security and law enforcement and know the rules and regulations related to personnel and property.
- Upon assuming duty at the assigned school site, inspect and brief each security officer assigned there, and report the status to the appropriate building administrator and office of security, as required.
- Ensure that all personnel assigned to the site are inspected at least twice per shift. Investigators with collateral or staff duties, such as operations officer or training coordinator, will conduct investigations and perform other duties as assigned by the office of security. Investigators will coordinate with field training officers and will

ensure that all assigned personnel are fully trained and instructed in their duties according to departmental procedures.
- Conduct security awareness, crime-prevention, and loss prevention training and counseling, and conduct surveys and prepare written survey reports.
- Be familiar with the following investigative techniques:
  - Seizing, evaluating, collecting, marking, tagging, and preserving evidence
  - Carrying out and recording effective interrogations and preliminary interviews with juveniles and adults
  - Apprehending suspects
  - Carrying out searches, inspections, and inventories of persons, vehicles, and places
  - Providing technical assistance in all areas of security and law enforcement investigation
  - Securing crime scenes and scenes of accidents for further investigation
  - Dusting, lifting, and recording fingerprints
  - Conducting thorough investigations and following through to a logical conclusion
  - Using approved methods for identifying individuals
  - Identifying narcotics and other dangerous drugs
  - Effectively communicating both orally and in writing
- Be knowledgeable in the following legal aspects:
  - Identifying jurisdictional authority
  - Interpreting investigative jurisdiction
  - Complying with the rules of evidence regarding statements, interviews, interrogations, searches, inspections, and seizures
  - Determining probable cause and reasonable suspicion
  - Enforcing the provisions of the _____ Rules and Regulations, as applicable to violations of the law
  - Enforcing state and local laws and ordinances as they apply
  - Developing strategies for dealing with trespassers and other security-related issues
  - Detecting weaknesses in building and property security, such as faulty locks, broken windows, inadequate lighting, and deficiencies in the intrusion-detection system
  - Providing assistance to administrators in preparing security contingency plans for their school or location
  - Maintaining surveillance of problem areas, particularly those areas known to be frequented by drug users or distributors or gangs, on or off school or location grounds, as appropriate
  - Attending after-school activities as assigned for security purposes (Compensation for all overtime worked will be in accordance with school board policy.)
  - Developing community contacts and conducting community relations initiatives so that the community's security concerns can be made known to the office of security and to the school administration
  - Participating in investigations and after-hour surveillance and response, as determined and scheduled by the office of security
  - Duties other than those relating to security will not be performed during regularly scheduled duty hours

School Supervisory Security Officer (Team Leader)
POST
This post, a *working* supervisory post, will be filled by an experienced individual who is knowledgeable in security or law enforcement and investigations and who possesses a mature and cooperative attitude in following regulations and guidelines. He or she must have initiative, tact, and skill in dealing with antisocial behavior.

HOURS
The hours of duty for a supervisory security officer assigned to a specific location will be determined by the principal and the office of security.

UNIFORM
Male security officers will wear civilian clothes of a professional nature, including dress shirt and slacks with a tie and issued badge, and other provided outer garment. Female security officers will wear civilian clothes of a professional nature or other provided outer garment. The officer's appearance will be neat and professional at all times.

EQUIPMENT
Supervisory security officers will carry a field notebook, pen, chemical spray and handcuffs (if authorized), radio, badge, and appropriate leather gear. They must be certified in the use of metal detectors.

USE OF FORCE
The use of force will be restricted to only the minimum force necessary to control and terminate unlawful actions and resistance and to preclude any further physical attack against others.

DUTIES
The following are the duties of the supervisory security officer:

- Upon assuming the duty, inventory all equipment and roll-call personnel assigned, inspect and brief each officer, ensure that preoperation inspections are made of all equipment, and report all discrepancies and the status of security personnel to the appropriate building administrator and office of security.
- Be thoroughly familiar with the contents of all instructions relating to law enforcement, security, and the rules and regulations of the assigned location, and enforce all rules and regulations in an effective, fair, and professional manner.
- Ensure as the field training officer that all security officers at the assigned location are fully trained and instructed in their duties and are completely familiar with all applicable laws, rules, regulations, and procedures.
- Personally inspect all assigned security personnel at least twice during the hours of duty, ensuring that they are alert and neat in appearance; report any discrepancies noted to the school principal and the office of security; and ensure that they are corrected as soon as possible.

- As a preliminary investigator, ensure that the proper methods of recording and investigating are employed, and notify the school principal and the office of security when a crime, theft, or other security-related incident occurs.
- Maintain a field notebook, and record incidents or suspicious activities.
- Ensure that the other assigned security officers are trained in the proper methods for apprehending and counseling violators and that they use the appropriate methods to prepare reports and notices.
- If any questions arise during the hours of duty concerning the performance of duties not covered by instructions or procedures, contact the school principal first, then the office of security.
- Review and revise, as necessary, all paperwork submitted by assigned security officers before it is submitted to the principal or office of security.
- When arriving at the scene of a crime or incident, make a visual inspection of the crime scene and ensure that the area is secured; note any item of evidentiary value, and if seizure is warranted, take precautions in handling the evidence to avoid disturbing fingerprints or contaminating evidence.
- Complete an Evidence/Property Custody Receipt for all evidence seized, and with the evidence turn it over to the investigator or police, as appropriate, when they arrive on the scene.
- Assume responsibility for reviewing, making entries, and promulgating "intelligence" and other information and forwarding it to the appropriate personnel.
- Conduct security awareness, crime-prevention, and loss prevention training and counseling, and assist in conducting and preparing written survey reports.
- Help develop strategies for dealing with trespassers.
- Detect weaknesses in building and property security, such as faulty locks, broken windows, inadequate lighting, and deficiencies in the intrusion-detection system.
- Help school administrators prepare security contingency plans for their school and assist in other matters pertaining to security.
- Attend after-school activities, as assigned by the principal or director of security for security purposes. (Duties other than those relating to the security of the assigned location will not be performed during regularly scheduled duty hours.)
- Perform such other security duties as deemed necessary by the school principal or director of security during and after normal hours of duty.

School Security Officer
POST
This post is a mobile or roving patrol covering specific areas, as assigned by the principal of the assigned school, the supervisory security officer, or the director of security.

HOURS
The hours of duty for a school security officer assigned to a specific building or location will be determined by the principal of the assigned school, the supervisory security officer, and the director of security.

UNIFORM
Male security officers will wear civilian clothes of a professional nature, including dress shirt and slacks, a tie and issued badge, or other provided outer garment. Female security officers will wear civilian clothes of a similar professional nature or other provided outer garment. The officer's appearance will be neat and professional at all times.

EQUIPMENT
School security officers will carry a field notebook, pen, chemical spray and handcuffs (if authorized), radio, badge, and appropriate leather gear. They must be certified in the use of metal detectors.

USE OF FORCE
The use of force will be restricted to only the minimum force necessary to control and terminate unlawful actions and resistance and to preclude any further physical attack against others.

DUTIES
The following are the duties of the school security officer:

- Upon assuming the duty, check all assigned equipment, and make a preoperational inspection of equipment assigned for individual use.
- Be thoroughly familiar with all instructions relating to law enforcement and physical security, and know the rules and regulations of the assigned location.
- Enforce in an effective, fair, and professional manner all regulations, rules, and laws pertaining to security at the building or location where assigned.
- Deliver all personnel detained or apprehended during the hours of duty to the school or location administrator (authorized representative) or the police for disposition.
- Operate off of the assigned location for other security functions when directed to do so by the principal or director of security.
- Complete security checks of buildings according to the approved checklist and complete routine patrol procedures at regular intervals during the hours of operation.
- Be especially watchful for unusual or out-of-place occurrences and suspicious activities, report them to the supervisor, and record them in the field notebook.
- Be thoroughly familiar with the procedures to be followed in the event of specific incidents, such as trespassing, discovery of weapons, bomb threats, disturbances, and so on.
- Treat everyone with the proper courtesy.
- Exercise extreme care and alertness while patrolling, and set an example for others; no smoking, chewing gum, or sitting (unless specified by assignment) while in the public view.
- When arriving at the scene of a crime or security-related incident, make a visual inspection of the crime scene and ensure that the area is secured; note any item of evidentiary value, and if seizure is warranted, take precautions in handling the evidence to avoid disturbing fingerprints or contaminating evidence.

- Complete an Evidence/Property Custody Receipt for all evidence seized, and with the evidence turn it over to the police or investigator, as appropriate, when he or she arrives on the scene.
- Complete all Security Incident Reports or other related reports properly and accurately.
- Help conduct security awareness, crime-prevention, and loss prevention training and counseling, when appropriate.
- Help detect weaknesses in building and property security, such as faulty locks, broken windows, inadequate lighting, and deficiencies in the intrusion-detection system.
- Help school administrators and supervisors prepare security contingency plans for their school and assist in other matters pertaining to security.
- Attend after-school activities, as assigned by the principal and office security for security purposes.
- Patrol the school and school grounds randomly, keeping fixed posts to a minimum.
- Perform any other security duties requested by the principal, supervisory security officer, or director of security.
- Duties other than those relating to the security of the assigned location will not be performed during regularly scheduled duty hours.

Hours of Work

Purpose. This section establishes the hours and system of operation for personnel assigned to the office of security and to the school-assigned security force.

Duty Hours. The following are the times of the duty:

- Staff Division, 0730 to 1600, or as appropriate
- Investigators, supervisory security officers, security officers at high schools, 0715 to 1445, or as directed by the school principal and office of security
- Investigators, supervisory security officers, security officers at middle or junior high schools, 0745 to 1515, or as directed by the school principal and the office of security
- Officers assigned to elementary schools will be scheduled appropriately

Duty hours may be changed or scheduled to suit the needs of the assigned school, as approved by the principal or director of security.

Reporting. Security personnel will report for duty on time and will not leave until their scheduled time unless approved by the principal or director of security. Tardiness and unexcused absences will be cause for disciplinary action.

Rotation. Security personnel will normally be assigned to a particular location to perform their assigned duties. However, they may be permanently reassigned to other locations or may be temporarily assigned as needed. Personnel may also be temporarily reassigned to other schools for training, to improve their professional skills, or to expose them to situations which give them experience they have not before been exposed to.

SECTION II: PERSONNEL POLICIES

Uniform and Grooming Standards

Purpose.   This section establishes the uniform to be worn and sets forth expected personal grooming standards.

Inspection.   The investigator or supervisory security officer (SSO) will inspect security personnel to ensure compliance with the provisions of this section. The SSO will bring to the attention of individuals any minor discrepancies; repeated offenses will result in disciplinary action. When the attire of an individual is of an unacceptable level for the performance of duty, the SSO will counsel the individual and give written notification to the principal and director of security.

Uniform.   Male officers will wear civilian clothes of a professional nature, including dress slacks and shirt with tie and issued badge, or other provided outer garment. It is recommended that tear-away ties be worn to avoid injury. Female officers will wear civilian clothes of a similar professional nature or other provided outer garment. Skirts and dresses will be of a modest length, and clothing will fit appropriately for a school environment. No other uniform may be worn without the approval of the principal and director of security. The appearance of security officers will be neat and professional at all times.

Equipment.   Officers will wear the following equipment in the manner set forth here:

- Badges will be worn on the left breast pocket or on the belt.
- Officers may also wear badges on a chain around the neck, when appropriate.
- Other approved and assigned equipment will be worn as appropriate.

Grooming.   Investigators, supervisory security officers, and security officers will conform to the following grooming standards:

1. Hair need not be a specified length but must present a neat, styled, and well-groomed appearance.
2. Hair will in no way interfere with the proper wearing of headgear that may be issued.
3. Sideburns will be neatly trimmed.
4. Male investigators, supervisory security officers, and security officers will be clean shaven, may have a neatly trimmed mustache that does not protrude beyond the corners of the mouth and does not grow over the upper lip, and may have a neatly trimmed beard.
5. Female officers will be groomed in a manner that projects a professional and responsible adult image in a school environment.

Leave Policy

Purpose.   This section establishes the leave policy for members of the security force.

Policy. It is the policy of _____ to allow employees to go on leave when they wish and for as long a period as they request. This policy must, however, be restricted to meet the needs of the location or department. By having a set policy and a good understanding of its operation all requests can be handled within reason.

Leave Request. Members of the security force will submit their leave requests to their immediate supervisor, who in turn will comment on the request and pass it through the chain of command to the approved administrator for approval. Leave requests will not be submitted more than ninety days in advance nor fewer than ten workdays before the beginning of the requested leave, except in an emergency. Leave requests will be considered on a first-come, first-served basis.

Leave Restrictions

- There will be no more than two employees (or appropriate number as determined) from the Staff Division on leave at one time.
- There will be no more than one clerk on leave at any one time.
- There will be no more than one investigator on leave at any one time at any one school or staff division.
- There will be no more than one security officer on leave from any single location at a time unless otherwise approved by the school principal and the director of security and in time to arrange for a substitute.

Empty posts due to official court appearances should be filled with a substitute, when possible.

Security Force Personnel Contact Information

Purpose. This section establishes the requirements and procedures for submitting and maintaining address and telephone number files for security force personnel.

Policy. Upon occasion, security personnel must be contacted at home for court appearances, training, emergencies, or other matters. For the protection of the individual as well as the efficient operation of the facility and department, addresses and telephone numbers must be kept current.

Establishing Files. A file or listing containing names, addresses, and phone numbers of security force personnel will be maintained in the appropriate school office and the office of security.

Responsibility. Each member of the security force will submit to the school office where assigned and to the office of security any change of address or telephone number within two workdays. The security secretary will update the address and telephone number files maintained within the office of security.

Divulging Contact Information. The home telephone numbers and addresses of security personnel will not be divulged for unofficial reasons. Individuals who desire this information may leave their number. The school office or office of security will pass this information on to the security force member.

Disclosure of Information

Purpose.   This section sets forth the policy and requirements for guarding against the disclosure of information.

Policy.   Employees assigned to security duties may come into possession of information of a sensitive nature, such as the name of a person who is being investigated for a criminal act; where the drug-detection dog team will operate; and common gossip that may be detrimental to an innocent individual. It is the policy that information learned by security personnel will not be disclosed to unauthorized individuals.

Disclosure by Loose Talk.   If a member of the security force repeatedly discloses information during casual conversation, corrective and disciplinary action will be taken.

Disclosure by Design.   If a member of the security force discloses information with the intent of hurting the organization or an individual, corrective and disciplinary action will be taken.

Disclosure for Criminal Purposes.   If a member of the security force discloses any information that is used, or may be used, to hinder or circumvent an investigation into a criminal act or an operation, he or she will be prosecuted as an accessory to the crime.

Disclosure to Release Criminal Record Information.   By June 1 of each year, each security force member will complete and return to the director of security the appropriate and approved form for authority to release criminal records. This release will be used for annual NCIC criminal records checks and is required to maintain peace officer status.

Use of Alcohol and Drugs by Security Force Personnel

Purpose.   This section sets forth the guidelines for the use of alcohol and drugs by members of the security force.

Policy.   Members of the security force provide services to all _____ personnel and to the public. As enforcers of the law and keepers of the peace, they are closely watched and are vulnerable to criticism. Members of the security force must not only abide by all laws and instructions, but must also give the impression that they are living up to the letter of all laws and instructions. The use of any item that would impede the operation of an individual's normal faculties will not be tolerated, not only because of public perception, but because of each officer's dependence on others during times of stress.

Alcoholic Beverages.   Alcohol and it's abuse has a staggering cost to society, particularly when it involves individuals in positions that effect public trust and safety.

Security personnel will be held accountable to the following standards as well as to other district policy where alcohol is concerned:

1. No person assigned to the security force will consume any type of alcoholic beverage while on duty.
2. No person assigned to the security force will consume any type of alcoholic beverages within six hours before reporting for duty.
3. Any person assigned to the security force who, by action, speech, or odor, gives the appearance of being or having recently been under the influence of any type of alcoholic beverage will be placed in a none-duty status, and the appropriate personnel action will be taken.

Medication.   Personnel assigned to the security force who are taking medication that may affect their normal faculties will report such use to their supervisor. It is the responsibility of individuals who are given medication by a physician to explain their function and ask whether the medication will affect the performance of their duties. If there is any question, the supervisor will contact the physician and ascertain the duties that the individual may perform.

Unlawful Drugs or Substances.   Not only is unlawful possession of or use of unlawful drugs or substances against the law but can also have a very damaging effect on individuals as well as others who depend on their actions and judgment. Security personnel will be held accountable to the following standards plus other district policy where the possession and use of unlawful drugs are concerned:

1. Any person assigned to the security force who is found in possession of or using unlawful drugs or substances will be prosecuted to the fullest and appropriate personnel action will be taken.
2. Any person assigned to the security force who has knowledge of any person possessing or using unlawful drugs or substances and does not voluntarily divulge such information will be disciplined to the fullest.

Enforcement.   Any supervisor who finds a member of the security force to be in violation of this instruction will relieve the individual from duty and have him or her report to the principal or director of security. In addition, the supervisor will file a complete report on the circumstances with the principal and director of security.

SECTION III: PROCEDURES

Care and Operation of Official Security Vehicles

Purpose.   This section establishes a procedure for the care and operation of official vehicles assigned to or for use of members of the security force.

Policy.   It is the policy of _____ that each vehicle assigned to a member of the security force will be well maintained and operated in accordance with state laws and district policy. In addition, it is the policy that all accidents involving a security vehicle will be investigated to determine negligence.

Inspection.   Each investigator assigned a vehicle will, at the beginning of his or her duties, inspect it, bringing any discrepancies noted to the attention of the director of security and the district transportation department.

Assignment.   Vehicles will only be assigned to an investigator of a division or to others as approved.

Repair.   It is the responsibility of the investigator to which a vehicle is assigned to establish liaison with the transportation department, review noted discrepancies, and schedule vehicle repairs and maintenance in accordance with district policy.

Turn-in.   If a vehicle breaks down during nonworking hours for the transportation department and it can be driven to the transportation department, it will be taken there. If the vehicle cannot be driven, the transportation department will be contacted, and the vehicle will be transported by approved means. Whenever a vehicle is turned in for repairs, a replacement vehicle will be drawn from the transportation pool, if possible.

Fueling.   All vehicles will be fueled in the approved manner at the appropriate location.

Cleaning.   Each investigator to whom a vehicle is assigned is responsible for the cleanliness of the vehicle. The investigator will contact the transportation department regarding the appropriate procedures.

Operation.   Security vehicles will be operated according to the following guidelines:

1. All accidents involving vehicles will be investigated by the transportation department and the police, as appropriate.
2. The abuse of a security vehicle affects not only the organization, but each security member on duty. No member of the security force will improperly drive, abuse, or negligently operate a vehicle. Anyone who observes any person improperly operating a security vehicle will immediately report the incident. A person who observes such operation and does not report it is as guilty as the person who actually commits the violation.
3. When an official security vehicle is on an emergency run, if so equipped according to state law requirements, the driver will obey the laws and operate the vehicle in a

responsible manner. The operator will not exceed the speed limit or fail to stop at a stop sign or red light. An emergency vehicle does not automatically have the right-of-way, but rather requests the right-of-way from other vehicles. Security vehicles will not engage in "hot pursuits."

Mileage.   The investigator to whom an official vehicle is assigned will record the daily mileage on the Security Employees' Daily/Monthly Activity Report.

Security Radio Procedures and Operation

Purpose.   This section establishes radio call signs and signals and provides information on how radio equipment is to be used.

Policy.   It is the policy of the director of security to use security radio equipment to its fullest capability, keeping it in good working order through proper maintenance and care. Members of the security force will use the radio procedures, call signs, and signals set forth in this section.

Radio Call Signs.   Radio call signs are numbers or names assigned either to individuals or to locations. The radio call signs used by the security force will be the last name of an individual or the name of a location.

Radio Signals.   A radio signal is a numerical code used to communicate messages expeditiously. The radio signals used by the security force will be a combination of plain language and standard- 10—codes, communications.

Radio Equipment
VEHICLE-MOUNTED
Each official vehicle permanently assigned to security will be equipped with a two-way radio. When a vehicle is turned in for repair and a replacement vehicle is drawn that is not equipped with a radio, a portable radio will be used.

TWO-CHANNEL PORTABLE RADIOS
All investigators, supervisory security officers, and security officers will have a two-channel portable radio. The radios of all investigators and supervisory security officers assigned to a school will be equipped with digital keypad frequency capability for emergency use. The SSO will train and supervise other security officers in the use of good radio discipline. The digital keypad with frequency capability will be used only for emergency 911 calls unless otherwise approved by the director of security.

Radio Operation
ON-OFF SWITCH
On vehicle-mounted radios, the on-off switch should always be placed in the "on" position. When the ignition is on, the radio will be on; when the ignition is off, the radio will be off. On portable radios, the on-off switch is incorporated into the volume control.

VOLUME

The volume control switch controls the loudness of what you hear. It has nothing to do with the radio's transmission strength. The volume need not be turned up all the way; in fact, when it is turned high, additional noise is received from the speaker. When the volume is adjusted to a pleasant listening level, the radio operates best.

SQUELCH

The squelch control is a mechanism that does away with static on the radio. Follow these procedures to set the radio to maximum receiving strength:

1. Turn the squelch knob until you hear noise.
2. Back it up slightly until the noise ceases.
3. Turn it back slightly until you hear noise again.
4. As the noise starts, turn it back very gradually until the noise stops.

If the squelch is cut down to beyond where the noise stops, the strength of the signal received is reduced.

CHANNEL SELECTOR

The channel selector on the dual-channel portable radio is a switch that changes the channel from 1 to 2.

Radio Procedures
CALLING

Radio procedure sometimes has a tendency to become very sloppy, and calls can be heard such as "One-one-three." Is that unit 11 calling unit 3 or unit 1 calling unit 13? The correct procedure is to announce the number of the unit being called and then to identify the unit making the call: "One. This is one-three."

Never make a call and give a message without waiting for a response. For example, do not say, "One. This is one-three. Request ten-nineteen," without ascertaining that you have the attention of the operator of station 1. Instead, say, "One. This is one-three," and wait for a response. When, "This is one," is heard, say, "One, this is one-three. Request ten-nineteen." If this procedure is followed, messages will go through the first time. If an immediate response is not received when calling another station, wait for a couple of minutes before calling again, unless it is an emergency.

In _____, radio call signs will be by name, not number, and radio call signals will be a combination of-10-codes and plain language.

SPEAKING

When talking on the radio, hold the microphone approximately two inches directly in front of your mouth. Speak slowly, distinctly, and clearly. By following this technique, we will be able to cut down on radio transmissions that have to be repeated because they are garbled. Think about what you are going to say before you speak, and then speak concisely.

INFLECTION

Inflection refers to how you sound to others. Do you sound tired, disgusted, mad, or aggravated? When speaking in the radio, none of these qualities should come through. Speak in a monotone voice. Some people can say "Ten-four" (I acknowledge) and make you mad simply by the inflection of their voice. Others indicate through their tone that they do not want to be bothered.

Investigative Jurisdiction

Purpose.   This section explains the cooperative responsibility of personnel of the Operations and Investigations Division and _____ Police Department in connection with crimes.

Policy.   It is the policy of _____ to investigate all crimes occurring on _____ property and to provide detailed, concise information as to the "who," "what," "where," "when," and "how" in reporting incidents.

Rules of Security Procedure.   It is understood that there will be some criminal cases that the security force will investigate in their entirety while others, after preliminary investigation, will be referred to the _____ Police Department. This section describes some of the different crimes and how they are to be handled.

The following are the general rules of security procedure in all crimes:

1. Obtain the names and the organizational or school affiliation of all witnesses and suspects.
2. Keep witnesses and suspects separated.
3. Do not accuse anyone of a having committed a crime, and do not take statements unless involved in an investigation. This is not a question of capability but one of time and the preparation of a case. Members of the security force have the right to detain a person whom they think may have knowledge of a crime.
4. Protect the scene of the crime.
5. If evidence is gathered, such as a gun, protect it for fingerprints and note where the item came into custody, from whom, and the date and time. If at all possible, leave an item of evidence where it was found, unless to do so would be inappropriate such as in the case of a gun or drugs.

Homicide, Suicide, Breaking and Entering, Robbery, Child Molestation, and Arson.   The officer will secure the scene and rope if off, if possible, to keep people out. In addition, the officer will obtain the names and organization or location of complainants, victims, witnesses, and suspects, detaining them and keeping them separated. The officer will notify the principal, the _____ Police Department, and office of security. A preliminary investigation will be conducted, as appropriate, and prepared for referral to _____ Police as required.

Auto Theft.   In case of auto theft, the officer will prepare an incident report, will search the grounds for the vehicle, and if vehicle is not found on the grounds will refer the complainant to the police. The local police will be called so that they can take a report. If the vehicle is found on the grounds without a driver, the officer will lock it up until the police arrive. If the vehicle is found on the grounds with people in it, the officer will detain the occupants of the vehicle and will notify the principal and the _____ Police.

Larceny of Personal Property.   The officer will make an incident report on all calls concerning larceny of personal property. If a person is caught in the act of stealing, the principal and supervisory security officer will be notified. The SSO will conduct investigations of larceny of personal property valued under $200 (or as agreed); all other cases will be referred to the _____ Police, as appropriate.

Larceny of School Property.   The officer will make an incident report on Form _____ on all calls of larceny of _____ property. If a person is caught in the act of stealing, the supervisory security officer will be notified. If the property is valued at $200 or more (or as agreed), the case will be referred to the _____ Police Department after preliminary investigation. If the property is valued at less than $200 (or as agreed), the case will be investigated by the SSO and discussed with the police as appropriate.

Assault and Fighting.   If two people have an argument that results in a fight, with nothing but their bare hands used (no weapons) and neither person requires medical treatment, the officer will make a report. If a weapon is used, medical treatment is required, or more than two people are involved, the officer will detain all personnel involved and will notify the principal and the supervisory security officer. Fights and assaults of a serious nature will be referred to the _____ Police Department.

Possession of a Gun.   The officer will safely confiscate the weapon, if possible, will detain the person, and will notify the principal, the _____ Police Department, and office of security. The school and the police will conduct the investigation, and the weapon will be turned over to the police department for prosecution after a receipt is obtained.

Discharging, Displaying, or Threatening with a Gun.   The officer will safely confiscate the gun, if possible, will detain the individuals involved, and will notify the principal, the supervisory security officer, the _____ Police Department, and other appropriate personnel.

Destruction or Vandalism to School or Private Property.   The officer will make the appropriate report and will conduct an investigation, as appropriate, after notifying the principal and the supervisory security officer.

Drugs, Marijuana, and Drug Implements.   If drugs or drug implements are found in common areas such as walkways, halls, bathrooms, and places to which many people have access, the officer will confiscate the items, protecting any possible fingerprints, and will make a report. All items will be turned over to the _____ Police after the principal and supervisory security officer have been notified. If a person calls anonymously and provides information on the use or possession of marijuana or other drugs, the officer will contact the principal and supervisory security officer for a decision on how to proceed. If a person contacts an officer, gives his or her name, and provides information, gained through personal observation, on the use or possession of marijuana or other drugs, the officer will notify the principal and the supervisory security officer and take appropriate action.

Other Offenses. All other offenses will be handled in the appropriate manner as decided by the principal and director of security in accordance with the law or rules and regulations. Additional guidance will be provided in future revisions to this manual.

Notification. All of the preceding incidents will be reported to the school principal in a timely manner and then to the office of security.

Search Procedures

Purpose. This section provides guidance for members of the security force when conducting searches of people and property.

Policy. It is the policy for _____ security force personnel to search criminal suspects for weapons and other potentially dangerous articles before turning them over to the police for transport. In addition, where appropriate and within the provisions of governing instructions and laws, searches may be conducted of individuals incident to arrest to detect evidence of suspected criminal activity and for self-protection, if warranted.

Definitions
ADMISSIBLE EVIDENCE
Evidence that has been obtained in accordance with the laws governing school law relating to search and seizure. The admissibility of evidence in court is determined at trial by a judge.

CONTRABAND
Illegal items, such as counterfeit money, certain firearms and explosives, and marijuana or other controlled substances and so on.

FRISK
A surface pat-down applied to the clothing of a suspect. A frisk is not a search, and it does not include emptying the pockets or closely examining articles found on the suspect. The security officer need not apprehend the suspect to conduct a frisk. The officer may decide to conduct a frisk based on suspicion of potential danger to the officer or others and professional observation of suspicious conduct on the part of the suspect.

FRUITS OF A CRIME
Items that can be identified as stolen articles or contraband derived by the criminal who committed the crime.

INSTRUMENTS OF A CRIME
Articles used to commit a crime, such as weapons, tools, and so on.

PROBABLE CAUSE
A legal standard against which many investigative procedures are measured. Probable cause is established as example when a reasonable and prudent person is convinced by reliable information or circumstances that the search of a specific person, place, or thing will reveal evidence of a crime. Only reasonable suspicion, rather than probable cause, is required to search students in school.

Search of a Person.   A suspect who is not under apprehension may be frisked, if warranted, to determine the presence of weapons or dangerous articles. If, while conducting a frisk, the security officer discovers and examines a suspicious bulge in the suspect's clothing and the bulge turns out to be caused by contraband and not by a weapon, the contraband may be seized. The evidence should later be ruled admissible in court because the purpose of the frisk was not to hunt for incriminating evidence or contraband, but to protect the officer and the suspect.

Once it has been determined that probable cause exists to place a suspect under apprehension, the suspect may be searched as thoroughly as circumstances require, including an examination of pocket contents and other items on the suspect's person. All individuals placed under apprehension will be searched for weapons and dangerous instruments before they are transported or turned over to the police. Evidence detected during this "search incident to apprehension" (for example, contraband or fruits or instruments of a crime) will later be admissible in court if the arrest itself was valid.

A strip search is not authorized. If deemed necessary, it will be conducted only by the local police department or other approved agency.

PROCEDURE FOR SEARCH OF A PERSON
In frisking a person, start at the top of the head and work to the feet, following this or other approved procedure:

1. Place the suspect in a position where he or she is at a disadvantage. Have the suspect lean against a wall or vehicle and spread the feet apart, placing the weight on the tips of the toes and the fingers.
2. Approach the suspect, placing one foot just inside the suspect's foot and resting your weight on the other foot. Positioned in this way, if the suspect makes a suspicious move, you can sweep your inside foot out from under the suspect, causing him or her to fall to the ground.
3. Using this routine, frisk one side of the suspect's body and then the other side.

Locker Searches.   The law recognizes that lockers are school property and can be searched by administrators at any time based on reasonable suspicion of contraband. Locker searches may also be included in an administrative random inspection program that uses metal detectors.

Room Searches.   Keep the following guidelines in mind while searching a room:

1. Carefully examine all desk drawers, including their bottom surfaces.
2. Check all items in lockers, but try to be as neat as possible, replacing items where you found them.
3. It is not necessary to unfold clothes while conducting a search, but do run your hands over clothing to determine whether there are any suspicious bulges.
4. When conducting a thorough room search, check light switches and electrical outlets, the legs of furniture, table drawers and bottoms, and the bottoms of chairs. Also check ceiling tiles. If any are askew, it may indicate that there is a hiding place overhead.

Crime Scene Protection

Purpose.   This section establishes a procedure with which security personnel will protect the scene of a crime.

Policy.   It is policy of _____ that the scene of a crime will be protected to preserve the physical evidence of the crime. In today's court system, all statements and procedures are suspect; therefore, it is essential that security officers protect crime scenes until investigating personnel have first had an opportunity to gather any physical evidence.

Types of Physical Evidence
PRY MARKS
When someone attempts to enter a building by prying a door or window open, the tool that is used to do the prying leaves a mark. Each tool has a different set of grooves or marks on its surface. When force is placed on the tool these grooves or marks are imbedded or transferred to the surface that is being pried. The tool can be compared in a laboratory to the surface that was pried, and in many cases, positive identification can be made. Marks that are not visible to the unaided eye can sometimes be raised in a laboratory.

FOOTPRINTS AND TIRE PRINTS
Security officers at a crime scene must be very careful where they walk to avoid destroying footprints or tire prints. Any prints that are found will be roped off. The investigating agents will photograph the prints and make plaster casts of them. In addition, soil samples may be taken from the area where the prints are found to compare any substances found on the suspect's shoes or in the suspect's vehicle.

FINGERPRINTS
Fingerprints are nothing but oil left on some surface by the ridges of the fingers. The hands and feet of a person are covered with ridges that can be used for identification. Anytime a person touches an object with a finger, palm, or foot, prints are left. Because they cannot be seen by the unaided eye, they are easily destroyed by carelessness at a

crime scene. In addition, every time security officers touch something, they leave their fingerprints, which must be eliminated. Officers will not use handkerchiefs to handle items at a crime scene. Although this technique does prevent new prints from being transferred to the item, it also destroys the prints of others.

BOLT CUTTER MARKS

Bolt cutters, like pry tools, leave marks. Both parts of the lock are important. If part of a lock is found, the officer will note its location but will not touch it.

OTHER ITEMS

The officer will not touch or remove any other items at a crime scene. The officer will leave them until the investigating agent ascertains their importance.

Authority.　The security officer will be in charge of a crime scene and will be responsible for its protection until the investigating officers or police arrive.

Entering the Scene.　Only the absolute minimum number of people required to accomplish the mission will enter the scene of a crime. In the case of breaking and entering, only two officers will enter. In the case of a possible arson, after the fire department has put out the fire, the security officer will ask the fire captain to remove the fire fighters from the scene as quickly as possible. The security officer will not allow the fire fighters to clean up the scene as they may destroy physical evidence in the process. In the case of a death or suicide, the security officer will not pronounce the victim dead but will call medical response personnel and let them perform that service. If they pronounce the victim dead, the security officer will have them leave the scene as quickly as possible and will not allow them to remove the body. If a major crime has occurred, the crime scene will be roped off as quickly as possible to keep people out of the area. The security officer will not allow more officers than needed to enter the crime scene. The security officer's responsibility for the crime scene ends when the _____ Police arrive. The officer will support the police as needed.

Criminals, Suspects, Victims, Complainants, and Witnesses.　Any person who is involved in or has any knowledge of a crime will be placed alone in an area where he or she cannot talk with any other person, particularly witnesses or victims.

Security Officer's Notes.　Security officers at a crime scene will make notes as to the time they arrived, what they did, who was on the scene when they arrived, who entered the scene later, the items that were touched and by whom, and any items they see that they believe may have a connection with the crime. In addition, they will obtain the names and addresses of everyone who has any connection with the crime.

Larceny of Private Property.　If an officer is conducting a preliminary investigation during normal working hours of the larceny of private property and there is physical evidence at the scene, the supervisor and the police, if appropriate, will be contacted to process the evidence. When an investigation is conducted after hours, the scene will be secured so that no one will have access to it until normal working hours or until all investigation is complete. If this cannot be done, the duty investigator, if assigned, will be contacted for instructions or the police will be called.

Importance. Security officers are generally the first on the scene of a crime. They can, by their actions, make or break a case. Security officers will practice the provisions of this section and will be the strong link in the investigation—not the weak one.

Control of Property

Purpose. This section sets forth the procedure for checking school property that will be taken away from a school or other location.

Policy. It is the mission of security force personnel to stem the unauthorized flow of property from school locations by checking for property passes and using Form _____, the Equipment Custody-Liability Change Authorization.

Control of Off-location Property Receipts

1. All persons and vehicles departing a location with school property must be checked, when possible, for a custody receipt, Form _____, which indicates authority to remove the property.
2. Upon presentation of this form, the security officer will note the name and time of departure in the field notebook or will examine the form to ensure proper completion by the office. Upon the return of the property to the location, the security officer will enter the name and time returned in the field notebook. This cannot be documented on all occasions but should be done when the security officer notices property being taken from or brought into a location.
3. An employee discovered with school property in his or her possession when leaving a location who does not have Form _____ should be reminded to complete the form. The security officer will note the incident in the field notebook, and then document the incident by notifying the principal and other appropriate people in writing.

On-call Investigator

Purpose. This section establishes the operating procedure for the on-call investigators or supervisory security officers, when applicable.

Policy. It is the policy of _____ to investigate all crimes committed on school property. To obtain a satisfactory level of investigative expertise at all times, an investigator will be subject to call twenty-four hours a day, seven days a week, as assigned and warranted.

Responsibility. The Investigations Division investigator is responsible for establishing a duty roster in accordance with this section and for ensuring that the duty is properly stood.

Tour of Duty.   One investigator will stand the duty (be on call) at a time. A different investigator will stand the duty each week or as appropriate, and an investigator will stand the weekend duty when appropriate. Weekend duty is from 1500 Friday until 0700 Monday.

Personnel.   All investigators assigned to schools or other locations will stand the duty as scheduled.

Page Radios and Cellular Phones.   The on-call investigator will be equipped with a page radio or cellular phone. The investigator will wear the page radio when away from home or the office. When at home or the office, the page will be turned off and placed in the charger, and the central alarm monitor or other appropriate monitor will be notified of the investigator's phone number and pager or cellular number.

Response.   The on-call investigator who calls to a location after duty hours will be guided by security instructions. If a question arises, the on-call investigator will contact the director of security or the Investigations Division investigator.

Conduct.   On-call investigators may travel anywhere within the area while on on-call duty as long as they have notified _____ that they can be reached by pager or cellular phone. They will guard against becoming involved in activities that will preclude their answering a page in a timely manner. In addition, they will not consume alcoholic beverages or take medication that will impair their faculties at any time while on call.

Changing of Duty.   There are times when social and family activities conflict with on-call duty. On these occasions, the on-call investigator should arrange with another investigator to stand by for him or her. The Investigations Division investigator will be notified and must approve the request. The investigator listed on the duty bill will be responsible for notifying _____ so that the change can be made on the call board.

SECTION IV: LOGS AND REPORTS

Security Desk Log

Purpose.   This section sets forth the procedure for maintaining the Security Desk Log in the office of security, when required.

Policy.   It is the policy of the director of security that all serious matters resulting in action by members of the security force be neatly and properly reported in the Security Desk Log.

Discussion.   The Security Desk Log is a chronological listing of matters of interest to the director of security. The combination of the Security Desk Log, the Daily/Monthly Activity Report, the field notebook, and various other reports tells the full story. The Security Desk Log is the starting point. It lists the security-related incidents that have occurred. How much time was spent responding to these incidents is found in the Daily/Monthly Activity Report.

Log Review.   The director of security will review the Security Desk Log each day and on completion of the review will make or coordinate appropriate changes or assignments. The log will be kept by the office of security secretary, when assigned, based on calls received or referred.

Log Procedures.   Log entries will be made as follows:

1. All entries will be printed.
2. A line will be skipped between entries.
3. A new page will be started at the beginning of each day.
4. Entries will be made only on one side of the page.
5. The division investigator, when assigned, will review the log.

Alarm Response Report

Purpose.   This section sets forth the procedure for maintaining the Alarm Response Report, when applicable.

General.   The Alarm Response Report provides information about how investigators, supervisory security officers, or other school personnel responded to an alarm, based on Form _____, Vandalism/Theft/Forced Entry/False Alarm Report, or other appropriate report.

Organization.   The Alarm Response Report will be organized into four sections: date, time, location, and remarks.

Alarms.   When an alarm annunciates at the central monitoring station, the investigator, school custodian, or any other designated school personnel who responds after notification will complete an Alarm Response Report to document the alarm notification, the response, and the action taken. A sample report will be provided when applicable.

SECTION V: TRAINING

Basic Security Training

Purpose.   This section establishes the basic training program for security officers.

Training Program.   The training program will consist of formal training, on-the-job training, and self-study. Each officer trainee will be assigned to an experienced supervisory security officer who will act as coach. The coach will be involved in each part of the training and will certify his or her involvement on the trainee's personnel qualification standards (PQS) upon completion of the training. The training requirements are set forth in this section. The PQS will be signed by the appropriate designated personnel and forwarded to the office of security upon completion for inclusion in the officer's training file.

All security officers will also complete and pass the Professional Security Television Network (PSTN) Basic Security Officer Certification Training (Section 5 of the PQS) within ninety days of reporting for duty.

Duration.   The training will begin on the first day of work assignment to the coach and continue for fifteen workdays. The trainee will take the same days off as the coach during the training period. The trainee must complete PSTN certification training within ninety days of reporting for duty.

Formal Training.   After the initial fifteen-day training program, the officer trainee will be assigned to work five days with another officer, if possible. The trainer will ensure that the trainee stands all posts during the time he or she is assigned to work. PSTN certification training will be provided by the office of security at an appropriate time and location within the trainee's first ninety days on the job.

Personnel Qualification Standards

Security Officer Personnel Qualification Standards School:

Security officer trainee:	Date:
Security officer coach:	Date:
School principal:	Date:
Training division investigator:	Date:
Director of security:	Date:
Training folder:	Date:

Personnel Qualification Standards (PQS)
Coach Date

 1. *Administrative*
  Briefed on Staff Division Investigators (if applicable)
  Briefed on divisions (if applicable)
  Briefed on criminal investigation

2. *Use of Force and Self-defense Training*
   Qualified with radio
   Qualified with handcuffs (if authorized)
   Qualified with chemical spray (if authorized)
   Use of force explained and form executed
3. *Special Area and Building Indoctrination*
   School perimeter and inside building
   Storage areas
   Doors
   Parking
4. *Local Security Regulations*
   Authority
   Admission to the location/signs
   Conducting of private business
   Property passes and custody receipt
   Access control
   Identification badges
   Visitor's badges
   Bomb threats
   Fires
   Administrative random inspections
   Drug- and explosive-detection dogs
   Locker searches
   Reasonable suspicion
   Temporary detention
   Decals for privately owned motor vehicles
   Parking regulations
5. *PSTN Security Officer Certification Training (Diploma)*
   Basic security officer training instruction
   Importance of the security officer
   Legal issues I
   Legal issues II
   Communications
   Patrol
   General duties
   Report writing
   Emergency situations
   Fire prevention and control
   Safety
   Other PSTN training tapes, as appropriate
   Security officer's role in crime prevention
   Tactical communications
   Crime scene containment
   Defense tactics
   Other topics as appropriate

6.   *Security Force Standard Operating Procedures*
Section I:
> Organization of the security force
> Jurisdiction, authority, and apprehension
> Hours of work

Section II:
> Grooming and uniform
> Leave policy
> Contact information
> Disclosure of information
> Use of alcohol and drugs

Section III:
> Vehicle operations
> Radio procedures and operation
> Investigation jurisdiction
> Search procedures
> Crime scene protection
> Control of off-location property
> Notification of occurrences
> On-call investigator

Section IV:
> Security Desk Log
> Alarm Response Report

Section V:
> Basic security training
> In-service training
> Self-defense tactics

Section VI:
> Numbering of reports
> Field interview and information report
> Security officer's log and Daily/Monthly Activity Report
> Administrative random inspection program

In-service Security Training

Purpose.   This section establishes an in-service training program for security officers.

Training Program.   The training sections will be conducted at roll call each day or during in-service days, as appropriate, during the school year. The following material will be used: International Association of Chiefs of Police (IACP) slide or video training presentations, PSTN tapes, Security Regulations and Security Force Standard Operating Procedures, and any other training material deemed appropriate to increase security officer professionalism and effectiveness. In-service training will usually amount to at least twenty-eight hours annually. Supervisors/investigators will have additional hours of training which will include separate supervisory training sessions.

Responsibility.   The Training Division investigator, when organized and staffed, and the field training officer are responsible for organizing the roll-call training and for the in-service training schedule. The training coordinator is responsible for executing the program scheduling with the support of the school principals.

Self-defense Tactics

Purpose.   This section introduces self-defense tactics training.

Classes.   Self-defense tactics training will be a part of the training program, as appropriate. The training will make use of PSTN tapes, the expertise of the _____ Police Department, and other available services. Self-defense tactics training must be given to security personnel frequently enough that they become proficient in its use.

SECTION VI: FORMS AND REPORTS

Report Numbering, Office Indexes, and Name Files

Purpose.   This section establishes a procedure for numbering reports and maintaining office indexes and name files. Other databased or computer-generated record keeping may be instituted or adopted when available.

System.   Each report will be numbered. Each number will contain two letters, two numbers, a dash, two numbers, another dash, and three numbers—for example, OS-96-06-001.

Letters.   The two letters *OS* indicate that the report number is assigned to the office of security. These letters will be preceded with a *J* if judicial or disciplinary action is involved—for example, J-OS-96-06-001.

Numbers.   The following numbering system will be used for all reports:

- The first two numbers will be the last two numbers of the current school year. For example, reports made during the 1996–1997 school year will begin with *96*.
- The first two numbers will be followed by a dash.
- The second two numbers will be a two-digit code for the current month. For example, June will be represented by *06*.
- The second two numbers will be followed by a dash.
- The last three numbers will be assigned to that particular case or report as it is received. For example, the first report received will be numbered 001.

Procedures

1. A log for each report will be used to keep an account of the numbers.
2. The number assigned to each report will be placed in the appropriate log book or listing and on each page of any report pertaining to that case.

Responsibility.   A secretary in the office of security will be responsible for seeing that reports are numbered as set forth in this instruction. The secretary will be responsible for maintaining the numbering system, entering the numbers in the logs, and placing the numbers on reports and index cards or other approved forms.

Office Indexes and Name Files.   Office indexes and name files will be maintained on 3-by-5 cards (or other approved cards) by the secretary in the office of security. Two separate card files will be maintained, and the format or other approved means illustrated in Figure A11.1 will be followed. The secretary will enter the required information for every investigation conducted.

Confidential Informant File.   A confidential informant (CI) file numbering system will be maintained by the office of security in a separate log book. If a secu-

1. Office Indexes

Title of Case:	File #
Type of Case:	X-ref. File #
V (Victim)	
S (Suspect)	
D (Defendant)	
Closed/solved/unsolved	

2. Name Files

Name (last name only):	File #:
Type of Case:	X-ref. File #
V (Victim) (One only)	
S (Suspect)	
D (Defendant)	

Figure A11.1 Sample Office Index and Name File Cards

rity officer needs to have a CI number assigned, the following procedure will apply:

1. Call the director of security.
2. Obtain a CI number.
3. Give the name, address, and telephone number of the confidential informant.
4. Refer to the confidential informant by number, not name, in all future discussion and correspondence.

No dealing with a confidential informant will be made without the initial approval of the director of security and information will be revealed when requested by the DOS.

Field Interview/Information Report

Purpose. This section establishes a standard for completing the Field Interview/ Information Report.

Policy. Information may be conveyed from the security officer of one facility to security officers of other locations when the need arises not only by telephone but also via the use of Field Interview/Information Reports.

Discussion.   On many occasions, security officers need to be made aware of information about noncriminal incidents or criminal incidents that occur in the schools particularly if it could effect other facilities. Information of this nature will be provided on the Field Interview/Information Report. The completed report will be forwarded to the appropriate school and security personnel and to the director of security. A copy of the report will be kept by the reporting school. The school principal will also be kept informed of appropriate information by the SSO.

Security Officer's Daily/Monthly Activity Report

Purpose.   This section establishes the requirements for a security officer's Daily/Monthly Activity Report and the procedure for completing it.

General.   The security officer's log serves many purposes. It relays information about where an officer was working and what he or she did. It protects the officer from false accusations and provides management with information to improve security services.

Requirements.   All security force personnel, including supervisors and investigators, will complete a report each day or month, as appropriate, accounting for their full hours of duty. More than one sheet of paper can be used. Investigators will complete the form daily. Other security personnel will complete the form on the last workday of the month and it will reflect their work and leave hours for the entire month.

Procedure.   The following information is provided to ensure the consistency of the complete report:

1. Name: Your last name, first name, and middle initial.
2. School/location: Where you are permanently assigned.
3. Location code: Your facility or location code by number or name.
4. Reporting period: The date of this report.
5. Employee no.: Your employee identification number.
6. Official car: The number of your vehicle, if assigned.
7. Odometer (start)
8. Odometer (end)
9. Total miles
10. Statement of duties: Times, places, and names that are significant to your duties or activities.
11. Activity: The times, in half-hour increments, of the different types of duties you performed.
12. Hours this period: List appropriate times in appropriate subject block.
13. Cumulative hours: List previous subject block hours.
14. Total hours: Add preceding blocks.
15. Other blocks: As specified.
16. Reverse side: To be completed when security-related overtime duties are performed. Hours will correspond to the date of the month when overtime was worked, and the type of duty performed will be indicated by numerical code.

Turning in the Reports.   The supervisor or investigator will collect the Daily/ Monthly Activity Reports on the last working day of the month or the first working day of the next month. He or she will review them for completeness and deliver them to the direction of security. A copy will also be provided as information to the principal of the school. The reports will be reviewed and retained for the current school year, or as appropriate. All reports must be completed and signed by the member of the security force submitting the report.

Administrative Random Inspection Program

General.   The administrative random inspection program was instituted to deter weapons from being brought into the schools. The degree and nature of the inspection will never go beyond what is necessary to allow the staff to discharge its responsibility. The number of forbidden objects that are discovered will never be used as the measure of the inspection program's success. A program that discourages students' testing of the detection efforts should be the goal. Random screening is an ideal solution because students can never be certain who will be inspected or when.

A request for use of metal detectors may include the request for randomly selected screening of students throughout the school day in the halls, entering or leaving a classroom or the cafeteria, exiting or boarding a bus, or any other randomly selected school building or grounds site. The random-selection method acts as a deterrent because students can never be certain just when or where they may be inspected for weapons. The selection for screening of just certain classes of individuals based on racial, ethnic, or similar characteristics is strictly prohibited, and the selection of individuals screened will always be truly based on random selection and not on any particular characteristic.

The random-selection technique has another deterrent value in that it helps combat the "pack-mule" technique in which known violators of security regulations coerce another student to transport weapons and forbidden objects into and around the school for them. These other students are usually docile, nonaggressive individuals who are easily manipulated by threats and intimidation. Female students are particularly susceptible to this tactic when threatened with physical or character attack or when friendly with the other student.

The operation of this inspection program will be in accordance with published procedures and guidelines.

Completion of Reports.   The required forms and reports (Request for Use of Metal Detector; Administration Inspection Log Report) should be completed by the supervisory security officer (SSO). The SSO should also ensure that other security officers are trained in completing the necessary forms and reports so that inspections can be properly conducted in the absence of the SSO.

Appendix 12

Sample Key and Lock Control Program

PURPOSE

This appendix establishes a sample key and lock control program in _____.
Included within this program are all keys, locks, padlocks, and other locking devices used to protect or secure facilities (such as schools and plants), facility perimeters, activities, critical assets, and valuable or sensitive materials and supplies. Not included in this program are keys, locks, padlocks, and other locking devices used for convenience, privacy, and personal or administrative use (including classrooms that do not contain valuable equipment).

RESPONSIBILITIES

Director of Security

The director of security will work with school plant facilities personnel and is responsible to the superintendent for all security-related key control and lock control programs in _____.

Administrative Heads

Directors, department heads, and principals are responsible for instituting the key control program within their facilities. They will appoint a key custodian or will assume this responsibility themselves, and they will provide the names of the key custodian and any subcustodians to the key control officer.

Key Custodians

Key custodians are responsible to the key control officer for the handling of keys, related records, investigation of missing keys, inventories and inspections, and the overall supervision of the key control program at their facility.

PROCEDURES

Key Issue

Keys for security locks and padlocks must be issued only to those who have a need for such and have been approved by the administrative officer of the facility. Convenience or status is not a sufficient criterion for issuing a security key. The key custodian will ensure that an access list is posted beside the key control locker in clear view. All sub-custodians will be aware of the list and will issue keys only to authorized personnel.

Key Storage

All keys covered by this instruction will be stored in the controlling facility's key locker when not in use. Keys will not be physically marked with location or name.

Key Checkout

Anyone who checks out a key will first sign the Key Control Log maintained by the key custodian or a designated representative. The key holder will also complete a Key Receipt Form (Figure A12.1).

Key Control Log

The key custodian will maintain a Key Control Log with each key locker. When not in use, the log will be kept under the custodian's control. When no personnel are available to oversee the log, it will be secured in an area qualified to hold valuable material. The log will contain the following information: keys issued, to whom, and the date and time when issued and returned. To account for all keys, the key custodian will check the log against the key locker at the end of each day or at some other appropriate time and will note the check of the status in the log.

Key Locker

The key locker will be kept in a secure area in the administrative office of the facility where reasonably constant surveillance is available. The locker will contain all applicable keys and their duplicates. An inventory list stating the quantity, use, and identification number of each key will be maintained within clear view of the locker—preferably taped to the inside door. The key locker will be closed and locked when not in use. The key custodian will maintain in an appropriate, secure place the master key that opens the key locker.

KEY RECEIPT

Date: _____

I acknowledge receipt of _____ key(s) to _____ school # _____.

I understand that such key(s) have been issued for use in connection with my duties at this school and that I am responsible for the security and proper use of these key(s).

I understand that upon transfer, termination, resignation, or retirement from this school, I must turn in the key(s) that have been issued to me before I can obtain final clearance and receive final termination or retirement pay.

Received: _____
Key holder / date

Returned: _____
Key holder / date

_____
School principal / activity head

_____
Director of Security

_____
Key custodian

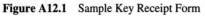
White copy: Facility   Yellow copy: Key holder   Pink copy: Office of Security   Blue: Key custodian

Figure A12.1   Sample Key Receipt Form

Duplicate Keys

No more than one duplicate key will be kept on hand. Duplicates will never be checked out for convenience. Before a duplicate key is checked out, the key custodian will establish the need for the duplicate and the disposition of the original. All requests for duplicate keys will be routed through the key custodian to school plant facilities or other arranged means for duplication. A record of the keys that have been replaced will be kept in the Key Control Log for future reference.

Lost, Misplaced, or Stolen Keys

In the event of a lost, misplaced, or stolen key, the affected lock or lock core will be replaced immediately or as dictated by established procedures and policy. Replacement or reserve locks, cores, and keys will be secured to preclude access by unauthorized individuals.

Lock Rotation

All padlocks and combination locks used to secure sensitive areas will be rotated (or the combination will be changed) at least once annually or as appropriate. A record of the locks changed, the date changed, and the personnel performing the task will be included in the Key Control Log.

Open Padlocks

When a door, gate, or other equipment normally secured by a padlock is open or operable, the padlock will be locked onto the staple, fence fabric, or nearby securing point. This precludes individuals from switching the padlock to facilitate surreptitious entry.

Gates

Gates that are inactive or infrequently used will be locked and will have seals affixed. Security officers or other appropriate personnel will check these gates frequently.

Security Applications

All locks and padlocks used for security applications will meet the minimum specifications for the level of security required.

Inspections

The key control officer will inspect all facilities once a year, or as appropriate, to ensure the proper operation of the key control program.

Administrative heads will enforce internal security in their assigned areas and will inspect external structures and facilities. They will report all violations to the director of security and will provide a statement of the corrective action taken or proposed.

Securing Buildings

All _____ buildings and spaces will be secured at the close of the normal workday and any time they are not occupied by assigned personnel. Unnecessary utilities will be secured, and all external doors, storage areas, and so on that are not frequently used should be locked with additional locking devices. Individuals who are assigned to work in buildings or spaces after normal working hours will ensure that all means of access to any area that is not under their immediate observation is closed, locked, or zoned for alarm.

Forced Entry

Anyone who discovers evidence of possible forced entry into a building or other space will notify the office of security, the police department, as appropriate, the administrative officer of the facility, and school plant facilities personnel, as necessary. They will not disturb the immediate area until the police department or other proper authority has gone over it. They will complete Form _____. Form _____ will also be completed when a school representative responds to the school after hours for a false alarm or theft.

Appendix 13

CPTED School Security Survey Form

SCHOOL SECURITY SURVEY FORM[1]

I. School Data
    A.　School
    B.　School number
    C.　By
    D.　Date
    E.　School level
        1.　High school _____
        2.　Junior high _____
        3.　Elementary _____
        4.　Vocational _____
        5.　Other _____
    F.　Student population _____
    G.　Premise type
        1.　Single story _____
        2.　Multiple story _____
        3.　Enclosed design _____
        4.　Tropical (open) _____
        5.　Fortress _____
        6.　Other_____
    H.　Hours _____
    I.　Busing % _____
II. Neighborhood Area
    A.　Neighborhood type
        1.　Commercial _____
        2.　Industrial _____
        3.　Residential _____
        4.　Other _____
    B.　Housing
        1.　Single _____
        2.　Multiple _____
        3.　High rise _____
        4.　Low rise _____
        5.　Public _____
        6.　Other _____
    C.　Businesses
        1.　Fast food _____
        2.　Convenience _____
        3.　Shopping center _____
        4.　Services _____
        5.　Other _____
    D.　Streets
        1.　Major arterial(s) _____

      2. Business _____
      3. Residential _____
      4. Mixed _____
      5. 2-Lane _____
      6. 4-Lane _____
      7. Signals _____
      8. Other _____

E. Institutions
      1. Church(s) _____
      2. Schools
            Public _____
            Private _____
      3. Social club _____
      4. Hospital _____
      5. Recreational _____
      6. Other _____

F. Police reporting area _____

G. Comments _____
                   _____

III. Interview Comments (Principal or Designer)

A. Problems
      1. _____
      2. _____
      3. _____
      4. _____

B. Needs
      1. _____
      2. _____
      3. _____
      4. _____

IV. Survey Items

A. Neighborhood

1. Contact	S _____	U _____	NA _____
2. Businesses	S _____	U _____	NA _____
3. Traffic flows	S _____	U _____	NA _____
4. Social	S _____	U _____	NA _____
5. Other _____	S _____	U _____	NA _____
6. Comments _____			

B. School grounds border definition

1. Fences	S _____	U _____	NA _____
2. Foliage/trees	S _____	U _____	NA _____
3. Gathering areas	S _____	U _____	NA _____
Informal	S _____	U _____	NA _____
Formal	S _____	U _____	NA _____
4. Bus (loading zones)	S _____	U _____	NA _____

    5. Police access   S _____ U _____ NA _____
    6. Furniture/amenities   S _____ U _____ NA _____
    7. Other _____   S _____ U _____ NA _____
    8. Comments _____

C. Parking lot(s)   *Teachers*
    1. Street(s)
        Access   S _____ U _____ NA _____
        Surveillance   S _____ U _____ NA _____
    2. Building(s)
        Access   S _____ U _____ NA _____
        Surveillance   S _____ U _____ NA _____
    3. Conflict with
        Bus zone   S _____ U _____ NA _____
        Gathering areas   S _____ U _____ NA _____
        Rec./DE   S _____ U _____ NA _____
        Other _____   S _____ U _____ NA _____
    4. Comments _____

         Students
    1. Street(s)
        Access   S _____ U _____ NA _____
        Surveillance   S _____ U _____ NA _____
    2. Building(s)
        Access   S _____ U _____ NA _____
        Surveillance   S _____ U _____ NA _____
    3. Conflict with
        Bus zone   S _____ U _____ NA _____
        Gathering areas   S _____ U _____ NA _____
        Rec./DE   S _____ U _____ NA _____
        Other _____   S _____ U _____ NA _____
    4. Comments _____

D. Building(s)   *Access*
    1. Roof   S _____ U _____ NA _____
    2. Windows   S _____ U _____ NA _____
    3. Entrances   S _____ U _____ NA _____
    4. Comments _____

         Surveillance
    1. Roof   S _____ U _____ NA _____
    2. Windows   S _____ U _____ NA _____
    3. Entrances   S _____ U _____ NA _____

E. Key control
    1. Great grand master   S _____ U _____ NA _____
    2. Grand master   S _____ U _____ NA _____
    3. Master   S _____ U _____ NA _____
    4. Individual   S _____ U _____ NA _____
    5. Zone control   S _____ U _____ NA _____

      6.   Assignment list   S _____ U _____ NA _____

      7.   Restrictions   S _____ U _____ NA _____

      8.   Other _____   S _____ U _____ NA _____

      9.   Comments _____

F.   Security Systems

      1.   Electronic   S _____ U _____ NA _____

      2.   Trailer   S _____ U _____ NA _____

      3.   Fences   S _____ U _____ NA _____

      4.   Locking systems   S _____ U _____ NA _____

      5.   Other _____   S _____ U _____ NA _____

      6.   Comments _____

G.   Classrooms

      1.   Windows   S _____ U _____ NA _____

      2.   Interior doors   S _____ U _____ NA _____

      3.   Exterior doors   S _____ U _____ NA _____

      4.   Windows in doors   S _____ U _____ NA _____

      5.   Proprietary space   S _____ U _____ NA _____

      6.   Multiple purpose   S _____ U _____ NA _____

      7.   Other _____   S _____ U _____ NA _____

      8.   Comments _____

H.   High-value areas (doors, windows, locks, location procedures)

      1.   Computers   S _____ U _____ NA _____

      2.   Business machines   S _____ U _____ NA _____

      3.   Audio/visual   S _____ U _____ NA _____

      4.   Shop/vocational   S _____ U _____ NA _____

      5.   Other _____   S _____ U _____ NA _____

      6.   Comments _____

I.   Corridors

      1.   Lockers   S _____ U _____ NA _____

      2.   Lighting   S _____ U _____ NA _____

      3.   Surveillance

            General   S _____ U _____ NA _____

            Classrooms   S _____ U _____ NA _____

            Offices   S _____ U _____ NA _____

      4.   Shop/vocational   S _____ U _____ NA _____

      5.   Other _____   S _____ U _____ NA _____

      6.   Comments _____

J.   Stairwells

      1.   Interior   S _____ U _____ NA _____

      2.   Exterior   S _____ U _____ NA _____

      3.   Fire   S _____ U _____ NA _____

      4.   Comments _____

K.   Restrooms

      1.   Location(s)   S _____ U _____ NA _____

      2.   Entrance design   S _____ U _____ NA _____

    3. Interior access   S _____ U _____ NA _____

    4. Other _____   S _____ U _____ NA _____

    5. Comments _____

L. Locker room(s)

    1. Location(s)   S _____ U _____ NA _____

    2. Surveillance

            Interior   S _____ U _____ NA _____

            Exterior   S _____ U _____ NA _____

    3. Doors   S _____ U _____ NA _____

    4. Windows   S _____ U _____ NA _____

    5. Equipment storage   S _____ U _____ NA _____

    6. Lockers

            Layout   S _____ U _____ NA _____

            Assignment   S _____ U _____ NA _____

    7. Other _____   S _____ U _____ NA _____

    8. Comments _____

M. Cafeteria

    1. Equipment   S _____ U _____ NA _____

    2. Storage   S _____ U _____ NA _____

    3. Queuing   S _____ U _____ NA _____

    4. Table arrangements   S _____ U _____ NA _____

    5. Surveillance   S _____ U _____ NA _____

    6. Patio/gathering area access S _____ U _____ NA _____

    7. Other _____   S _____ U _____ NA _____

    8. Comments _____

N. Other areas

    1. Portables   S _____ U _____ NA _____

    2. Athletic/recreational   S _____ U _____ NA _____

    3. Storage   S _____ U _____ NA _____

    4. _____   S _____ U _____ NA _____

    5. _____   S _____ U _____ NA _____

    6. _____   S _____ U _____ NA _____

    7. Comments _____

O. Administrative

    1. Inventory control   S _____ U _____ NA _____

    2. Facility management   S _____ U _____ NA _____

            Scheduling   S _____ U _____ NA _____

            Hours   S _____ U _____ NA _____

            Functional layout   S _____ U _____ NA _____

            Productivity   S _____ U _____ NA _____

            Surveillance   S _____ U _____ NA _____

    3. Maintenance   S _____ U _____ NA _____

    4. Programs   S _____ U _____ NA _____

            Incentive   S _____ U _____ NA _____

            Student patrol   S _____ U _____ NA _____

Other _____   S _____ U _____ NA _____
   6. Comments _____
V. Priority Recommendations
   A. Physical space
      1. Remove   _____
         _____
      2. Repair   _____
         _____
      3. Replace _____
         _____
      4. Install   _____
         _____
      5. Reallocate   _____
         _____
      6. Other _____
         _____

   B. Management (policy, procedure, personnel allocation,
      neighborhood programs, or other)
      _____
      _____

VI. Security Plan
   A. Neighborhood   _____
      _____
   B. Perimeter _____
      _____
   C. Grounds   _____
      _____
   D. Parking (vehicle and bicycle) _____
      _____
   E. Building access _____
      _____
   F. Building exterior _____
      _____
   G. Building interior (classrooms, corridors, restrooms, offices)
      _____
      _____
   H. High-value areas   _____
      _____
   I. Protection of persons _____
      _____
   J. Special events _____
      _____
   K. Other _____
      _____

VII. School Incident Map

		Last year	Year-to-date
A. Target incidents			
1. Breaking and entering		_____	_____
2. Vandalism		_____	_____
3. Theft		_____	_____
4. Arson/fire		_____	_____
5. Staff assault		_____	_____
6. Assault/battery		_____	_____
7. Sex offense		_____	_____
8. Drugs/alcohol		_____	_____
9. Bomb		_____	_____
10. Weapons		_____	_____
11. Other		_____	_____

---

[1]Adapted from School Security Survey Form, TDC Associates. Reston, VA, 1982.

CPTED Matrix

Location	Advantages	Disadvantages	Precautions	Recommendations

Bibliography

Broder, James. *Risk Analysis and the Security Survey.* Boston: Butterworth—Heinemann, 1984.

Crowe, Timothy. *Crime Prevention through Environmental Design.* Boston: Butterworth —Heinemann, 1991.

Crowe, Timothy, "Safer Schools by Design." *Security Management* (September 1991): 81–85.

Fay, John P. *Encyclopedia of Security Management.* Boston: Butterworth—Heinemann, 1993.

Fennelly, Lawrence. *Effective Physical Security.* Boston: Butterworth—Heinemann, 1992.

Garrett, Charles. *School Security Screening.* Dallas: Ram Books, 1991.

Healy, Richard, and Timothy Walsh. *Protection of Assets Manual.* Santa Monica, Calif.: Merritt Press, 1993.

Landon, Walt. "Violence and Our Schools: What Can We Do?" *Updating School Board Policies* 23 (February 1992): 1–5.

Murphy, Patrick V. "Policing and Effective Law Enforcement." *Intergovernmental Perspectives* 19, no. 2 (Spring 1993): 26–28.

Ninety-nine Ways to Upgrade Your School's Security. New York: Rusting Publications, 1992.

O'Block, Robert, Stephen Doren, and Joseph Donnermeyer. *Security and Crime Prevention.* Boston: Butterworth—Heinemann, 1991.

"Playing It Safe." *American School and University* (October 1993): 28–32.

Post, Richard. *Security Administration.* Boston: Butterworth—Heinemann, 1991.

Quinnones, Nathan. "Creating the Climate for Safe, Effective Schools." *School Safety* (Winter 1985): 4–6.

Rotondo, Diane M. "Curbing Crime." *American School and University* (October 1992): 40–48.

"The Ultimate Test." *Security Management* (September 1991): 89–93.

Weber, Thad. *Alarm Systems and Theft Prevention.* Boston: Butterworth—Heinemann, 1985.

Index

access control, 33–39, 87
accountability, 17, 19
activities. *See also* facilities
    administrative officers' responsibilities, 6
    definition of, 1
    in leased spaces, 4
    nonschool hours security for, 25
    security plans for, 11–12
administrative inspections, definition of, 1.
    See also random inspections
Administrative Random Inspection Report,
    107, 110, 112, 207
administrative officer, definition of, 1
administrative posts, 30. *See also* posts,
    security
admissible evidence, definition of, 193. *See*
    also evidence
Alarm Response Reports, 199
alarm systems. *See also* intrusion-detection
    systems
    fire, 149–150
    local, 58
alcohol
    testing equipment, 82–83
    use of by security personnel,
    186–187
annunciators, 60. *See also* intrusion-
    detection systems (IDS)
area protection/control, 25–29
    post considerations for, 30
assessments. *See* security audits; security
    surveys/assessments
assaults
    investigative jurisdiction of, 192
    and personal safety, 159
audiovisual equipment, securing, 25

authority, delineating lines of, 177,
    191–192, 196
auto theft, 191–192

badge systems, 33–37
    characteristics of permanent badges, 36,
    37
    construction of badges, 36
    control of, 38
    "exchange," 35
    expiration dates in, 34–35
    lost badges and, 34, 38, 39
    rebadging in, 34
    recovering badges, 37
    standards for, 35–36
    temporary badges, 35, 38
    visitors and, 35, 37
barricaded captor situation plans, 167–173
barriers, 43–50
    and clear zones, 48
    determining type required, 43–44
    and emergency entrances/exits, 44
    fences, 20, 44–47
    inspection of, 47
    natural, 43
    openings in, securing, 48–50
    and patrol roads, 48
    as perimeter controls, 20
    posting of, 44
    purpose of, 43
    in security/loss prevention plans, 88
    structural, 43
    temporary, 47
    vehicle, 47
    walls as, 47
    and water, 44